AUTHORITY

*The Most Misunderstood Idea
in America*

EUGENE KENNEDY
SARA C. CHARLES, M.D.

THE FREE PRESS
New York   London   Toronto   Sydney   Singapore

_f_P

THE FREE PRESS
A Division of Simon & Schuster Inc.
1230 Avenue of the Americas
New York, NY 10020

Manufactured in the United States of America

10   9   8   7   6   5   4   3   2   1

Library of Congress Cataloging-in-Publication Data

Kennedy, Eugene C.
    Authority : how Americans can regain the satisfaction they miss at
home, at work, and in public life / Eugene Kennedy, Sara C. Charles.
        p.   cm.
    1. Social institutions—United States.   2. Social structure—
United States.   3. Authority.   I. Charles, Sarah C.   II. Title.
HN65.K473   1997
306'.0973—dc21   97-5502
                                                              CIP

ISBN 0–684–83665–3

To

JOSEPH CARDINAL BERNARDIN

1928–1996

Who possessed authority but
was not possessed by it

The issue of authority has such a bad reputation that a philosopher cannot discuss it without exposing himself to suspicion and malice. Yet authority is present in all phases of social life . . . Why is it that men so mistrust so intensely a thing without which they cannot, by all evidence, live and act together?

—Yves Simon, *A General Theory of Authority*

 *aug*

Increase. Greek, *auxesis*. Latin, *augment, auction, auxiliary, author, authority, authorize; augur,* from whom the celebrant hoped divine increase; *augury, inaugurate; august,* favorable; the month was named for Augustus Caesar. Germanic, *eke;* a nickname was "folkchanged" from an ekename; *wax:* to grow, opposed to *wane, waist*—too often seen to expand. The young Nathaniel Hawthorne (born 1804) wrote to his mother: "I don't want to be a doctor, and live by men's diseases; nor a minister, to live by their sins; nor a lawyer, to live by their quarrels. So I don't think there's anything left for me but to be an author."

—Joseph T. Shipley, *The Origins of English Words*

Contents

1

Why We Need to Rediscover Authority

Americans do not distinguish authority, which is something good, from authoritarianism, which is something bad. The idea of authoritarianism has been so fused with that of authority that, like massive rust married to the *Titanic*'s hull, they seem inseparable in our imagination.

The failure to understand the difference between the two entities makes it hard for Americans to diagnose what troubles them. They have a vague but pervasive sense of disconnectedness—of things not working well—that makes them anxious. The era in which we live, according to the *New York Times,* is "toxic. . . . The boundaries of the body feel as vulnerable as the borders of our country. Invisible, unknowable threats have replaced nuclear bombs as the source of collective fear."[1]

We habitually use such vague terms in describing our general unease. That is because authority is close to the core of the problem, and we do not talk about authority or examine its meaning. Our ignorance about authority and our confounding it with authoritarianism constitute the phantom cause of our poorly described malaise.

Because we do not distinguish clearly between authority and authoritarianism, authority is confused with power when power is actually a function of authoritarianism. Authoritarianism, with its impulse to control everything about our lives, makes us fearful; authority does not. The stabilizing character of healthy authority is what has been missing. Its return is what will make us more confident and less anxious in managing our lives.

What Authority Is

Natural authority is a positive, dynamic force ordered to growth. Authority's essentially dynamic character is obvious from its root, shared with "author" and "augment," in the Latin *augere:* "to create, to enlarge, to make able to grow."[2] Authority generates life. It is a living substance that frees the possibilities of other persons as, for example, in parents who "author" the growth of their children.

Authority is a function of, and if not found outside of, human relationships, such as those of mothers and fathers with their children, teachers with students, pastors with their flocks, or even executives with their workers. The philosopher Iredell Jenkins suggests that authority depends on and is transmitted only through human relationships.[3] There is a trinitarian character to authority-bearing relationships. They all contain three essential elements: the author, the agent of energy; the recipient of that creative energy; and what is authorized, the creation or achievement beyond both agent and recipient. The parents endow their children with the growth that makes them good parents to a further generation. The music teacher encourages the talented student to compose a symphony.

The dynamic of authority does not settle for or remain within the relevant relationship but unbalances and breaks it open so that something new comes into existence. Thus parents author their children out of their own love, committing themselves to their growth into productive adulthood. General Colin Powell, for example, acknowledges his parents as the authors of his ability to become a commanding authority in American life.

Everyday illustrations include health authored by physicians in relationship to patients, learning generated by teachers in relationship to their students, and spiritual growth authored by pastors in relationship to the members of their flock. The crucial work for all those achievements is done in and through the relationship. Generative authority may be identified by its context of human relationships and by the positive accomplishment that flows from it.

We sometimes use the phrase "strike a new chord" to describe such three-part generative achievements. It reflects the three-tone nature of a musical chord, that is, elements authored in new relationship to each other resulting in a new sound. That is a common experience for people when they fall in love and sense deeply that together they author something that transcends their separate selves, that something new has come into being and that there is more to them together than there is to them as individuals. We may also find healthy authority by tracing our way back to it from observing its effects. Encounter a happy couple, productive students, a magnificent symphony orchestra, or a great work of art and you will be able to draw a direct line to an agent or agents of healthy authority.

In our own lives, for example, we may be able to relate what we have become to a teacher who opened us up as no other had done and whose relationship sustained our ongoing development. Such teachers had authority, we realize, for we grew positively out of our relationships with them. The triangulation is always there: somebody outside of us who helped us to achieve some good outside ourselves.

If the balance among them is not preserved, or if any one element is disrupted or missing, then authority, as Jenkins notes, "vanishes to be replaced by despotism, anarchy or apathy." Like love and hope, authority is psychological and spiritual in nature. Like good health and good humor, it cannot be faked without causing itself to collapse from within.

Not only does natural authority inhere in and provide the energy for all generative human activity, it also specifies the responsibilities and rights that flow from authorship, whether of children, a painting or a play, a sermon, a class, or a crop. Every one of those needs nourishment and ongoing attention, the discipline of correction or refinement, the continuing pledge of the author's attention until they reach their own fullness. The violation of the authoring relationship—by the state, for example, in usurping the parental role in family life, by the deconstructionist academic in dismissing a writer's intentions, or by a later hand in altering an art work—is experienced as a sacrilegious assault on the binding ties between the creator and the created. Such interference breaks the intimate spiritual connection that is the essence of generative authority.

Nor can morality exist without authorship. Virtue depends on our ability to author for ourselves what we do in our daily lives and work. Virtue is the something new, the expanded good we bring to life. Being responsible requires that we acknowledge authorship of our actions and their consequences. Moral authority belongs to those who are willing to write their signature on their lives.

Authority's effects are as positive as its instincts are moral. It nourishes the sound development and maturity of the individual, but it also exists to enhance the common good, that is, to build communities to accommodate a broad range of citizens. Authority is not authority unless it enlarges the healthy freedom of men and women. In the same way that breathing, curiosity, and the need for love are intuitively understood as natural, so too is authority, as the impulse to give and enrich life in and for others.

Authority supports those institutions, such as the family, good schools, medical services, and government, that are hospitable to and promote human growth. Its natural setting is in the close quarters between human beings. Authority may be understood as energy expended not for its own sake but to be transformed through the process of its transmission into growth in others. Such authority is both medium and message—the line, the electric surge, and the light that comes on in the distant dark—bringing illumination and expansion of and through itself to others.

There are some things that authority is not. Authority, although powerful in its effects, does not use manipulative power to achieve its ends and cannot be identified with that concept. Natural authority is not a function of laws, rules, slogans about empowerment, or public relations. It is not law or regulations but views them as a means to its goal of human growth. Authority employs them in a careful and disciplined manner.

Natural authority is therefore the opposite of the authoritarianism with which it has become identified. Because Americans do not generally understand what healthy authority is—and so frequently confuse it with what it is not—generative authority must be rediscovered if we are to define accurately and deal successfully with our pressing national problem.

What Authoritarianism Is

Authoritarianism, authority's ghostly doppelgänger, is not dynamic but essentially static. It imposes a template of conformity on people to restrict and control their individual development. Its meaning is revealed in the growth it hinders because of its repressive and controlling tactics, which systematically reduce human freedom. Freedom is, however, intertwined inextricably with the exercise of authority. Hannah Arendt has suggested that the reason we no longer understand the idea of freedom is that we no longer understand the meaning of authority.

The base of authoritarianism lies not in love but in power. Much like a derisive laugh, it delights in force, manipulation, humiliation, revenge, and winning by any means and at all costs.

Authoritarianism serves the purposes of the few who would dominate the many. To that end, authoritarianism promotes bureaucratic structures and casts an ever finer net of laws and regulations over the lives of ordinary people. Authoritarians diminish the sacredness of the history-tested institution of law by making laws and regulations ends in themselves.

The fruits of authoritarianism, therefore, serve not the interests of the men and women involved but goals unrelated to them or their welfare. Authoritarianism is not ordered to the growth of others from within but to the control, censorship, and delimiting of their growth from without. It is, as noted in Adorno's *The Authoritarian Personality,* essentially antidemocratic and fascistic in spirit. Authoritarianism's frequently negative outcomes are a function of its amoral techniques.

Any totalitarian state, for example, that would classify parents as neutral breeders from whom children could be separated indifferently and with no consequences would be breaking a natural link. People would recognize this as an authoritarian transgression against human nature, an attack, as authoritarianism always is, against the very essence of generative authority.

Why Authority Doesn't Work Any More

Authority does not work well now because authoritarianism has a hard time working at all. Authoritarianism has a hard time working because hierarchies no longer function well. Authoritarianism expressed itself largely through hierarchical structures, which, for complex historical reasons, no longer reflect, symbolize, or mediate reality. Authority, long misidentified with authoritarianism, has been the innocent victim of the latter's default.

It seemed natural for most of our great institutions—such as religion, law, and government—to use hierarchy as their structural model. Over the centuries the goals of social institutions, businesses, and the broad span of human endeavors have been ordered and facilitated by the presumption of some form of underlying hierarchy. Such hierarchies became the roosting places for authoritarianism. Their pyramidal configuration, placing one person with absolute power over all others as a divine plan, obvious in the nature of things, was the accepted interpretation of reality for hundreds of years.

If authoritarianism's grasp was so overwhelming, how has authority survived at all? Authority maintained itself as humans do in dehumanizing circumstances. As with faith and love in a totalitarian state, authority lived in the human relationships that flourished despite the shadows of the rigid social conventions that fell across them. Authority depends for its life on healthy people maintaining healthy relationships in their personal, work, and communal lives. It survives wherever people try to help each other grow.

At present, however, authoritarian forms seem less natural than they once did. They are still found in many settings, even though their ability to function well has been impaired. Neither kings nor university presidents can make any authentic claim to divine rights. To understand how authoritarianism lost its claims we must examine where we get our ideas about our personalities and our social structures. Our pictures of ourselves follow the lines we see in the environment, reflecting back our images of nature as surely as Monet's rivers reflect the skies of nineteenth-century France. Our earliest cities and states, much like tribes, read their own natures in nature itself. The hierarchical ordering of the universe and of human personality derived from the skywatching priests of Mesopotamia, who first made out this design in the heavens. To them, the hierarchy they thought they could see in the sky seemed to be the divinely established construction of reality. Thereafter, everything human was plotted along hierarchical lines: the universe, kingdoms, personality itself. The king had unquestioned authority at the top of the secular pyramid, as the Pope did over the ecclesiastical world and the father over the family. The mind presided over the lesser creature of the body, the spirit over the flesh. Hierarchy was the only network along which authority could be understood.

The idea of hierarchy arose from our perception of space, from the star-filled skies into which human beings have gazed with wonder, fear, and curiosity as long as they have left signs of their lives on earth. Some 3,500 years ago, in the very land where American guns lit up the skies during the 1991 Gulf War, Sumerian priests first observed and made records of the passage of planets through fixed stars. As Joseph Campbell puts it, the Mesopotamian skywatchers were struck by "the perception of a cosmic order, mathematically definable, with which *the structure of society* should be brought to accord. For it was then that the hierarchically ordered city-state came into being, which stands as the source, and for millenniums stood as the model, of all higher, literate civilization whatsoever. Not economics, in other words, but celestial mathematics were what inspired the religious forms, the arts, literatures, sciences, moral and social orders, which in that period elevated mankind to the task of civilized life."[4]

Divine will was thought to be discernible in this hierarchical framework of reality. The heavens, in which the gods lived, were above, and the earth, the habitation of humans, was below. The earth presented a fixed flat stage from which the panorama of the transforming constellations could be observed and with whose movements

such events as victorious battles, the birth of great persons, and boun-
tiful and bleak harvests could be correlated. In the star signs one
could read a personal destiny. It was a time for astrologers and
prophets, for soothsayers and others to whom were granted authority
and privilege because they could read nature's messages.

Kings sat at the top of the triangle, serene above the descending
and broadening steps of the privileged to the base on which huddled,
as in a caste system, those of the lowest social state. The prerogatives
of royalty were God-given, an arrangement formalized as the Divine
Right of Kings. That concept provided the controlling spirit of authoritarianism, the absolute power of the topmost hierarch over the
tiers of people spread below.

It was possible for kings who enjoyed hierarchical privilege to exercise natural authority nonetheless, enabling healthy human growth to
occur in their courts and their realms. Yet their divinely appointed capacity to decide the fate of millions remained undiminished. The last
Tsar of All the Russias sealed his own fate by perceiving the defense of
his royal privilege against democratic initiatives as his sacred mission
to carry out God's will. Kings were characterized by authoritarianism
far more than by natural authority.

Who could doubt that life on earth was so arranged when the heavens themselves reaffirmed the truth of hierarchy each night? Every social edifice and organism, including human personality, was thought
to be drawn according to this cosmologically inspired and theologi-
cally endorsed blueprint. Everyone's destiny was frozen in place and
was inescapable. So natural did the hierarchical ranking seem in,
among other locales, Egypt, Sumer, and China, that when the
monarch died, as described by Joseph Campbell, his entire court was
buried alive with him.[5] The Council of Trent (1545–63) reinforced
the idea of a divinely established hierarchy: *If anyone says that in the
Catholic Church there is not a hierarchy, instituted by divine ordination
and consisting of bishops, priests, and deacons, let him be anathema.*[6]

Because hierarchy seemed to be consistent with the pre-Copernican grasp of the universe, it went without serious challenge until the
Polish astronomer transformed our picture of earth in relationship to
the heavens. That intellectual idea was not, however, emotionally

confirmed for most people until we entered the Space Age. Hierarchy has come apart not because of the rational application of the Copernican theory—the replacement of a false idea by a true one—but by a slow incorporation of the concept because of historical experiences.

The Copernican Revolution ousted the earth from its privileged place at the center of the cosmos. It has also changed people's imaginative sense of living in space very slowly. The metaphor of an *up* and *down* universe still maintains a grip on the popular consciousness. But it is precisely this platting of heaven and earth as hierarchical structures that has been shattered by what we may call the Space/Information Age. This period views as outmoded and unuseful the archaic engraving of earth and heaven divided against each other. As the unity of the universe is rediscovered in and through the Space/Information Age, so, too, is the unity of the person, once thought to be sectioned hierarchically into higher and lower faculties.

As hierarchy loses its conceptual power, authoritarianism loses the housing it depended on for its very existence. Scattered across culture are its shells and hulks, Tara-like ruins after the evil spirit of slavery had been exorcised by civil war, symbols now of a once-accepted but dead way of life. Hierarchy, and the authoritarianism that flourished within its structure, no longer functions as an explanatory idea of the universe, a blueprint for human institutions, or a model of human personality.

Without quite recognizing or naming it, our perceptions of our universe and of ourselves are dissolving and recrystallizing. The ongoing, ineluctable transformation of our way of looking at and structuring reality is comparable to the literal sea change in perception begun half a millennium and more ago that was gradually shaped by ocean voyages, as ours is now by those into space.

The then novel experience was of the earth's roundness, a sphere endlessly yielding horizons to those who sailed its waters. That perception was gradually incorporated and emotionally ratified by the testimony of ocean voyagers. It rendered the previously held model of a flat earth unbelievable and untenable. Horizons as the boundaries of the world are now dissolving as we enter more deeply into the Space/Information Age. Perceptions of a universe without horizons are reinforced with each launching of a spacecraft or transmission of its pictures back to earth. Indeed, all the reference points by which we structure our physical and spiritual geography are being transformed in this new age. If there are no horizons, neither is there an up or a down.

How the Space/Information Age Reshapes Our Perception of Reality

The historian Paul Johnson says that "the modern world began on 29 May 1919 when photographs of a solar eclipse . . . confirmed the truth of a new theory of the universe." His reference was to Einstein's theory of relativity, first proposed in 1905. For most people, Johnson suggests, the theory of relativity meant that "the spinning globe had been taken off its axis and cast adrift in a universe which no longer conformed to accustomed standards of measurement. At the beginning of the 1920s the belief began to circulate, for the first time at a popular level, that there were no longer any absolutes of time and space, of good and evil, of knowledge, above all of value. Mistakenly, but perhaps inevitably, relativity became confused with relativism."[7]

The breaking down of familiar standards has been accelerated by the effects of the Space/Information Age. It was born on a date shared by two events linked to Einstein's genius. On July 16, 1945, the first atomic device was exploded at Alamogordo, New Mexico, marking a triumph for physics and initiating a period of dazzling transformation in our practical view of ourselves and the universe. Twenty-four years later to the day, on July 16, 1969, Apollo 11 was launched from then Cape Kennedy in Florida to bear human beings to the moon and back. Through television we were able to see the earth in space, a milestone in the conceptualization of time, space, and communication.

In space all our familiar reference points vanish. The single image of "Earthrise" transmitted from the surface of the moon at midsummer 1969 reveals that the earth is not divided from the heavens but is in the heavens. We now see that reality is not hierarchical, not shaped like a pyramid or divided into higher and lower grades of being. That revelation of the unity of the universe is reworking our sense of place within it. It is also changing our ideas about our personalities and institutions. Hierarchy is no longer a useful model for any of these.

As if a fraternal twin, the Information Age was born at virtually the same time as the Space Age. In 1972, three years after Apollo 11 reached Tranquility Base, three young engineers in an unknown California startup named Intel invented the microprocessor and changed the world. Fused together, those remarkable advances created the new environment of the Space/Information Age.

In the Golden Age of hierarchy, information was perceived as power and was reserved to very few at the highest levels. It was sacred, an expression and source of power, reserved like the Holy of Holies, with access for the elect alone. Technological advances democratize information so that it is now instantly available to everyone within a country or an organization. It cannot be kept or controlled at the top. The top is no longer separate from the bottom.

This change also takes away the middle, eroding hierarchy by eliminating the graded intervening steps between the highest and the lowest. Without intermediate levels, hierarchy collapses as a person would who suddenly lost his skeleton. The realities of the Information Age contributed to the end of the Soviet Union as an authoritarian state, because news, such as the 1986 nuclear accident at Chernobyl, could no longer be embargoed at the top. Thus the pyramid necessary for hierarchy disappeared.

Because this insight is so little understood—as are the revolutions of this century, each of which is an effort to overthrow or reestablish authoritarian hierarchy—its impact on every institution, commercial, ecclesiastical, and social, is bewildering. Yet this perceptual transformation moves forward, gradually but relentlessly reworking all institutions.

Life is essentially free-flowing, but it is poured into, contained by, and dependent for its expression on the social forms of a particular era. Until the twentieth century, existence had been processed largely through powerful hierarchical structures. Like fertile soil for a crop, they offered the ideal conditions for the cultivation of the authoritarian style that characterized monarchy and other institutions. This worked until we entered the Space/Information Age, not just by way of our intellects as we had with Copernicus, but as pilgrims affected throughout our personalities by its impact. This is the difference between having theoretical knowledge about a far country from books and being personally changed by living in it, thinking in its language, grasping its customs, and locating ourselves properly in its geography.

In the Space/Information Age, the center of the universe can be anywhere and everywhere. The familiar markings, the notches we made in the trees to follow on our way home, have vanished. It is hard to tell where true north is, or if it exists any more. Although Buckminster Fuller prophesied a quarter of a century ago that "all humanity is about to be born into a new relationship to the universe," the dominant human institutions give little evidence of insight into this new reality. This period may be thought of as an interim bereft of the structures of hierarchical authoritarianism. In it we encounter a kind of formlessness and must search for ways to stabilize ourselves and our institutions. Success at that depends on the rediscovery of the concept of healthy authority.

As noted, such elements of true authority as hierarchical structures tolerated, basically spiritual in nature, were expressed against the grain of, and in spite of, the pervasive authoritarian network. When its hierarchical sheathing wore out, authoritarianism sputtered like a downed wire that could no longer transmit power.

The result is the power outage that we now observe. The order and standards that were unquestioned and largely unquestionable when hierarchy was in place and authoritarianism remained functional have been shortcircuited because of the latter's broken wires. The idea and exercise of genuine authority, obscured by the glare of authoritarianism in its ascendancy, are now obscured by its blackout.

The healing arts are a good example. In the heyday of hierarchy, their intrinsic natural authority to bring wholeness to others became subordinated to and identified with the privileged level reserved for professionals in the larger social structure of society. Physicians were called to exercise generative authority in their practice, but they often lived on a plane above that of most of their patients. Now that hierarchical authoritarianism has crumbled, everything about doctors, including their genuine authority, has come into question if not under siege. Doctors are routinely criticized for once having aspired "to be gods."

Removed from their pedestals, it is not easy for them to rediscover real authority in the age of managed care and competing health providers. Yet the authority of knowledgeable and highly trained professionals in any field remains a prized and genuine entity. It is radically different from hierarchical authoritarianism. In the present protean period, people and organizations are looking for and experimenting with ways to manage post-hierarchical life. They are really searching for what emergency crews seek beneath the fallen walls and cracked foundations after a disaster: the precious sounds of life that give hope that what is healthy about humans and inseparable from them—in this case natural authority—may yet be rediscovered and brought back into life.

Characteristics of the Post-hierarchical Period

This period is characterized by *authority's moving away from the center, accompanied by a purge of hierarchs and hierarchies.* In many places, from board rooms to monasteries, central authority has been replaced with nonhierarchical and more diffuse schemes of management. Old hierarchs, such as Chrysler's Lee Iacocca, have gone out of style; such companies as General Motors have allowed outside directors to lead their reorganization. Knock on a convent door and you are more likely to find a "coordinator" than a Mother Superior. The business expert Kenichi Ohmae has advocated "getting rid of the headquarters mentality" and "decomposing the center" of the enterprise.[8]

This seeming fulfillment of Yeats's poetic insight that "the center cannot hold" is exemplified in the common question, "Who's in charge here?" Americans express their discontent with leaders through their suspicion of public officials and their desire to vote on limiting their terms in office. Leaders, accustomed to the set lines of hierarchy and quick obedience to their directions, now cannot easily find their way in such a featureless and unfamiliar environment. Nor can they automatically lead others in such circumstances.

In the murky twilight of these times, it is very difficult to identify effective leaders, that is, those persons who can distinguish between outmoded authoritarianism and natural authority. A symptom of the times is the lack of heroic or visionary leaders. That is, however, a common complaint of many ordinary Americans who, as a result, have withdrawn much of the faith they had invested in society's institutions.

This post-hierarchical time is also marked by *widespread experimentation with authority forms.* This is essentially pragmatic, expensive, and ambivalently received, and it has had mixed results. Thus the Roman Catholic Church shifted away from hierarchy to collegiality in Vatican II (1962–65), by which the authority of individual bishops was recognized as theirs by right rather than as something delegated from the Pope. The basic structure of the Church was to be collegial rather than hierarchical. Pope John Paul II began to reverse the collegial structure almost immediately after his election in 1978 and has since worked to restore the model of authoritarian hierarchy. Before the board room purge of the 1990s, General Motors attempted unsuccessfully to implement broad psychologically based efforts to dismantle hierarchies in the 1980s. A library of books has been written on new decentralized management styles, which have been applied as well in other fields, including education and law enforcement. Even the Army, the original source of the command and control concept adopted by American big business as it emerged after the Civil War, encouraged delegating broad authority to field commanders during the 1991 Gulf War.

This era also witnesses *the transformation of the purposes of institutional authority.* Schools, for example, have faltered in carrying out their traditional task of teaching language, mathematics, and history. Instead, they have tried to author noneducational goals. The basics have been replaced by two major curricular objectives: the achievement of "psychotherapeutic" goals, such as self-esteem, and political indoctrination, often based on Marxist principles, such as class warfare and the elimination of elites.

The means and goals of generative authority—human growth through human relationships—*have been monetized.* There has been an effort to translate every value, including that of spirituality, into the vocabulary of capital markets. Bureaucracies, for example, monetize human experience in the widespread application of cost-benefit ratios to the allocation and delivery of various services, from law enforcement and health care through guidelines for urban investment and large-scale waste disposal. That tendency is reflected in the monetization of the law, through its academic reinterpretation and professional application according to purely economic principles. It is impossible to author justice when outcomes are decided on the basis of what is the least costly settlement, the most profitable outcome, or who can hire the "best" and most expensive lawyers. Religious responses, including martyrdom, have been subjected to monetary analysis. Rational choice theorists, such as Richard Posner, apply monetary analysis to morality, human sexual behaviors, and the disposition of the aged.

Perhaps most strikingly, monetization becomes a substantial measure of fundamental human ethical problems, especially in making medical decisions. The transformation of health care into a for-profit business has resulted in cost's superseding clinical judgment in health care practice. For example, cost often determines the mode of therapy available to patients, such as the use of social workers instead of psychiatrists to treat the mentally ill. The merits of the therapies and the training or expertise of the therapists are often irrelevant in this market-based decision. It is, of course, commonplace, as in the lectures of Deepak Chopra, to link the pursuit of virtue with capitalistic success.

As authority fragments, *standards fade because they are cut off from their roots and pulled out of their nourishing soil.* When moral principles are decapitated from their tradition, they lose authority. The result is that nothing can be called good or bad, virtue or sin. No better or worse behavior exists, no better or worse performance occurs in any human universe because there is no basis on which to evaluate them. The only measure of an action's probity is whether it meets political or ideological expectations. The preservation and flourishing of standards depend on identifying natural authority and its claims.[9] As long as they remain unclear in the post-hierarchical darkness, standards cannot easily be restored.

When the nature of true authorship is obscured, *increased social turbulence, marked by centrifugal forces fleeing from the fragmenting center,* destabilizes society even more. That is observable in the commonplace reports of random violence and crime, such as shootings out of the now unbound night; the disintegration of whole communities;

the increase in illnesses associated with lessened standards in personal behavior, including drug use and sexual activity. According to Hannah Arendt, this also creates a psychological field ripe for paranoia and scapegoating, such as anti-Semitism and racism.[10]

In the post-hierarchical period characterized by default at the center, *bureaucracies swell along the continuum.* For example, many mayors of American cities complain about the "micromanagement by federal and state government" of their authority over their budgets. Mayor Richard M. Daley of Chicago relates how the bureaucratic stranglehold prevents money designated to help students from reaching them because administrators devour it along the way. "We spend $80 million a year on busing," he says, "moving children from school to school, doing nothing for their learning and practically nothing to solve the social problem. But the bureaucracy will not modify this in any way."[11] In every institution, the torte-like layers of administration have little to do with the primary purpose of the institution.

Signs of work dissatisfaction multiply as people find that increased experimentation, expanding bureaucratic regulations, and the transformation of their work's purpose during this post-hierarchical period make it more difficult for them to "author" what they do, that is, to bring their work product into being without interference or distortion. Widespread complaints arise that "work isn't fun any more."

The period is also marked by a frustrating dynamic: *Instead of rediscovering genuine authority, many people reinvent authoritarianism instead.* This is obvious in educational institutions that jettison their standards and their traditional role of *in loco parentis.* Trying to create something like authority *de novo,* they construct instead codes and regulations more complicated and far less human than anything in the Talmud. Those are characterized by the unforgiving intricacies that flow from attempts to define and monitor hate speech, sexism, racism, and sexual harassment. The rules are absolute, often demand draconian punishments such as expulsion, rule out free expression for any but "politically correct" views, and, in pale imitation of Soviet tactics and American fads, demand psychotherapeutic transformations for dissidents through "sensitivity training."

The culminating sign of this era is found in *institutions that adver-*

tise their own loss of authority by their massive efforts to use the authority of the law as a surrogate for the authority they can no longer generate of themselves. The law and the courts come to be viewed as the sources, interpreters, and enforcers of even such fundamentals as ethics and morals. The authority of the law itself is debated theoretically even as it is piled high with burdens that it cannot and should not carry. The environment comes to be characterized by the adversarial, confrontational ethos and practices of the law. Everything is translated, often inappropriately and with confounding results, into the legal vocabulary. When every American must "think like a lawyer," no American can author life naturally, spontaneously, or freely any more.

I

The Institutions of Intimacy:
Rediscovering Authority at Home

2

The De-authorization of Marriage

As the twentieth century began, hierarchical authoritarianism, the control of the many through the exercise of unmitigated power by the unembarrassed few, was, except in the United States, commonplace across the world. Authoritarianism seemed to be the natural energy for the hierarchical pattern adopted, again as a seemingly natural choice, by civilization's developing institutions. The latter aimed to maintain a world whose good order would mirror the universe's own good order by drawing their own blueprints according to the hierarchical cosmic design. Typified by those of monarchy, such pyramidal structures strengthened institutions while guaranteeing their own survival as the intuitive, indeed divinely ordained, way of looking at and running things. Unlimited power roosted at the top of hierarchies. While they were intended to be vehicles of authority, they were ideal mechanisms for the absolute control that is the nuclear dynamic of authoritarianism.

Institutional enhancement and preservation, rather than individual development, became a principal objective of the control mechanisms of both dynasties and papacies, whose heads wore crowns as symbols of their all-embracing authority. Ordinary people experienced that extraordinary control through the double threat of losing not only their earthly possessions but their eternal rewards as well. Control rather than freedom meant that authoritarianism overwhelmed authority in classic hierarchical/authoritarian forms.

We may understand this impulse to dominate as primary authoritarianism and appreciate how, through their vast, often interrelated bureaucracies, church and state extended their control to even the intimate aspects of life. The uses of sexual control are various and powerful. Sex in marriage was supervised carefully by the agents of hierarchical authoritarianism through the long partially dark ages during which it was important to guarantee a stable population for the kingdom or empire. Celibacy in organized religion was emphasized as a way of leading a life of sanctity, but it also provided large numbers of dependent, economically efficient personnel to serve and maintain the ecclesiastical institution. Marriages were arranged for royalty and for commoners with an eye to the acquisition of property and a guarantee of the dynasty or the family line. The virginity and inviolability of the bride were regarded as conditions in enforceable agreements rather than as ideals of the virtuous life.

Such primary hierarchical authoritarianism expressed itself by focusing on marriage as a contract rather than a human relationship and was unconcerned about individual feelings or sentiments. The authoring of their marriage by individual men and women—the exercise of their human authority, recognized by the Church as the essence of marriage—fell under the shadows of the property-oriented contract. Nonetheless, natural authority and other healthy signals of the human spirit survived, even as wildflowers did, within those walled kingdoms.

The Loss of Common Sense

How does the overall decline of the primary culture of hierarchical authoritarianism, which pulled down sensible authority with it, manifest itself to average Americans in the areas of sex and marriage? What cultural symptoms occur in the zone of intimacy when an older age passes and a new one slouches uncomfortably toward a thoroughly modern Bethlehem?

The transmission of hard-bought wisdom about sex, marriage, and childraising from the older to the younger generation has suffered a major breakdown. It may seem like common sense to learn from the past in those sensitive areas, but many contemporary people act out a resentment toward traditions, often ascribed to the outlook of the 1950s, that seem to grow out of and encourage an incurious and un-rebellious conformity. Yet they feel a profound ambivalence about whether to plunge even more deeply into a world without limits or to recapture the contentment that appears, in retrospect, to have charac-terized the now fashionably rejected past. A 1993 *USA Today* survey shows that, if given the choice, Americans would select the 1950s as the most desirable decade in which to raise a family.

The chronic uncertainty shows through, for example, in the story of "Linda, twenty-seven, [who] has just moved in with her fiance. She talks wistfully of the romance—sans sex—that existed in those days of yore. 'My grandparents were engaged for nine years; part of the time, my grandfather was away fighting in World War Two,' she recounts. 'They didn't sleep together, but my grandmother told me they came to know every other nuance of each other. Their engagement was like a jigsaw puzzle they were piecing together, starting from the border and working their way in. They found out that she enjoyed walks at the shore, that he wanted his own business. Gradually, they filled in the middle with more intimate knowledge. And when they finally made love,' Linda concludes, 'well, they made the puzzle complete.'"[1]

Linda longs, as so many younger people honestly do, for the kind of romance and love she knows existed in the past. And yet she rejects it, going against her own and a larger common sense at the same time. She and other young people may feel the future in their flesh even as they recognize a yearning about the past in their souls. Popular cul-ture, which ironically identifies itself with what it terms "freedom" in every venue, is in fact an amorphous authoritarianism that, like Robert Frost's ice, moves on its own melting. It insists on—and pos-sesses the power to drown out or ridicule other approaches—an agenda that opposes and suppresses personal authority as totally as any long-gone monarchy. Linda and her age-mates are caught in the conflict between longing to author their own lives and the insistence of the countervailing culture that they conform to a new authority-free, tradition-cleansed life-style. The popular culture is broad but shallow and fits the postauthority interlude as a mask through which, as by actors in ancient theater, the message of the protoplasmic, standard-shy interim is incessantly proclaimed.

It is very difficult for young people to recover their own capacity to author their lives—their own natural authority—when the we-never-close, highly authoritarian popular culture constantly bombards them with its lack of reference points and its general sense that, as long as they "choose" it themselves, nothing they do differs very much from anything else they might do. It is small wonder that the young find it difficult to resolve their ambivalence. Small wonder, too, that older men and women are bewildered and frustrated that their experience and judgment, although envied, seem to a younger generation part of an unusable past.

The Institution of Marriage

Institutions exist to stabilize public and private life even through periods of general cultural turmoil. At their best, they identify, preserve, and ritualize the deepest truths about the human condition. Constitutionally, institutions operate in just the opposite way from popular culture. As if by immediate osmosis, popular culture filters change rapidly, passing it through its slender membrane to the public on a broad scale. Institutions absorb and diffuse change, slowing it down, processing it through layer upon layer of their being, distilling its impurities, modifying its effects, and handing them on like time-release medication to the people. There is always an immense lag between real-time change and institutional acceptance and adjustment to it. For example, the sentiment for the abolition of slavery, as we shall note later, bloomed inside human hearts long before the institution of the law and the Supreme Court caught up with and validated that moral insight.

Institutions are nonetheless capable of sheltering within their thick walls the assumptions about human nature, such as those concerning fundamental rights, necessary for the reform of retrograde social practices and policies. Institutions provide the forum for serious dialogue on the central questions of any age. Marriage is just such an institution. It exists in and through other great institutions, such as the state and religion. Within them, and despite the ponderous but accidental hierarchical authoritarian forms they wore much as noble knights did their regal armor, they cherished indispensable convictions about the true nature of authority in itself and in marriage.

For example, the Church, weighed down by hierarchical, institutional encrustations and practices, never wavered, in the deepest vaults of its deliberations, in its conviction that freedom was an essential condition for entering a valid marriage. It also recognized and supported with its sacramental rites the fact that it is the husband and wife, rather than the Church, who author the marriage. The Church only witnesses what, in the prime meaning of authority, spouses create of themselves when they choose and promise their lives to each other. It was understood that, in the long absence of a priest in some regions, couples could enter marriage on their own. That does not mean that churches, like other institutions, cannot mistake their hierarchical-authoritarian style for the substance of their true authority. Indeed, institutions, including ecclesiastical ones, are currently in disarray because they have not distinguished between their historical forms and their transcendent substance. That would be mistaking the clothes we wear in any historical period for our souls, from which our individual authorship flows. In the same way, their outmoded structures no longer constitute adequate vesture or voice for their deep and necessary activity.

In this tradition, marriage is not a convenience or an easily terminated arrangement but rather an authoritative institution that validates and supports faithfulness as the bedrock condition for men and women who want to share a life together. Faithfulness, like faith, is a commitment to the unknown and unknowable future, summoning men and women to create, or author, a unique life and family together. Marriage transcends honoring the public legal contract, allowing spouses to go beyond themselves for the sake of each other and for their children. Fidelity is essential to protect and express the dynamic field of generative authority.

With the decline of the effective functioning of hierarchical-authoritarian institutions, the notion of marriage as a sacrament solemnized by religion, symbolized in its rites, and supported by the laws of the state has been seriously compromised. That, of course, is because no distinction has been adequately made, either by institutions or by others, between their transitory historical forms and their basic social coding and stabilizing function. Their authority still breathes, of course, beneath the fallen turrets and domes of hierarchical authoritarianism, but its cries of life are either unheard or ignored. That resembles getting rid of the golden monstrance, the spectacularly overdecorated vessel for the Eucharistic wafer used in the Catholic rite of benediction. The ornate monstrance is the elaborate hierarchical-authoritarian structure that only held but was not the Eucharist itself. Emphasize only the monstrance, empty of the Eucharistic bread, and we have the exact parallel to emphasizing the filigree of authoritarianism over the essence of natural authority. The empty monstrance cannot be raised in blessing because it no longer bears the authority of the sacrament. That is exactly what occurs when a church proposes its hierarchical structure as its central source of authority and classifies that hierarchical form as an object of faith.

That is the condition of this interval period in which, because authority in general and the authority of marriage in particular remain confused with the detritus of hierarchical authoritarianism, marriage is gradually being radically redefined. That is exactly what one would expect during the interlude in which, now that its authoritative character has been obscured, marriage can be pragmatically analyzed and endorsed on the basis of other principles, such as those of economics.

Hence in such documents as the Lutheran draft on sexual morality there is a clear call for the quasi-sacramentalization of homosexual relationships. Many other religious groups have encouraged a similar institutional affirmation of relationships that would operationally broaden the theological definition of marriage and its purposes. That, along with cultural, business, and legal willingness to grant official recognition to "domestic partnerships" that sometimes include the adoption of children by homosexual couples, comes across to the ordinary American as a drastic revision of their understanding of relationships, sexuality, and generativity.

Good moral sense does not wish to ignore or to degrade the love and fidelity that often exist between human beings in circumstances or settings that make traditional marriage impossible. Recognizing and accepting such situations does not, however, demand the de-authorization of traditional marriage by a massive shift of the locus of its expectations. Marriage has perennially stood as an institution whose ends serve those of individuals and the human race, buttressed by the true authority of Church and State. Their interest in and their duty to preserve and enlarge life also make demands on the couples entering marriage. The married state is the authorized source of expectations, so identified and seconded by ecclesiastical and civil authority rather than authoritarianism, that men and women would change themselves to honor its character.

In the new and revised version, the couple, howsoever composed, are the source of expectations, progressively identifiable and enforceable by civil law and approved by broadening ecclesiastical opinion, that marriage will change itself in order to allow almost any combination to enter and claim its title and benefits. The presumption is always made that older ideas of marriage no longer make sense and that such changes unquestionably exemplify enlightenment or an acceptance of the way things are in the real world. People are so estranged from the idea of natural or healthy authority that the notion of authorization and its healthy function never even enters the conversation. That is a classic and quite understandable interim phenomenon: the effort to improvise, on the basis of economic and other considerations, quasi-standards in a world in which authority's inherent role has been cut out of the script.

The great institutions contribute to this interval confusion because, not reading their own condition correctly, they continue to present their viewpoints in a hierarchical-authoritarian language that no longer commands attention, much less ready obedience. But they often believe that the problem lies, not within themselves as speakers, but within their flocks as listeners. Obedience, it should be noted, comes from the root *obedire*, "to listen to." Obedience is not slavish submission to authoritarian controls but rather the intuitive response to natural authority. In a discussion where participants un-self-consciously turn toward and give their attention to the one who makes the best sense of a matter, we recognize the person who speaks with authority. Such "natural obedience" is not given to false authority. Indeed, people turn away eventually from false claimants to authority; no matter how skilled they are at manipulation, they finally de-authorize themselves by their falseness and people stop listening to them.

In large part, we have stumbled into this ill-defined interlude because the great institutions that identify their authority with their hierarchical structure are, in effect, raising an empty monstrance and demanding that people accept the receptacle as if it were the sacrament. They thereby de-authorize themselves. When such de-authorization occurs, people lose faith in and turn away from institutions. Freed from their burden, they enter the void like an army that has overthrown an oppressive regime. They begin to experiment, as people are now obviously doing, with extra-institutional, trial-and-error efforts to reestablish guidelines for living. That gives rise to a companion set of shadow institutions, ranging from domestic partnerships to New Age religion, including do-it-yourself law and folkloric medicine, each making a claim on our attention. In such periods, as after the downfall of the autocrat of all the Russias, Tsar Nicholas III, the experiments with a classless state give way to a dictatorship, the reinvention in drab clothing of the autocrat.

The interlude is therefore fertile ground for the quick growth of religious organizations that are as improvised in their own way as new conjugal arrangements are in another way. They are often seemingly institutionless, such as storefront churches, or are quasi-institutions, such as the Moral Majority or the Christian Coalition. The latter are often fundamentalist and literalist in temper and practice, that is, operationally authoritarian. They reveal in their actions the interim characteristic of heavily politicized authority by their deep immersion in elections at every level. Although they are critics of the popular culture, harshly indicting the media and entertainment, they may not see how they, by reinventing moral authoritarianism, actually express and promote the conditions of the void.

Authority thereby passes out of the institution and into the hands of the masses, much as authority does from every overturned government. This provides an operational definition of how an institution, in this case marriage, may be de-authorized by the removal and diffusion of its authority during a period in which authority is itself undervalued and so easily subject to such transformation.

Sex and Marriage

Ordinary people recognize that, by a combination of institutional decay and populist improvisation, sex has been effectively separated from marriage. In the interlude, sex does not now conform itself to institutional expectations, as noted, as such institutions strive to conform themselves to sexual practices. Little thought is given to the cost to the institution of marriage or to the possibility that this may, as a weakened president undermines the presidency itself, have baleful long-term effects or that rootless experimentation may be a function of larger historical changes. Experiments such as the widespread failure to marry are, according to David Murray, "a sign of impending disaster. Cultures differ in many ways, but all societies that survive are built on marriage. Marriage is a society's infrastructure, its bridges of social connectedness. The history of human society shows that when a people stop marrying, their continuity as a culture is in jeopardy."[2]

Loosening the authoritarian grip of institutions such as the Church over sex may be understood as an overdue release of the control promoted by the generation of guilt that made people feel they were sinners for being only human. Yet there are side effects to such victories, especially when what is good—natural authority—is cast out with what is bad—hierarchical authoritarianism. Those unnamed effects tingle in the void. Marriage is separated from even its own intrinsic natural authority. That has led to the formless landscape of the interval in which, in effect, everything is the same and anything goes.

Greater sexual freedom, in and of itself, is viewed as the fruit of a noble rebellion against inhuman and repressive forces. Such a thing is validated in popular culture as an end in itself. Unqualified sexual liberation, that is, sex detached from human relationships, becomes a central tenet of the popular wisdom. Nonetheless, ordinary citizens cannot understand how the things they continue to cherish are so devalued and treated with lessened respect—that is, de-authorized—in the dominant vocal culture. They are troubled that "liberated" sex has taken such a hold, despite the side effect shower of problems it has precipitated, in the present moral vacuum.

Most men and women understand the necessity of fidelity and trust in marriage. Those elements give creative authority to relationships and enable healthy persons to transmit and enlarge life. They may not use the word "authority" in this context, but they recognize that their own emotional links need stabilizing weight, that marriage is an ongoing working out of a serious commitment to each other, to their children, and to the mystery of life itself. Such men and women sense that something is missing, but they do not clearly recognize that it is an indispensable human energy and its name is authority.

Without substantial content, that is, without expectations, obligations, and sacrifices, marriage and its intimacy deliver no rich fulfillment. "Fulfillment" is, of course, a justifying sexual revolutionary goal for individuals, but, because it is so often achieved temporarily and in a shallow and largely self-referent fashion, such activity de-authorizes itself and becomes even more elusive for those who seek it outside of the institution of marriage. "Fulfillment" is, sadly, one of the formerly great, now largely debased, American words. It is presently the promise associated as much with commodities, such as cars, underwear, or fragrances, as with human relationships. "At last," the woman sings as the Jaguar drives up in the commercial, "my love is here to stay."

Absent demanding human content, marriage is not marriage; like all things lighter than air, it easily drifts away. The sharply increased divorce rate and the rise in illegitimate births, along with their harvest of intractable emotional pain, is a sign not so much of a triumph of freedom as of the loss of the internal authority of marriage itself.

The separation of sex from marriage, achieved early in the Sexual Revolution, was made possible, in part, by the development of the birth control pill, which made far more certain and predictable the operational distinction between sex and procreation. That enhanced the already developing possibilities for financial independence for women through their more general incorporation at every level into the world of work. Breaking the link between sex and marriage, however, also severed its connection with the human capacity and need for authorship, that is, the creative and generative core of traditional marriage.

The isolation of sex from genuine human purposefulness transforms it into a "recreational" activity. "Recreational" sex is essentially de-authorized sex because it is separated from generativity and the very idea of "authoring" another life. We are not speaking of sex as the powerful expression whereby people affirm and nourish their love for each other. Such sex is integrated into the relationship, and through it people re-author their commitment to each other and give energy to their marriage. Such sex is naturally authoritative and needs no other justification.

If "recreational" sex means activity that does not promote mutual growth and serves only the subjective desires of the individual, it cannot serve those of either the partner or the community. But ordinary men and women cannot live happily or successfully if sex is little different in its possibilities and meaning from any other activity. If sex is a free-market expression, then no objection can be raised or judgment made about it in any circumstances, and it dwells in a self-constructed void.

Men and women therefore struggle to fill the moral void. They are handicapped in this effort, however, because they have also been separated from the moral principles that disappear when sex is set free of all institutional demands and traditional understandings. That is why the resulting struggle to restrain sexual behavior, or to write rules for it, is so disconnected, ineffective, and, at times, ludicrous.

On the one hand, fundamentalist religious groupings attempt a restoration of authoritarian, literalist control of sex to save society's soul. If their hierarchical-authoritarian language, like that of certain extinct tribes, can no longer be understood, it cannot be heeded by the confused masses. On the other hand, professed inhabitants of a world from which authority and standards have been exiled clumsily attempt to invent codes to govern sexual behavior that seems, in an explosion of assaults, rapes, and misunderstandings, to be out of control. Their effort to reinvent something like morality leads to a heavy, generally authoritarian, politicization of sexual behavior, as in the multistep solicitation of consent at every stage in a scenario of old-fashioned seduction that has been issued at Antioch College in Yellow Springs, Ohio.

It is not surprising that de-authorizing sex also demystifies it, obliterating its communicative possibilities. The popular culture—the mask of the formless interval—reinforces the de-authorization of human sex around the clock on television and through other media. Sensible people do not buy into the de-authorized frenzy, but it is difficult for them to escape the sex-drenched environment of this interim time. They often feel intimidated because they seem so out of step and out of sympathy with sex that has been drained of everything but a flickering eroticism. They need encouragement to trust their own feelings—the true sound of natural authority within themselves—as reliable guides to their choices in life.

In fact, most people cannot live for long in a directionless and undifferentiated sexual confusion. The complaint of lack of desire on the part of those seeking sexual therapy in the 1980s was a poignant symptom of this de-authorization, a way that the culture had of talking to itself about itself. It is ironic that in the postliberation era impotence, frigidity, and a wide range of sexual performance problems have become so commonplace. It is possible that when sex is not integrated into a loving relationship, with its resources of continuity, understanding, and forgiveness, the elements of performance, self-worth, and self-consciousness are intensified, increasing anxiety and leading those affected to seek professional help. Depersonalized sex becomes machinelike, with a demand for a uniform and reliable response. That, of course, is impossible for human beings because it omits human authorship which gives life and meaning to sexual activity.

No more revealing signal could be given. That is also why, as we shall note, power has supplanted authority as a principal variable in human relationships. Deprived of an understanding as well as an exercise of natural authority, people feel impotent throughout their beings. There is not much, they feel, that they can do about events that threaten to overwhelm them. It would be unnatural if this frustration did not show up in the sensitive indicator of sex itself.

Finally, people are exhausted by the demand to find so much in and to prove themselves through their own performance outside the authorizing and supportive context of marriage and family. Sex without love, like life without work, sounds better than its gradually dulling edge turns out to be. Meeting and committing oneself to another remains the best environment for sharing life, including sexuality, in a healthy and profoundly human manner. Missing from many reinterpretations of marital intimacy is the person, the human being or self, the author who must grow and give growth through sexuality or stumble into the poignantly echoing emptiness of this interim period.

Mistaking Power for Authority

Although "empowerment" is currently hailed as their central positive ingredient, successful marriage and family life are presumed to be unending contests for dominance. In intimate matters, healthy couples should be skeptical of power-based notions of sex and marriage. Power and authority are very different notions. Authority in intimacy is an open and freeing agency of relationship, while power is a competitive striving for franchise rights. The current emphasis on power as a desirable personal attribute should be understood as a symptom of our culture's estrangement from healthy authority.

With such confusion of vocabularies, giving people power—empowerment, as it is termed—is widely thought to be a remedy for a serious contemporary personal and social difficulty. Power's indiscriminate use as a supposedly positive and necessary endowment is, in fact, not an indication of enlightenment but a symptom of confusion. Power, not hope, was the last thing left when the Pandora's box of modern times was opened. With natural authority not yet recovered from the tangled heap of hierarchical authoritarianism, only primitive power remains as the energy and its transfer mechanism in marriage and other relationships. Power is essentially indifferent to the subtleties of love and trust. Proposed as a touchstone for happiness, it can only lead to greater frustration within and between human beings.

This explains the emphasis in popular culture on one or the other partner's need to "get the satisfaction they desire" or "get what they are looking for" out of the relationship. The focus on self-reward destroys the understanding of marriage as something to which each spouse gives to the other in a surrender that is not only of the body but of the spirit. No marriage can succeed when husbands and wives keep separate emotional accounts, looking out for their own gratifications rather than the creation, or healthy authorship, of a life together. Tension is the necessary condition of balance-of-power constructions of human relationships. That is the very opposite of the delight lovers find in being defenseless together within the precincts of intimacy.

Authority and power are easily distinguished in human relationships. Power is indifferent to whether an act is beneficial or harmful to human growth whereas authority defines itself by nurturing positive personal and communal development toward properly human goals. The objectives can be something practical, like learning a language or holding an election, or something less easily measured, such as fidelity, honor, or integrity, the true experiences by which we grow in our humanity.

Power is numb to human feeling and manipulates persons by any available means, including bribery, seduction, deceit, and blackmail, to get what it wants. The very lexicon of power reveals its true nature; we speak of power brokers, influence peddlers, and "powerful" lobbyists as predators of our institutions. Power is used in legislatures not to promote the lawmakers' possible virtues but to capitalize on their probable vices. Power's end always justifies its means. For authority, the means must be as good as the goal in view.

Power is essentially amoral, sets its own standards, is indifferent to its agents, and is wedded to the instant out of which it flows. Authority is necessarily moral, reflective, and ordered to a future outcome that represents growth in itself as well as for the human beings affected by it. Perhaps, in the human condition, the use of power in governmental and political operations is understandable as a function of such pragmatic flawed environments. There are circumstances, however, such as marriage and family life, in which the concept of power, with its aggressive and competitive connotations, is incongruous and ultimately destructive. Therefore to characterize sexual relationships as contests for the prize of power, as some sociopolitical movements have, is to make war, not love.

If love is interpreted as a function of power, then men and women must ever be on guard against each other. Not only must husbands and wives feel safe with each other, but children deserve a sense of being safe in their families, of growing up without being on guard. Healthy authority matches the needs and goals of serious intimate relationships, because its concern is not to overcome others but to fuel the growth of people who feel safe with each other.

Power may deliver big deals, but authority is made more for the small, off-peak moments of living and growing together. Authority infuses those seemingly routine moments, enlivening incidents that seem forgettable but that people ultimately treasure. Those include living at close range with each other not just in bed but in a thousand settings that range from winter breakfasts to summer vacations as well as the milestone events of anniversaries, birthdays, graduations, weddings, and funerals. Power does not know its way in these magical places in which healthy authority is completely at home.

Natural or traditional authority, the source and affirmation of time-honored principles governing sexual and marital conduct, has been pulled down like the Tsar's symbolic eagle, making it possible for the sexual revolutionaries to clatter through the great gates above which it once sat as a seal. This relic of authority has not, however, been hauled away. It remains a majestic ruin on which lesser life forms have sprung into existence. Like the islands of moss creeping along a fallen monument, efforts to supplant or make up for the irreplaceable but lost authority of morality are pathetic and ineffective substitutes.

Perhaps the most obvious strain in such development is what is called Sexual Correctness, a feeble effort to supply a surrogate for morality. In sexuality, as in every field in which "correctness" applies, it is an alternate version of hierarchical authoritarianism. Sexual Correctness prescribes orthodox beliefs and punishes those who do not accept them as vigorously as the Inquisition did with religious dogmas and dissenters in another era. As with the larger Political Correctness movement that prevails in education, this represents a shadow effort to institutionalize beliefs and practices of a pseudo-moral nature during the interim that has followed the disfranchisement of explicitly authoritarian institutions.

The "correct" sexual attitudes include the acceptance of homosexual marriage as well as the broadening of acceptable sexual behavior outside of marriage, such as teenage sexuality, living together, and casual sex. It insists on abortion rights and rejects antiabortion programs as outdated extremism. Politically correct sexuality identifies AIDS as a kind of external enemy, a function of traditional religious and governmental repression, to the cause of whose cure all other medical investigation must be subordinated. In its most extreme form, it confidently indicts every man as a potential rapist, as at the University of Maryland in the spring of 1993. A group calling itself the Women's Coalition for Change took all the identifiably male names from the student telephone directory and, as part of an antirape project, posted them as potential rapists.[3] Politically correct sexuality thus changes the focus, and thereby the subject, and in so doing sidesteps the real issue, which is the longing for moral standards, banished because they were identified with oppressive hierarchical authoritarianism rather than understood as functions of healthy authority.

Such pseudo-morality is to genuine morality what blackened stubble is to healthy wheat. Its blight suggests how far it falls short of what it is supposed to be. That is the natural consequence of detaching sex from authoritative morality and traditional values. Yet those flawed ethics are sown as good seed in the popular culture, where they flourish unexamined and are displayed regularly on television sitcoms, talk shows, and at times on news programs. Largely because of such prominence, those fragile hypotheses still intimidate people and challenge their common sense. It is not surprising, therefore, that the effort to live by pseudo-morality has left many persons less than happy and in fact puzzled, angry, frustrated, and often deeply disappointed. That, sadly, is the mood of interim life.

3

Rediscovering Authority in Marriage: Recommendations

Healthy people must not be intimidated by a culture from which they feel estranged. To reclaim natural authority in sex and marriage, healthy people must realize that there are no lobbyists for the cause of being normal. It is time for sound Americans to defend their vital constituency and to take back for themselves the healthy authority that has been ignored or usurped by the less-than-healthy for almost two generations.

But how can we tell if people are healthy? What is it about them and their ways of living together that validates a claim to psychological and spiritual integrity? Physical health is an insufficient measure of overall human health. Many remarkable physical specimens lack the balance, the judgment, or the unself-consciousness that are found in the overall fitness we recognize as signs of wholesomeness. Indeed, common sense is that spontaneous, shared appraisal that arises unbidden from within healthy people when they are confronted with excess, as in people who distort their lives, their looks, and their dispositions in pursuit of the perfect diet or the perfect workout.

When we speak of that overlooked majority, we find that the vocabulary, unlike the ever increasing classifications for physical and psychological pathology, is limited to a few words, the principal one being the term "healthy" itself. That is because healthy people are unique and cannot be readily placed into some classification shared with others showing the same symptoms of a disorder. Healthy people do not think about themselves the way the self-concerned constantly do. They are marked by freedom of judgment and action; they ride easily in the saddle of their lives. They do not behave defensively, are not always explaining themselves, seek relationships with a wide group of people, can observe and forgive their own imperfections, and have a good sense of humor. Health comes from the Old English word *hal,* which means whole; in a very real way, that notion of wholeness—of integrity of life, of fitting together well as human beings—describes them well. Even if they lack physical beauty, their wholeness makes them attractive to others. Indeed, healthy people recognize each other and become friends easily precisely because they share so much even before they meet. Love at first sight is a common experience of healthy people who fall in love with *each other* rather than get encumbered with the tangled wiring of each other's needs.

Basically healthy people can also be identified readily because they strive to live according to standards and ideals outside themselves. They do not view the pursuit of their own desires, cut off from ethics and morals, as self-justifying. They continue to live this way even though popular culture does not reward but at times ridicules them for doing so. The great problems of society—the one-third of American children born out of wedlock, the rates of sexually transmitted disease, the widespread crime and violence—generally come not from their households but rather from those already harmed by some social pathology. Healthy people survive in a popular culture controlled by the few and aimed at the lowest common denominator of the rest *because* they are healthy, that is, strong enough to survive external pressures because of their internal convictions. Popular culture presents existence in a domed stadium whose ceiling has been painted to resemble the sky. That does not fool healthy people who barely glance at the tawdry show under way but head instinctively for the exits to find the sunshine and fresh air again. That is how they feel in American culture—on the outside of it, offering and drawing support from what is healthy about each other.

Basically sound people come to agree on life's fundamentals. That is the common sense that Hannah Arendt says "regulates and controls all other senses and without which each of us would be enclosed in his own particularity of sense data which in themselves are unreliable and treacherous."[1] Common sense, for example, tells ordinary people that it is better and easier in the long run of life to tell the truth than to lie. That same insight, expressed in fidelity and honesty, holds in sex and marriage as firmly as in any other realm of life.

Such principles express their moral and spiritual ideals and serve most good people in very practical ways as well. Sensible people find that when they affirm their own moral assumptions, they are often regarded as hopelessly old-fashioned and out of synchronization with the times. The rock concert called modern culture drowns out average citizens, leaving them two uncomfortable choices: to surrender themselves to the rhythmic will of the crowd or to go into internal exile, trying to live as best they can while the band plays on around them.

As a result, healthy people feel out of place in a media-driven environment whose trends and mores do not match those of their own convictions, consciences or common sense. That healthy people experience chronic intimidation by popular culture is both quite common and quite healthy. To feel that they are different, somehow psychologically diminished, and in a real sense embarrassed by, for example, the bogus sexual personae of Madonna and Michael Jackson is actually an appropriate reaction to the shallow values of a profoundly conflicted culture. It is healthy to be repelled by the nonnegotiable insistence by dwellers in the superficial culture that traditional values in sex and marriage such as fidelity, truth, and standards can be rejected without doing emotional and spiritual harm to anyone. Emotional immaturity or illness always makes healthy people uneasy in one way or another. Indeed, the reactions of the majority of good people provide one of our most consistent and reliable measures of the human soundness or moral acceptability of any opinion or behavior.

When ordinary men and women share a negative reaction to some evidence of psychopathology masquerading as sexual sophistication, such as vile pornography, they usually pull back from the activity or the persons promoting or politicizing it. Their revulsion prompts them to return to their own lives and places, to withdraw rather than try to pick their way through an environment with which they feel so little sympathy. What they are doing, of course, is separating themselves from the craziness in culture because they find that there is no room for them inside it. That is the instinctive response of reasonably healthy people, akin to backing away from raging flames. This is how health makes itself known from within: Trust your deepest instincts, those that have proved their soundness before and are shared by other good people.

Life is not an illness for which a cure or treatment must be sought, nor is birth into the human race a trauma from whose impact we spend our lives in recovery. Neither is it a meaningless aberration to be indulged or a puzzle to whom somebody else has the answers. America's veneer culture, however, glories in the pathological like a talk-show host and speaks about it in terms of failure such as "cheating" or "infidelity," or in therapy's lexicon of "victim," "denial," "addiction," and "recovery." In such a pathology-bounded environment, nobody is allowed to be "normal" in any really healthy sense. People who think that marriage and family arrangements are neutral to personal growth are often shocked at or downplay research findings that confirm that commonsense morality is crucial to the overall development of good citizens.

Normal as a category has been pried so wide open in reference to sex and marriage that practically all diagnoses from bestiality to necrophilia now fit into it. So blurred is the term "normal" that it has lost its authority. Now protoplasmic, it reflects the fluid nature of a subjective popular culture that does not allow the existence of healthy, self-determining authority. It binds itself awkwardly together with a new brand of secondary authoritarianism, a transaction, invisible to many beneath the relativistic culture's liberating claims, in which authority is replaced by power.

This secondary authoritarianism energizes the manifestoes of the Sexual Correctness movement that, imitating the strenuous efforts of ancient religious orders, controls its adherents by manipulating the regulations they must follow to achieve perfection. A lack of "modern" sexual ideology becomes the sin against the spirit, the offense that cannot be forgiven in this supposedly sexually redemptive dispensation.

Living life humanly, that is, imperfectly, remains the only way it can be lived at all. Real authority—the ability to author one's own life and family—belongs to those who understand that in sex and marriage the imperfectly human is the only sure path. Being imperfect *is* the human condition, to be inhabited rather than cured. Sensible people intuitively understand that about themselves and everything else important in life, including sex and marriage.

Resist fads at all costs. Life's oversimplification by slogans and fads is a perennial problem for pragmatic America. Genuine faith and love that feed a family are dense transactions, never programmable, cost-efficient, or manageable by "experts." The things that count inside the world of true human intimacy are far beyond the reach of such approaches.

Rich generative human authority does not resemble a product in any way. It is never, in fact, expressed twice in exactly the same fashion. Like any truly human experience, such as the enjoyment of good weather or a magical off-the-interstate detour, the spontaneous authoring of life cannot be planned and cannot be repeated or recaptured by any formula. Nobody outside the relationship through which they occur can tell men and women how to author the best things that go on between them and within their families. Being free and natural is not the same as being impulsive and animalistic. It is a function of health and remains the essential but mysterious and unpredictable condition for authoring both a marriage and a family.

No one can write regulations for or give suggestions on how to be healthy. It comes from the inside. Nonetheless, advice is constantly and abundantly given about sex, marriage, and raising children. What are good people to do to preserve their own inner authority from being confused or overwhelmed by those voices telling them what they should believe and how they should act? As though biting on a proffered coin, they should test this advice against their own reactions to it. Through such reactions their own authority speaks to them. In sex, marriage, and family life, people make few mistakes when they follow Thomas Aquinas's centuries-old advice: "Trust the authority of your own instincts."

One can recognize healthy instincts because they lead to healthy actions. Such outcomes can be assessed by asking a few questions: Does this contemplated action promote my growth or the growth of others toward a positive goal? Will there be more of me or less of me in existence if I follow this instinct? Does the action follow the commonsense judgment of most good people as being emotionally healthy and morally sound? If I follow this instinct what am I really authoring, something praiseworthy or something questionable, something that will validate my honor or cause me to feel guilty and remorseful? Am I willing to let everyone know that I am doing this, or do I want to keep it partially or wholly hidden?

Good instincts should not be confused with random impulses, such as those that motivate people on the spur of the moment to steal or commit assault. Good instincts are bolstered by their commonsense results. Unruly impulses are followed by negative real-life consequences. Good instincts are instruments of authority, delivering outcomes that of themselves command respect; therefore, they extend and enlarge the individual's healthy authority. Acting on impulse may produce consequences that are shaming and shameful. Impulses can eat away at authority, personal and public, and must be monitored and controlled by mature persons. Unmodulated impulses, prized by popular culture, never lead to the maturity that results from humanly authored activity.

"More communication" is the current all-purpose prescription for almost any difficulty in the intimacy of marriage and family life. That vaunted "communication" is, however, no simple process nor is it an undifferentiated good. Communication is not "information," although the two are sometimes confused. Communication is related to the word communion, to that intermingling at all levels, conscious and unconscious, that least inadequately defines how spouses sense and talk in a variety of human languages to each other and to their children. Advice about communication that emphasizes the transfer and switching of intellectual freight misses the human depths and subtleties of living relationships.

Although there is a place for it, there is not enough authority in the superficial notions of communication, such as posting itineraries on refrigerator doors, to support what is required in marriage and family life. Itineraries offer useful intelligence about the physical whereabouts of family members. Communion is not so external or automatic but it provides a much deeper and far more significant sense of their spiritual whereabouts. The latter must be consulted to discover the authoritative record of the intensity of family life. Communion is the channel through which spouses author themselves, their marriage, and their families.

Healthy married persons should flee all killer bee buzzwords. The best test of such phrases or popular aphorisms is how they stand up, as noted, to a couple's own human experience: Are people really like that, can they live, for example, as if fidelity were unimportant? Does this principle emphasize a whole relationship or only a portion of it? By asking and answering such questions, men and women automatically reassert their own authority and take advantage of their commonsense immunization against the intimidation of the reigning culture. Listening to themselves, they can hear whether the advice rings deep and true or in a tinny, shallow, and untrustworthy key.

Spouses should view suspiciously any counsel about their marriage that excessively employs such concepts as "sharing," as if that were an activity between adults requiring no more of the self than a kindergarten "show and tell." If advice on "sharing" causes people to feel self-conscious, they should disregard it immediately and completely. In that way their healthy instincts assert their unmistakable authority. Invitations to "share," as if this were the easy magic or cheap grace of living, do not match the dignity of human beings. Healthy people can tell the difference between manipulations of their sentiments and true movements of their hearts and souls in their relationships with each other.

"Sharing" in this superficial sense is easy to identify: It lacks the authority that inheres in processes that are deeply anchored in human experience. No earth clings to such shallow roots. People never communicate or love each other better or improve their sex lives because they "share"; they share automatically because they already love and unself-consciously speak the many languages of intimacy in their communion with each other.

The authority of advice about sex and marriage can also be evaluated according to whether it adds to or detracts from the healthy growth of the people involved. Ideas are unhealthy when they treat the man and woman as *objects,* impersonal chess pieces to be moved to and fro on the board of intimacy. Objects are *its,* lacking gender, while subjects are always *hes* and *shes,* males and females in the fullest human sense. Recommendations are healthy when they conceptualize individuals as *subjects,* that is, as sensitive, responsible human beings whose inner states and external actions have moral and psychological effects on others. By rejecting or ignoring movements, fads, or widely accepted cultural imperatives that deal with human beings as objects, men and women rediscover and reinforce their own authority over the intimate areas of their lives.

Substantial relationships speak with a distinctive hard-won authority of their own. The television critic Walter Goodman wrote of the couples married more than fifty years chronicled on a Public Television *POV* documentary, "For Better or for Worse": "Hearing aged men and women admit they have never slept with anyone other than their spouses may strike one as quaint, particularly on television, where promiscuity is a commandment, but whatever they may have lost in sexual variety seems trivial compared to what they have built and sustained."[2] Goodman is describing the inner commanding authority of proven relationships of love and trust.

That psychologically hardy persons hold convictions different from those of the people rushing wildly past them is a signal of their inner health just as a favorable lab report is of good physical health. "Commonsense Pride," though a less-than-adequate formulation, might serve as the ennobling motto of the least-supported cohort of our citizens. No movement so named exists, however, because common sense generates self-esteem of itself. These people are not preoccupied with themselves, they are not forever analyzing themselves, they do not feel "victimized," they have little time to be "in recovery," and they manage their way through love, sex, and marriage with honesty and good humor. Their "self-esteem" is not something for which they must campaign, nor a "right" they demand from society; it is a function of their fundamental healthiness.

The surprises that sexual intimacy holds for loving couples arise from within themselves, their lack of self-consciousness and their undiminished capacity for playfulness. The spontaneous psychological strategies authored by ordinary men and women validate the general principle that imperfect, healthy people lead sex lives that are also imperfect and healthy.

Such people recognize that the intimidation they feel from prevalent modern culture is the sensible reaction of the best and most reliable aspects of their own personalities. The healthy read themselves as if they were thermometers plunged into the simmering society around them. That they feel "out of sync" is a measurement not of their own condition but of the disorders in the fad-driven universe outside them. They are definitely not the ones who are crazy. Holding on to that encompassing insight provides the indispensable and natural setting for rediscovering their healthy authority over sex and marriage.

The advice columnist Ann Landers has written, "Sooner or later all the good people in the world get to know each other." She is describing one of the small miracles of everyday life. Good people, as previously noted, *do* recognize each other and respond effortlessly in neighborliness and friendship. They often feel that they have been friends all their lives, just waiting to meet each other. They can do so because they are not defensive and make themselves instantly available to others who are not defensive. They commune right from the start. Their sense of what they hold in common is a feature of their common sense. Such unprompted communion erases every element—religion or race, for example—that often divides people.

Good people can identify with and support each other in validating their judgments about what is morally and emotionally right in sex and marriage. Bolstered within, their alienation from culture is immediately reduced and their confidence in their own authority is instantly expanded. As a result they feel more comfortable following their common sense to make common cause with other sensible people on every level in following and promoting undefensively the values in which they believe and by which they try to live. The essential and indispensable core of the moral authority of common people is found in its imperfection, its utter humanity, its matching instead of undercutting or overruling the way men and women actually are. Breaking out of the Custer's Last Stand formation into which the media-dominated culture has driven them, healthy people find that, possessing genuine human authority, they are not surrounded by, but themselves surround, the forces that have de-idealized, de-institutionalized, and de-authorized sex and marriage.

Health is not so much perfection as striving to live by the best parts of one's self and to live up to the highest ideals rather than to live down to the meanest or crudest possibilities of existence. Through those simple options, men and women rediscover and reclaim authority over the intimate geography of their lives.

Build communities based on common convictions. Buoyed by the confidence their own good health gives them, people readily affiliate with others who share their convictions. Such a group will vary enormously as to race, creed, and political party. That is part of what makes its members healthy and gives enormous strength to their common cause. Such banding together, which may be strengthened through their prodding of such institutions as churches, schools, and local governmental resources for support of various kinds from meeting halls to family-friendly policies, ends their sense of isolation and their feeling that they lack the platforms from which to make their voices heard.

Forming effective alliances depends on the quality that is always present in such healthy cohorts, authority itself. Among sound people, authority to give voice to and lead a specific movement to secure a common good is very different from the power struggles that characterize groupings in which individual ambition is primary. Some person speaks with authority on some matter, and other healthy people recognize and, in the fundamental sense of obedience, willingly "listen to" them. That is the dynamic that can be counted on to provide the energy and direction for organizations that want to accomplish, in line with authority's philosophical purpose, a good that lies outside and beyond each of its members. Such groups, then, "author" themselves; while not immune to minor disputes, as no one is in the human condition, they are healthy enough to overcome them in order to push toward a common good. Those alliances may be as small as a neighborhood or as big as a nationwide or global network. The Space/Information Age makes it easier for such people to find one another and join together even across otherwise daunting geographical divides.

Americans who take a stand against the forces that belittle traditional attitudes toward sex and marriage in favor of new, improvised arrangements are often dismissed, as we have noted, as captives of right-wing conservatism or fundamentalist Christian zealotry. In fact, most of those unsung and unchronicled Americans are hostage to no extremist group. They represent the great center of the nation, and their instincts are strongly validated by a flood of research reports on family life. Those results should encourage them to make their case together against the marginal superficial culture whose "power" shrivels in the light of their authority. Such men and women were in the novelist George Eliot's mind when she wrote, "for the growing good of the world is partly dependent on unhistoric acts; and that things are not so ill with you and me as they might have been, is half owing to the number who lived faithfully a hidden life, and rest in unvisited tombs."[3]

Realize that authority's moment has come. The not accidental coincidence of the decline of hierarchical-authoritarian structures and the birth of the Space/Information Age suggests the arrival of a great opportunity for healthy people to manifest their authority and to provide the kind of leadership for which America sorely yearns. The interval drags on, marked by halting and at times bizarre experimentation with standards and organizational forms. Authority's moment has come, but it depends on healthy persons' taking leadership in defining freely the meaning of natural authority and showing how it can serve as the basis for institutional and cultural revival. Success depends on clearly distinguishing repudiated authoritarianism from healthy authority and helping other struggling elements of the culture to grasp and incorporate those understandings in their own efforts at rehabilitation. The Space/Information Age, as observed, provides the nonhierarchical means to communicate such insights to those hungering and thirsting for new ways to manage the chaotic features of the interim period. This is no easy task for people accustomed to surviving against the odds and in a world that, however desperate for new leadership, does not yet grasp the difference between authority and authoritarianism. If healthy people took as their task nothing more than making that distinction clear, they would change the world.

4

The De-authorization of the Family

Understanding, transmitting, and supporting natural or healthy authority is the fundamental responsibility of the family. It is critical as well, as Tocqueville noted, to the success of democracy.[1] The effective pursuit of happiness, an active rather than a passive occupation, is made possible through the human growth that takes place within an intact family. The entire country is strengthened if the basic unit of its culture, family life, is strengthened. Out of self-interest alone, Americans cannot afford to misread or misinterpret the relationship between the progressive collapse of family life and the deterioration of the common life of the republic.

What happens to a country happens first in its families. Along with the structures of other institutions, family structures have suffered damage and have been the subject of widespread experimentation in the current interim. Research confirms what ordinary people already observe: the fever spike of family problems during this period of marital disruption. The tale is told in melancholy fashion in small-town newspapers that print new marriages on one page and recent divorces on another. Nationwide statistics support the commonsense impression that many marriages, begun in hopeful celebration in one listing, pass, often in less than a year, to the second sad display. Three of every five first marriages now end in divorce.[2]

After the enormous dislocations of two world wars and the Great Depression, America regained its balance at midcentury and witnessed a higher proportion of its children living in stable two-parent families than at any other time before or since. When John F. Kennedy was elected in 1960, 9 of every 10 children lived with two parents at home. A generation and a half later, when George Bush entered the White House, only 7 of every 10 did so. Almost three-quarters of the Kennedy-era children lived with two natural parents who were married only once. On the eve of the 1990s, the figure was just above half. As America passes into the shadows cast by the advancing millennium, half of the country's children can expect to spend at least some time in a single-parent—usually the mother—family, almost all because of divorce.

Of the children born between 1950 and 1954, only 19 percent of whites and just under half of blacks spent some time living in a single-parent family by the time they reached seventeen. In 1960 only 9 percent of all children under eighteen lived with a lone parent. For white children born in 1980, the estimate has grown to 70 percent and, over 90 percent for black children. The fastest-growing new family type, the evidence of interim experimentation with institutional forms, is single-parent households, 9 out of 10 of which are headed by a woman.[3]

While some argue that this is evidence of evolutionary growth, common sense, bolstered by research, suggests that to call this progress is naïve at best and propagandistic at worst. Those outcomes are indications of a lost sense of authoring, or natural authority, and a blindness to its well-documented consequences. Children in single-parent families are two to three times as likely as children in two-parent families to have emotional and behavioral problems. They are more likely to drop out of high school, to get pregnant as teenagers, to abuse drugs, and to be in trouble with the law.[4]

During this post-hierarchical-authoritarian interlude the diffusion and dilution of natural authority have issued into an unparalleled deterioration of the health of the family as a social institution. Families have lost their natural authority over their members and, as a result, a measure of their social and generative functions. Like a genetically damaged infant, the family is smaller in size, is less stable or healthy, and can expect a shorter life span. Social analysts confirm the self-concern or narcissism that cripples natural authority by poisoning people's capacity to commit themselves to persons or causes that do not gratify their own needs. As a result they cannot author new lives or foster future generations; when they do have children, they often congratulate themselves as if they were brave pioneers in a previously unexplored land. Unfamiliar with authority as a generative concept, such persons are found to be less willing to invest time, money, and energy in family life and more likely to turn instead to investments in their own satisfaction through pursuing material things, bodily fitness, and other strategies of self-enhancement.

There is no substitute for the family in carrying out certain functions critical for the waxing rather than the waning of children and society. The family makes a home together, a sacred yet profoundly human place, the one, as Robert Frost says in the "Death of the Hired Hand," that "when you have to go there, they have to let you in." These nontransferable functions include giving birth to and successfully socializing children; the free rather than calculated provision of care, affection, and companionship to its members; the sharing of economic resources, especially shelter, food, and clothing; and, as vitally essential for developing authorship as it is rarely discussed, healthy monitoring and regulating of sexuality so that it is integrated successfully as human, rather than random, inconsequential behavior, whose meaning and purpose enhance the growth of persons and society.

Childbearing's decrease over the last thirty years is linked with a loss of the very sense and mystery of authoring, that is, the generative and authoritative functions of fatherhood and motherhood. The weakened embrace of parenthood as a satisfying role in life matches the bleaching away of the stigma that was once associated with childlessness. When having children is valued less, "life" is reserved, like the best of the wine, for adults. The result is that in America children now constitute a much smaller proportion of the population than ever before, dropping from one-third in 1960 to a little more than one-quarter near the century's end.

Instead of signaling evolving life, such changes resemble those that occur after death, the progressive loosening of the organism's grasp on life. Like the body, the institution gradually decays and stiffens as the family's ties and natural authority dissolve because of the dilution of the relationships between the parents and children. The vacuum of parental authority is quickly filled by the influence of peer pressure and the mass-media culture. So much has been bet on contemporary marriage's delivering happiness to the man and woman who enter it that some expect it to deliver the growth and satisfaction by itself and suppose that they need not strive to author it from within themselves. Inevitable problems and crises are therefore less acceptable and much more difficult to manage. A grim inevitability attends the separation and divorce that rise spectrally as the next choices. Indeed, this is the one path most traveled during the interim period.

The steady century-long decay of hierarchical-authoritarian structures is a common observation in social and historical analysis. But the work of natural authority in family life—the nurturance and growth of the next generation—has remained urgent and, where successful, has been carried on through the healthy authority that has survived in healthy parents. As noted before, natural authority has gone largely out of style but it has not gone completely out of existence. It survives in and through the relationships that healthy people author even when the culture barely acknowledges and seldom rewards them for doing so. The very namelessness of the overall problem hampers good parents because authority is hardly mentioned in any national conversation on our cultural dilemmas. Still lumped with the remains of hierarchical authoritarianism, natural authority is considered a negative force rather than a positive energy in the work of raising children. The renewal of family life and its expansive effect on society depend on distinguishing the freeing effects of natural authority from the stifling impact of controlling authoritarianism.

Barbara Dafoe Whitehead captures a national dilemma when she observes that "the debate is not simply about the social-scientific evidence. . . . It is also a debate over deeply held and often conflicting values. . . . If we fail to come to terms with the relationship between family structure and declining child wellbeing, then it will be increasingly difficult to improve children's life-prospects, no matter how many new programs the federal government funds."[5]

Nobody, however, sets out to fail at marriage, family life, or child-rearing. Divorce and single-parenthood touch almost every citizen in some way or other. Righteous indignation or moral condemnation is a reaction as inappropriate as automatically endorsing those changes as progress.

Whitehead concludes that "not only does the intact family protect the child from poverty and economic insecurity; it also provides greater noneconomic investments of parental time, attention, and emotional support over the entire life course. This does not mean that all two-parent families are better for children than all single-parent families. But in the face of the evidence it becomes increasingly difficult to sustain the proposition that all family structures produce equally good outcomes for children."

The present neglect of natural or healthy authority in family life is a bitter and unanticipated effect of the rejection, spurred by progressive system failures within them as well as revolutionary assaults from without, of any authority that seems related to, or dependent on, hierarchical-authoritarian institutions. Democracy itself is construed by many as a movement against social hierarchies or elites of any kind, to be constitutionally pitted, without distinction, against authority. Democracy's franchise is thought to arise from a primordial battle in which the dragon of external control was slain by heroes whose return we still cheer as our closest claim on glory.

Whitehead situates the crisis of the family within the present culture of democracy itself. In America, the breakup of the family has "been greeted by a . . . triumphant rhetoric of renewal [depicting] family breakup as a drama of revolution and rebirth. The nuclear family represents the corrupt past, an institution guilty of the abuse of power and the suppression of freedom. . . . In short, family breakup recapitulates the American Experience."

That produces what the political philosopher William Galston terms the "regime effect," by which the original political values of the country—individual rights, personal choice, and egalitarian relationships—have come to define social relationships as well. Those American values define the conditions under which we want to live. They can also produce side effects. Under the regime effect, Whitehead observes, "the family loses its central importance as an institution in the civil society, accomplishing certain goals such as raising children and caring for its members, and becomes a means to achieving greater individual happiness—a lifestyle choice."

Children are cast as equals in the new family scenario. Dependent children cannot "express their choices according to limited, easily terminable, voluntary agreements [or] act as negotiators in family decisions, even those that most affect their own interests. . . . Perhaps more than any other relationship, the parent–child relationship—shaped as it is by patterns of dependency and deference—can be undermined and weakened by the principles of the regime."

Quoting Tocqueville's shrewd observation that an individual society depends on a communitarian institution like the family for its continued existence, Whitehead concludes that it is impossible and self-defeating to model the family on the liberal state or to attempt to govern it by that state's principles. Ironically, the family in which natural authority is exercised is the critical seedbed for the very virtues required by a liberal state. A good family authorizes the characteristics on which that state depends. They include responsible independence, self-restraint, responsibility, and moral conduct, each a star in the flag of a free, democratic society.

"The erosion of the two-parent family," Whitehead notes crucially, "undermines the capacity of families to impart this knowledge; children of long-term, welfare-dependent single parents are far more likely than others to be dependent themselves. Similarly, the children in disrupted families have a harder time forging bonds of trust with others and giving and getting help across the generations. This, too, may lead to a greater dependency on the resources of the state." As she had noted, "If the family fails, then the entire experiment in democratic self-rule is jeopardized."[6]

The healthy family is the keystone in the arch of American liberal democracy. At present the government, like many before it, has yet to commit itself to supporting the natural authority of intact families so much as it has to the elimination of smoking and other health hazards. The failure to address the results of the de-authorization of family life is a function of the long-term failure to distinguish between the healthy authority that is so good for children and the liberal state, and the hierarchical authoritarianism that is so bad for both. Authority has fallen victim to mistaken identification. As a result the land that prides itself on individualism and choice cannot understand that they flourish only if natural authority also grows vigorously. Thus, the great corrosive problem remains without a name and without a voice during the long gray interim.

The family is essential to individual and democratic health because it is the primary environment, as the charged atmosphere is for lightning, for the discharge and transfer of the positive energies of authority. We live at a time in which the invisible impact of our way of treating each other is increasingly being realized. The crime of sexual assault committed on the child, for example, lingers like a just-inflicted wound, unaffected by time's passage, deep in the psyche of the individual. This unseen world is that of family life. If its psychological field is damaged, untended, or planted with weeds, the yield will inevitably be stunted and bitter. What happens between family members, especially between spouses and between them and their children, is psychologically decisive. This cannot be an area to which we, or any democracy interested in its own survival, can long remain indifferent.

5

Rediscovering Authority in the Family: Recommendations

Real authority—the capacity to author their marriages and families success-fully—lies, like the Kingdom of God, within people themselves. Natural authority, as previously discussed, exists only in and through relationships between human beings. The living family, not the handbook or the flow chart, is therefore its ideal medium. Social policy legislation may support families trying to achieve authentic values, but it cannot create them.

The moments in which healthy authority touches and enlarges others are usually undramatic and, in the course of busy days and years, go unremarked and unnamed. A keener realization that the occasions for natural authoring constitute the serviceable lining rather than the fancy trim of ordinary life deepens the confidence of parents in their spontaneous, intuitive and unself-conscious expression of their personal authority in every seemingly commonplace incident, such as maintaining the underrated but vitally important stable routine of intact family life.

For couples, the focus must be on their own marriage relationship through which they author, nourish, and oversee the growth of their continuing marriage and the family to which they give life. Through their marriage and family, rather than through becoming rich or famous, they fulfill their profound human need to be generative. That is another way of saying that healthy authority is a distillate of healthy, loving, less-than-perfect relationships. Some of what is healthy makes up for most of what may be lacking of perfection in the un-self-conscious ways in which average men and women author their family lives. Exercising authority is fundamentally spiritual work.

"Marriages," Ann Landers once wrote, "may be made in heaven but the maintenance work is done down here on earth." The maintenance work of keeping marriage and family alive and healthy is done by the husband and wife as they function together, without thinking much about it, in the easy ways of old friends, that is, confidently and simply, almost without looking up, within their intimate world. In short, being a creative human author includes the self-monitoring, self-discipline, and homely hard work of growing in tandem with spouse and children. Unlike writing a book or carving a statue, such open-ended authorship consumes and gives birth to itself across time but never exhausts itself, never, in a real sense, ever finishes its work or reaches its goal. There is a hint of the eternal in the never ending cycle of authorship.

Healthy marriages resemble healthy individuals; they are harder to describe, as we have noted, than unhealthy relationships or pathological personalities. Nonetheless, the richness of emotionally healthy couples can, in very broad terms, be described, as can their role in giving birth to and nourishing a happy family around their own relationship. "All happy families are the same," wrote Tolstoy quite accurately. In every case their authenticating watermark is a true loving relationship between the spouses. That is their energy source for authoring their children and for creating with them something that transcends yet contains them, this third spiritual entity, the happy family.

Families are a prime example of how authority thrives even within a roughly hierarchical design that could easily express authoritarianism instead. In healthy families it is found that natural authority flows from the parents who exercise it as it is meant to be, in relationship to their children to inspirit their growth to full-term adults. They are in charge and do not yield their ultimate authority to the children. Healthy parents are not "heavy handed," the psychiatrist Jerry M. Lewis writes. "Rather they provide . . . a quality of easy leadership. . . . Rarely did the parents [studied] appear authoritarian. . . . In this way, the differences between the roles of parent and child were clear. There was a generation gap, but it was not an angry, conflicted one."[1]

While such families experience the garden variety of troubles and misunderstandings built into the human situation, these are not the conflicted, never resolved center of their common life. Trusting their own instincts, such parents avoid the disruptive collateral alliances or chronic ineffectiveness often observed in troubled families.

Freedom is the condition that people seek to provide for those they love. Much like the earth's atmosphere, healthy freedom is a mysterious but necessary condition for human life, except that it is not chemical but psychological in nature. Freedom connotes a peaceful region or a place of safety, which is perhaps as good a definition of the atmosphere of family life as we are likely to find. It is the safe place or "space" where human beings need not be on guard and so can become their true selves. Far from being a vague, unwatched, or wild space, freedom refers to the safe place that people who love each other strive to create for each other.[2] It is exactly what many children are denied in homes shattered by conflict.

Curtailing freedom, tyrants destroy the space it needs, crowding people ruthlessly together, degrading them by denying them privacy and intimacy. Authoritarianism is here clearly distinguished from authority; authoritarianism seeks to eliminate freedom's space while authority seeks to expand and safeguard it. As Hannah Arendt notes, totalitarianism's terror "destroys the one essential prerequisite of all freedom which is simply the capacity of motion which cannot exist without space."[3]

Albert Camus writes of what we feel when we enter the space of fully authored freedom: "Freedom is not a reward or a decoration that is celebrated with champagne. Nor yet a gift, a box of dainties designed to make you lick your chops. Oh no! It's a chore . . . and a long-distance race, quite solitary and very exhausting. No cheap champagne, no friends raising their glasses as they look at you affectionately. Alone in the prisoner's box before the judges, and to decide in face of oneself or in the face of others' judgment. At the end of all freedom is a court sentence; that's why it is too heavy to bear, especially when you're down with a fever, or are distressed, or love nobody."[4]

Such freedom implies trust, vigilance, and concern as well as structures and expectations; in short, it necessarily reflects responsibility for another person's safety and wellbeing. That is a critical aspect of the sacred work of the family. Absent such responsible freedom—far different from the random "anything goes" distortion—all family members lose their safety, especially the children, who, as if uninoculated, are then vulnerable to every social ill. Although freedom is *the* necessary condition for the exercise of healthy authority, it is also a function *of* healthy authority. Freedom cannot exist without authority any more than the one who is loved can exist without the one who loves.

Parents should recognize the great value of even the smallest rituals as the reinforcers of health in family life. As the sacraments of ordinary life, rituals not only symbolize and express, for example, important truths about marriage and family but contain within themselves some of the latter's essence and true mystery.

Neither a menu nor a nourishing diet describes the profound ritual of eating together through which a family symbolizes its unity and recapitulates its history by authoring, in the very moments of sharing the meal, a revised edition of their life together. It possesses the healthy tension and reward of a live performance in which, although it is unrehearsed, each member understands his or her evolving role.

A lot of the work of a family is done around the dinner table. For a family's essential work is to be in relationship, member to member in almost infinite combinations that constantly transform themselves. In a healthy family it is also its play, its field of delight. The meal together is far more than a representation of a family. Sharing their daily bread, its members enter such moments together, living in that intimate veil of relationship that is changed by the presence of an outsider, or changes the outsider.

The evening meal is the setting, in a variety of religious traditions, for its most sacred gatherings. The Passover Seder, for example, brings the family together precisely to recall its members' ties to each other and to the Jewish people that authored them. The history of that people is recalled and symbolically reenacted through a ritual meal. Furthermore, the feast is sunk deeply into seasonal rhythms by being set according to the first full moon after the vernal equinox, the celebration of new light and new life. The Christian Eucharist builds on that tradition, thereby incorporating its mythological underpinning as its own as it reenacts the sacrifice of Christ under the symbols of bread and wine shared by his followers. Throughout history, inviting others to take a meal has meant to bring them into the circle of intimacy, into one's family, into one's life.

Rituals, even those turned as silvery dull as driftwood through routinization, are never fully dead because they carry the cells of living memories and possibilities within them. They may be cleansed and polished until at least some of this life within them glows again. Rituals match the needs of human beings.[5] If they are deprived of them, men and women miss, and may not be able to make up for adequately, what rituals carry, as the heated iron does fire, as both fact and mystery, about what it means to author and be authored in that free and safe environment of family life. Natural rituals, such as eating together, are powerful and fundamental occasions of life. They are therefore beyond organization and efficient systematization. Their mystery resides in and to some extent depends on their quality of never being finished and their resistance to being used up. That is why their effects do not wear out. Rituals break open the timelessness that inheres, of all places, in the passing moments of family life. The meal therefore offers, as the right word does, the completed meaning of the experience that everyone brings to the table. A family authors itself—discovers, acknowledges, affirms, and takes emotional possession of its own creation—through such rituals.

Unexpected or inexplicable changes differ from healthy or spontaneous modifications of the ritual. The former may interfere with the authoring of family life or life in any other ongoing structure of relationship. "Somebody's been sitting in my chair" echoes from the fairy tale as a human protest about the importance of rituals as reflective of the proper ordering of relationships at a family meal. Remove the mother and father, the authors of the family, and the atmosphere is less free, the space is not as safe as it is when they are there.

Loss through death, divorce, or unavoidable absence is not without impact, and a reordering must take place, as, for example, when a single parent must preside alone. But the place of authority must be filled by a parent who understands that occupying it is a necessary aspect of a life-expanding ritual. That is why children, supervised by an older sibling or a stranger while parents, or a parent, are away, are happy to see them return to reclaim their proper chairs at the dinner table again. They make the family whole, restoring its integrity by replenishing the vital energy of their authority to this central ritual.

Meals are also the setting for the sensible socialization of children. As Joseph Campbell puts it, rituals, such as family meals, are occasions of social imprinting. "Myths," he writes, "are the mental supports of rites; rites the physical enactment of myths. By absorbing the myths of his social group and participating in its rites, the youngster is structured to accord with his social as well as his natural environment, and turned from an amorphous nature product, prematurely born, into a defined and competent member of some specific, efficiently functioning social order."[6]

Recent research on family rituals reinforces their relationship to the successful socialization that flows from good family life. It suggests that if you grow up in a family with strong rituals, you're more likely to be resilient as an adult.

Without directly making it a goal, self-esteem is found to be higher in parents and children who view their family rituals as positive. College students from such families are better able to handle the stresses of college. In investigations of the families of alcoholic parents, the continuity of family rituals is correlated with the decreased likelihood that the children will become or will marry alcoholics. For members of families in which at least one parent is an alcoholic, but which place high value on rituals, the latter seem to channel off anxiety.[7]

Rituals as Agents of Socialization

The social nature of the ritual must be preserved against the fragmentation caused by clashing schedules or people casually feeding themselves alone. Other sources of distraction and disintegration include phone calls and television viewing, which leave the family members physically present but spiritually and psychologically removed from each other. If the rite itself is gutted, it quickly becomes a condemned building that does not invite life or offer shelter and cannot be safely inhabited. The meal is the family classroom in which children learn such lessons as sensitivity to the needs of others and how to postpone their own gratification, that is, how to wait for the sake of others or for the importance of the ritual itself. It is at the family meal that children learn manners, the lesser but profoundly important rituals that make life with others possible. Such basic grounding in the ways of civility are not insignificant in the maintenance of civilization. One of the most important functions of parental authority is to ensure that the principal family ritual—sharing the main meal—is observed so that it can fulfill its many functions in as healthy and un-self-conscious a way as possible.

The observance of birthdays, anniversaries, graduations, and weddings provides a sequence of rituals that both memorialize and restabilize, as well as redefine, families as they develop. Even such occasions as the death of grandparents become extraordinarily important as moments in which a family gathers unto itself, the eldest and the youngest, to reset its clock, so to speak, and to readjust its internal relationships—in short, to rediscover itself and its authority.

Parents should rediscover and reinstate without apology the stories, symbols, and celebrations of the feasts of their distinctive religious traditions. These rites and symbols bear enormous positive authority. They recapitulate the ideals, customs, and expectations of a family that, after all, has come from other families whose members share not only the same genetic traits but the same spiritual aspirations as well. Healthy authority delivers a sense of identity through symbols that, like great art, music, or literature, speak directly to the spiritual depths of human beings in ways that nothing else can. A diet of American culture, with its noisy emphasis on surfaces, starves people spiritually. Parents who wish to strengthen their authority should see their religious tradition as a fundamental and indispensable source of assistance.

If you want to author adults, be an adult and make a renewed act of confidence in your good instincts and common sense. As noted, common sense may be understood as the sense of the healthy community, that is, what the majority of sensible people feel is the right that should be chosen and the wrong that should be rejected. The judgments of common sense are transmitted on everyday wavelengths: in neighborhood life, casual conversations, and the ethos of communities bound by the same moral traditions. Such opinions are not easily swayed by what is "in the air," although at times they are drowned out by the white noise of the surrounding culture.

Children need their parents to function at the adult level of development, to resist their constant manipulations and to frustrate their minor rebellions. Children cannot grow unless some healthy and constructive tension exists between them and their parents. As with the research on learning, neither absolute unrelieved tension nor complete relaxation promote learning. Some moderate tension is required for learning to take place effectively.

Children learn self-control through the experience of being sensibly controlled by their parents. Parents who place healthy expectations on their children express their constructive authority in a living rather than an abstract way. They help children learn to exercise authority over themselves by being adult, a state that allows them to communicate health unself-consciously throughout their families without looking for or contriving artificial ways to do so.

Being and remaining an adult does not depend on perfect execution but on homelier virtues, such as consistency, self-control, and understanding. It is a challenge that is best met by two parents working cooperatively to meet its demands. Authority shared sensibly by a mother and a father is far easier to maintain than it is when it must be sustained for whatever reason by one parent.

The "generation gap" is not a regrettable chasm of separation but a necessary and helpful reality. Parents cannot author their children in a healthy manner if they are not distinguished in a number of natural ways from them. Their capacity to do authority's first work, that is, to be generative, is correlated with their preservation of and capitalization on the generational difference between them and their children.

Friendships outside the family circle become a possibility because children first experience successful trusting relationships inside the family. These prepare children for the adventure of friendship but they are not themselves friendships, which are reciprocal discoveries of each other's qualities by equals. The relationships of parents and children are never realistically equal. William Safire expresses a father's longing this way: "We want our intrinsic authority back. This essential prerogative of fatherhood has been stolen from us by children who want us to be their friends and by those children's mothers who insist on shared paternalism."[8]

A question to Ann Landers from a mother who discovered that her daughter, an eleven-year-old sixth-grader, was having sexual relations with a fifteen-year-old boy, is illustrative. Not wanting to appear "old-fashioned," she wonders, "I'm not sure it would be a good idea to confront her with the evidence and insist she abstain from sex until she is more mature. I don't want to ruin our good relationship." The columnist's response is characteristically sensible and direct: "Woman, are you out of your mind?"[9]

Denying children the experience of the healthy and confident authority that is necessary for their own growth limits their capacity for human intimacy, the work, as Erik Erikson has suggested, possible only after adolescence is completed. He suggests that it is only after a reasonable sense of identity has been established that real intimacy with the other sex (or, for that matter with any other person or even with oneself) is possible.

Many American children are denied the free experience of their childhood by parents who demand that children become what they want them to be rather than themselves in such areas as athletics, studies, and career choice. Allowing children to be themselves rather than little grown-ups is one of healthy authority's best gifts to them. Allowed to be themselves, they become themselves.

Some parents, in thrall to the regnant culture, mistreat their children subtly, not by physically abusing them but by psychologically mishandling them. They blur generational distinctions, regarding the children as deliberative partners instead of dependent and immature human beings. For example, they discuss and reason with offspring long before they are capable of such activities, forcing the children into adult roles that they cannot handle. Parents who refuse to discipline their children because that would be "to use violence" against them are also plagued with modish and unhelpful ideas.

Parents who expect their children to live on adult schedules put their own gratifications first and do not fully understand and cannot respond to their children's needs. Including infants, for example, as companions at late dinners at restaurants or at night football or baseball games is not uncommon in a self-centered culture that does not encourage parents to be adults and does not allow children to be children.

Parents cannot author their children by expecting the children to be co-authors with them, discussing their diet and daily schedule at length with them. That takes away the opportunity they have to be children in need of sensible control and hundreds of decisions made about their lives in which they have no vote. Authority cannot be delegated to a child for it remains ever the task of, and anchored in, the parents.

Such fads are largely middle-class temptations, made possible by a degree of affluence and access to the popular magazines that serve as the fad-bearers of the culture. Indulging in these fads is a luxury. Far more stark for children is the near chaos of families so deprived and ill-managed that fads are an unimaginable indulgence. Yet chaos correlates not with material poverty but with spiritual poverty. Many poor parents are rich in natural authority and hand that on as an imperishable legacy to their children. Being adults, comfortable with the exercise of natural authority, is the prime way parents guarantee that their offspring will become adults themselves.

Impose your values on your children. Parents author their children. Rather than retreat to a neutral corner to "let their children make up their minds for themselves," they must nourish them and educate them in the tradition into which they were born. That is not an authoritarian undertaking but the work of healthy authority that seeks to promote the physical, emotional, and spiritual development of its subjects. It is never accomplished by indifference or by laissez-faire parenting, the ill-founded and dangerous idea that, left on their own, children will flower in these crucial areas totally from within themselves.

The mass of research points to an ineluctable conclusion. Parenting, that is, the ongoing authoring of the young, is a complex process that demands the physical, emotional, and spiritual presence and attention of adults. Popular culture makes "the imposition of values" a prime danger and a social quasi-felony.

Good parents have no choice if they wish to author their children in a healthy manner except to be authorities and models to them. They are not thereby necessarily authoritarian or fascistic. "Impose" may seem an unfortunate word, because it tingles with an aura of negative connotations, of forcing something unreasonably on others. In this context, however, it refers to the active and positive work of authority in parents' handing over, at least as carefully as they would their physical assets and estates, their convictions and beliefs to the next generation.

It is, in fact, child abuse to neglect or fail to act according to a set of principles in which you actually believe. It has not been uncommon in recent years for certain thoroughly secularized parents who have abandoned their own religious practices to find their children seeking those practices out to revive and adapt them once more. Often stringent dietary and other practices of a demanding and penitential nature are involved. The younger people act as if they were making up for tradition deprivation, as if they had a specific hunger for what their own tradition could authoritatively hand on to them.

Such adult children are telling the parents who raised them in tune with a spiritually barren culture that they desperately miss something that their mothers and fathers should have given them when they were growing up. Judge Abraham Lincoln Marovitz of Chicago has said of such parents, "They were so anxious to give their children the things they did not have that they forgot to give them the things that they did have."

Good parents who make every effort to author their children in

commonsense ways may find that at certain ages the children will examine, question, and test the limits of their authority and their traditions. That is a much better situation than that observed in families
whose basic structural flaw is that they provide no structure, beliefs,
or boundaries with any content worthy of examination or any expectations sufficiently defined to be subjected to testing.

Good parents, anxious to bolster their authority without becoming
authoritarians in the process, should not, therefore, hesitate to make
demands on their childrens' behavior, to set expectations and rules,
and to use both rewards and punishments in helping their children to
acquire discipline over themselves. Healthy parents need not be harsh
to be consistent in the ideals they propose and in their anticipation
and monitoring of the ways in which their children pursue them.

Parents need to be present in the home physically and psychologically.
Among the fondest memories that people carry into adulthood are
those of working as members of the same family on projects of common interest. Whether it is sharing in home chores, doing the dishes,
or building a porch, a summer house, or a model railroad setup,
working together binds family members in a way that few other
things can. That involves the generations in shared authorship, thus
bringing into play all the positive energy of authority, enhanced because it is shared and because it creates something that stands free of
them but is a function of their cooperation and a symbol of their relationships and their vital family life.

If undifferentiated television constitutes, as many insist, the culture
of America, mothers and fathers must work hard not only to supervise
what their children watch but to turn it off in order to read the books
and stories that reinforce their own healthy parental authority while
also broadening and deepening the character development of the
young. Christine Hoff Sommers makes a strong case for the role of literary classics in moral education: "To understand 'King Lear,' 'Oliver
Twist,' 'Huckleberry Finn,' or 'Middlemarch' requires that the reader
have some understanding of (and sympathy with) what the author is
saying about the moral ties that bind the characters and that hold in
place the social fabric in which they play their roles. . . . I am suggest-

ing that . . . children become acquainted with their moral heritage in literature. . . . The best moral teaching inspires students by making them keenly aware that their own character is at stake."[10]

Such refreshing common sense makes a good library, linked with the other institutions of faith and tradition, an extraordinary vehicle for expressing and expanding the natural authority of parents. Most mothers and fathers have books they cherish from their own childhood and adolescence. Handing them on is a way of transferring not only their moral content but the spirit and tradition of the family itself. As Jim Trelease puts it, "I read because *my* father read to *me*. And because he'd read to me, when my time came I knew intuitively there is a torch that is supposed to be passed from one generation to the next."[11]

The choice of good books is therefore one of the prime ways in which parents can express their authority in a positive, creative, and generative way. Many reading lists reflecting the best in literature and the finest in works that contribute to moral development are available.

The successful socialization of children cannot be done by remote control nor, for that matter, by day care arrangements, although the latter, in the universe of our transformed work habits, have become a salient feature of American life. Day care is an ironic necessity for working mothers even in two-parent, intact families. It may seem cultural heresy to ask whether it is an adequate substitute for direct parental care, yet this question must be explored by parents who want their authority to be effective in helping their children to grow.

Despite the delicacy of the issue, data on this subject are hardly reassuring for those interested in the welfare of the nation's children. Day care is so diverse in character that it lacks a professional coherence or central instrument or code to establish or to monitor standards. Serious questions about the quality of day care have therefore been raised repeatedly in recent years.

There may well be ways in which parents who must commit their children to such care generously supply what day care does not. Somebody must provide the stability and consistency that is so vital for children if they are to form some sense of the world as a trustworthy environment. That task, according to overwhelming research, is still best carried out by two parents working at it together under the same roof. Christopher Lasch has written about the ongoing stress of parenting: "Without struggling with the ambivalent emotions aroused by the union of love and discipline in his parents, the child never masters his inner rage or his fear of authority. It is the reason that children need parents, not professional nurses and counselors."[12]

Parents should make investments of healthy authority beyond their own walls; these areas can include the homes of their childrens' friends. The point is not to interfere unnecessarily in outside environments but to know what is going on there and to exercise control over their own childrens' presence and participation in such settings. They should know whether and how activities are supervised, what kind of programs are allowed on television, and whether, in general, the standards support the values they are trying to reinforce in their own homes.

Parents should take an active interest in their childrens' schools, not hesitating to look into curricula, special programs, and textbook selection. That can be done in a way that is not at all extreme or radical. In many settings the teachers themselves appreciate the interest and support parents can give them in sensibly fulfilling their own obligations as authors, that is, in helping children to grow intellectually and morally under their care.

Parents should take an interest in the neighborhood in which the family lives. Some parents, to reduce the amount of crime in their neighborhoods, have organized, patrolled the streets at night, and taken down license plate numbers of cars cruising for drugs. With the cooperation of the police, a series of arrests have been made and children now play safely in the streets. Parents and children together can participate in neighborhood celebrations and other communal activities that not only increase the safety of all but contribute greatly to the quality of life and further the work of healthy parenting.

Remember that the healthy family lets other families grow out of it. The healthy family, true to the essential character of dynamic authority, is a self-dissolving unit, that is, it yields itself up for the sake of the growth it generates, giving way to the families that grow out of it instead of trying to dominate them in imitation of some authoritarian monarchy.

Thus life surrenders to death in a thousand ways in any good marriage and in every good family. Generative authority, that which is ordered not to self-maintenance but to the growth of the next generation, is exemplified in those gentle uncouplings, not accomplished without sacrifice, effected, for example, by grandparents when they encourage their married children to establish and give first place to their own family rituals instead of insisting that they continue to observe those of their families of origin.

That does not mean children and grandchildren never exchange visits on lesser and greater occasions. It does suggest that a prime characteristic of generative authority is the way it respects and grants freedom for new life and new lives to grow on their own. Adults unself-consciously teach a fundamental lesson about love's true nature when they know how to "let go" of their children. Authoritarian parents, on the contrary, bind their children and grandchildren to themselves, denying them freedom in their strenuous efforts to control their choices and destinies.

In a culture where so many homes are broken and their occupants are in need of ongoing emotional support, there are many ways in which the deposits of sound authority in the human family in general can be tapped for infusion into disrupted human families in particular. This is work that can be done only one by one. Yet these personal transfusions from the bloodstream of natural authority to individuals also affect the common good, resulting in far greater and more permanent social change than many well-funded and well-regulated interventions by the government.

People can do family work outside of their own family. An ex-convict named Charles Ballard anticipated by several years the 1995 Million Man March through which black men publicly professed their commitment to fatherhood and its potent natural authority. Ballard, who never knew his own father, has given leadership (the most common way we have of describing the exercise of healthy authority) to the National Institute for Responsible Fatherhood and Family Development. In less than ten years he has, according to the syndicated columnist William Raspberry, touched the lives of nearly two thousand young fathers.

"Well over half of them," Raspberry explains, "have 'legitimated' their children—gone to court to acknowledge their paternity and signed documents giving the children their names, inheritance rights, etc.—and many have married the mothers of their children." He quotes the fifty-five-year-old Ballard as saying that his work is an outgrowth of his experience at a Cleveland hospital maternity ward: "I kept noticing all these mothers and babies, and no fathers. So I started collecting the names of the fathers and visiting them after work, just to talk to them. Before I knew it, I had six different groups of these young fathers in various parts of Cleveland meeting and talking about everything from parental responsibility to childhood development and reproductive health." As Raspberry observes of the program's growth, it now involves "other family members—grandparents, aunts and uncles—to help the little ones get a sense of belonging and stability."13

Instead of spending his leisure time playing golf and fishing near his Naples, Florida, home, Roderick Graham, a retired meteorologist, became an afternoon tutor in a program organized by the city's black leadership. He uses his extensive computer knowledge to train young students in their use. His "Saturday Girls," as they are described by his daughter Ellen, a *Wall Street Journal* reporter and editor, are the first of an ever growing number of students who respond enthusiastically. This is a double accomplishment, for it not only addresses their individual needs but the racial divide in a retirement center in which African Americans live in a highly segregated enclave far from the condominiums of the largely white retirees and vacationers.

"Over the years," Ellen Graham writes, "Dad chose to go it alone—without a commission, a panel or a committee behind him. He didn't wait for legislative mandates or government grants. . . . Now he's reaping the only reward he ever sought. Twice this month—at the age of 78—he drove to Northern Florida to attend commencement exercises." The last of his Saturday Girls, we are told, would graduate from college later in the year.

Ms. Graham's conclusion fits all such efforts to infuse the sluggish bloodstream of society, even when positive results do not seem likely, with the plasma of generative authority. "My parents," she writes, "would be the first ones to stress the girls' accomplishments are their own. But there was a sustained effort on both sides. Connections were made and promises kept. I like to think that made a difference."[14]

Authority as a Life Calling

Sentimentalization is the ironic tribute that an authority-deprived public pays to its most potent and crucial institutions. Sentimental-ization, like a tear-filled retirement dinner, seems to discharge our du-ties toward its subjects. Otherwise we would need to take them more seriously and transform our attitudes toward them. Motherhood—half the franchise of authorship—and home—the site of the hard work of authoring a family—are prime subjects for this emotional fix in America. But sentiment is often a form of self-indulgence and fails to honor the sacrifice and dedication that marriage and family life de-mand of us. Making a home, as with authoring anything, is not a ca-sual activity but a lifetime calling. It is Everyman's and Everywoman's Sistine Chapel ceiling, the great work that, at a great price, they were born to do. Authoring's pigments are not, however, somber and gray but, as with those of Michelangelo's recently restored masterpiece, colors filled with a light that does not fail. Making a home, the most creative challenge people face, demands burning off their generative energies so that other families and homes may flow out of it, strong enough to do history's hard work of realizing and enlarging hu-mankind's possibilities.

II

Authoring the Self:
Rediscovering Personal Moral Authority

6

Rediscovering the Source of Authority

Bob Dylan's "Blowin' in the Wind" was enormously popular in the 1960s because it spoke to the unconscious of people, putting into words their experience that old social structures and personal restraints were splintering. It was indeed the appropriate anthem for the era that followed the breakdown of hierarchy both as an institutional framework and as a language for moral dialogue. Robert Jay Lifton suggests that even the structure of our personalities evolved into a sense of self, which he terms "protean," that reflects the restlessness and flux of our times.[1]

Although everything was indeed adrift in the wind, many of the notions that presented themselves as progressive steps in "sexual liberation," such as "open marriage," now look impulsive and even foolish, the kind of thing people try out and ruefully put aside because they find they cannot live humanly, or very happily, according to its dictates.

In the same rush of post-hierarchical history, a wave of experimental movements swept through moral education during that era. Housing neither authoritarianism or healthy authority, they taught variants on moral themes without any moral foundation or content. While these have largely failed to work, traditional morals, still lacking a modern translation from the language of hierarchical authoritarianism, remain culturally diluted or dissipated and lack, in that outdated form, the authority to engage our attention, much less our unified response. As a result, many ordinary people feel that recourse to communal moral standards has been superseded by the subjectivity by which individuals, seemingly shorn of the guidance of tradition, must find all authority within themselves for their moral choices.

Authoritative Morality, Law, and Ethics

In this foggy interval, how can we recognize authoritative morality and distinguish it from the concepts of law and ethics, with which it is often confused? Morality refers to the basic convictions about right and wrong quarried out of human experience over many centuries. These fundamental persuasions do not come from rational analysis or arguments. They arise from a sense of the rightness or wrongness of certain actions agreed upon by what we have referred to as the healthy majority of human beings. Such moral insight does not come full-blown; it evolves slowly and may be inflected in slightly different ways in varying cultures.

Slavery's elimination in the United States was the outcome of a great crusade energized not by ethics or law but by the authority of the moral insight into its evil shared by large numbers of individuals. Indeed, its elimination followed a brutal civil war. The laws against slavery and the relevant constitutional amendments followed, as true law always does, on moral convictions whose seeds lay folded in the original prerational intuition. The moral authority arose from the insight and was the basis for the later laws, not, as some suppose today, the other way around.

Among the root meanings of law is "that which is set down."[2] Something passed by a legislature may be a regulation or a statute that concerns arbitrary situations, such as speed limits, and can be morally neutral. It is reasonable to expect general legal codes to be consonant with basic moral principles, but they can, like those passed in Nazi Germany to facilitate the expropriation of Jewish property and the extinction of the Jews, make sacrilege of a moral tradition. If the Devil can quote scripture for his own uses, he is even better at passing laws to further his own interests. For our purposes, the authority of good law depends on its ultimate reference to basic human insights into moral truth. The law never creates these but it can give voice to them in specific circumstances.

Ethics may be understood as principles of right or good conduct, or a body of such principles that codify the ideals and behavioral expectations of specific groups, such as the codes of ethics of physicians and lawyers. The root of the word ethics is the Greek *ethos,* "moral custom," and is grounded in the social entity; its derivatives include "self" and "custom."[3] Ethical principles arise from a sensitivity, within particular social settings, to the meaning, values, and implications of specific incidents analyzed in the light of general moral principles. Ethical principles are not the same as morals or laws. They reflect the ethos or spirit of a group, what it strives to do, and what its members agree upon as the fitting ways to do it.

Ethical codes are developed by the professions, for example, to guide their members in behaviors that may not constitute moral questions or be covered by any law. The medical doctor, when examining a patient, is ethically expected to provide an environment with as much privacy for the patient as can be afforded by the circumstances. It is not immoral to do otherwise, nor is there a law against it. The ethical sense of medicine, however, demands it. So too, lawyers must ethically reveal conflicts of interest, and journalists are expected to seek independent corroboration of the important "factual" information they report.

No effective defense against either immoral or unethical behavior begins with the statement, "I have done nothing illegal." Neither can the morality or sound ethics of an incident be inferred merely because some behavior, such as slavery at the birth of this nation, was considered legal. When, as during the present interval, a moral tradition goes into eclipse because of changing social perceptions or fresh insights, its authoritative voice can no longer be heard. Great confusion about the meaning and use of these terms ensues. It is not surprising that the law and the courts are then looked to by individuals and groups as the combined source of both morality and ethics they cannot deliver.

In such an oxygen-deprived interval, jet-trail trends possess illusory substance. Social fashions that de-authorize traditional concepts of marriage and family life have themselves become amorphous standards. Thus the authority of once commonly held positions is easily resisted or is dismissed as extreme or outdated. Meanwhile, extensive experiments with new modes of seeking subjective moral authority, much like the one-night bloom of the sea hibiscus, flourish brilliantly but briefly.

Trial-and-Error Moral Experimentation

Classic among the experiments is Sidney Simon's method of "Values Clarification," which has been adopted in school systems almost beyond counting. It seeks to make students aware of "their own feelings, their own ideas, their own beliefs . . . their own value systems." In an exercise termed "values voting," students are asked "How many of you like to take long walks or hikes?" "How many like yogurt?" "How many of you approve of premarital sex for boys? for girls?" "How many of you think we ought to legalize abortions?"[4] This approach does not instill values but elicits them on the same level as tastes and feelings.

Simon's own values are clearly on display as the verbs change from "like" about walks and yogurt, to the "approve" of premarital sex, and the "ought" for the legalization of abortion. Professor Thomas Lickona cites an eighth grade teacher who queried a low-achieving class about the four activities they most prefer. Their response was "sex, drugs, drinking, and skipping school." The values clarification method failed to give the teacher a way of persuading them about alternative "values."[5]

Experiments such as "Values Clarification," with their uneven amoral neutrality, have contributed to the moral illiteracy of many young Americans: students in ethics classes who report that there is no such thing as right or wrong but only good or bad arguments, or ones who can find no moral referent in the Holocaust.

Rediscovery is the necessary approach to reestablish the authority of morality, because it has not vanished from the universe but has rather been obscured by the dust clouds still mushrooming out of hierarchical authoritarianism's collapse. As a result, authority in exile is not remembered as a healthy component of life but is treated as an emigré count after the Russian Revolution, an advertisement for lost royal claims in threadbare evening clothes. Authority is what people thought they wanted to get rid of. And they did, with such magnificent thoroughness that it is almost impossible to mention authority without making people defensive, especially about its relationship to morality.

Healthy authority is, however, the natural energy of moral standards. To understand its plight in another way, imagine the decline of authoritarianism as the corrosion of the pipeline through which natural authority once flowed. Both the pipeline and the energy resource it transports have been abandoned.

It is as if America, after an oil spill or some other breakdown, were to abandon fossil fuels altogether and embrace synthetics, corn derivatives, colored water, or any other device or substance fabricated in the nation's garages, to supply the energy for its ravening economy. It would soon be obvious that improvisations, some of which might seem workable, would not, indeed could not, fill the gap, and that breakdowns, frustrations, and social changes would rapidly occur.

That is how life proceeds in this period of interval trial-and-error moralizing. In the entertainment industry during the same standardless interim, everything has been tried, that is, everything once restrained by morals, taste, or artistic judgment has been set loose. The result is an expensive landfill of lookalike and soundalike movies. Hollywood has also turned to remaking classic movies of a previous era, but, because their makers lack the internalized standards of the earlier time, their failure rate here is also high. Thus in morals, the Age of Temptation has been ended with Wildean irony. By giving in to them in such palely human ways, virtue and sin become indistinguishable, resulting in an appropriately purgatorial intermission in which people find that they lack the moral energy to author either good or evil. They therefore become victims. And traditional morality, much like classic old movies, cannot be successfully remade from the outside, although that is what literal fundamentalists attempt on morals during the same period.

The post-hierarchical interval can be identified because of its conspicuous lack of creativity and its dependence on mimicry and imitation. Society sails into the doldrums whenever natural authority is misunderstood or misplaced. Nothing can be authored well, there is little generativity, and even in the fine arts, creativity is becalmed. Interval moralists, like younger directors who say they are paying "homage" when they are copying from older moviemakers, reveal their lack of authority in what they produce. When something lacks creative authority it does not command our attention. As a result, interim morality does not generate confrontation or comfort.

Characteristics of Interval Morality

Interval morality is essentially narcissistic. The frustrating experiments in interval morality, like so many modern movies, are a narcissist's dream. They are marked by a self-absorption that asserts that merely by making a "choice" one makes an action moral. Such self-referent behavior often masquerades under claims for "rights" that are usually code names for infantile impulses or urgings. They include the right to urinate anywhere one pleases and the right to be a cheerleader even though pregnant in violation of high school standards. Narcissism, armed with threats of lawsuits, expands the claims and debases the notion of genuine human rights.

Such explorers of the interval moral terrain may deserve more sympathy than condemnation; they certainly do not merit idealization. They are like children playing in the ruins of social institutions whose purpose still exists even though their hierarchical forms have fallen into decay. The overseers of the these afflicted institutions resemble a museum director who equates his burned-down museum with the art it once displayed. They have so identified their institution's purpose with its structure that they mourn the ruins rather than build a freshly formed structure to serve its lasting purpose. Thus the children scuffing through the rubble rightly feel abandoned. They can only consult their own awakening needs for the fonts of some kind of morality. Unaided in growth, they naturally fixate more on the needs bubbling out of whatever level of human development they have reached. They cannot be other than narcissistic.

Narcissistic self-absorption matches a very early plateau of growth and is marked by primitivity. Its diversions, including rock concerts, television as confessional, and the advocated vulgarity and violence of rap and other formulations, are heavily narcissistic. That they are evidence of stunted growth does not make them evil. Those experimenters, at play in the interval's column-strewn fields, lack the matured inner structures necessary to achieve and express the moral form of an adult.

In this period of interlude morality, rewards are distributed not to those who try to grow up or be good but to those who reject growth and remain petulantly childish. In fact, the petulant child has been transformed into a winsome treasure known as the "child within." He is cultivated as the innocent victim of malign forces, especially of the parental generation. The parents symbolize the once powerful authoritarian structures that, when oversimplified, for example, as "white male Western culture," are the historical source of all present evil. Even on the part of the Church, there is less emphasis on acquiring virtue or becoming a saint than on changing the world through political action and social policy. Saints and heroes constitute elites that are intrinsically unacceptable on the level plain of the interval.

Interval morality is subtly authoritarian. One can easily observe the highly controlling character of improvised modern liberal codes. The best example remains the richly authoritarian Antioch College policy on Sexual Violence and Safety. Step three of the "consent" for sexual activity states: "Verbal consent should be obtained with each new level of physical and/or sexual contact/conduct in any given interaction, regardless of who initiates it. Asking 'Do you want to have sex with me?' is not enough. The request for consent must be specific to each act."[6] Even the current fad of companies' allowing workers to "dress down" on occasion in order to increase productivity is, according to one observer, "breeding a spooky Maoist conformity." In one company everybody, men and women alike, showed up in a blue button-down shirt, cardigan, khakis, and loafers.

The new guidelines illustrate the interval's deficient sense of humor, underscored in its defense by Andy Abrams, described as a "community manager," and Kristine Herman, a senior student who is "educational-activities coordinator for the [Antioch College] Sexual Offense Policy." They explain that "when verbal communication is not a central part of the sexual encounter, false assumptions may and do occur. Misreadings of body language may prevail. In undefined situations, one person may be experiencing a 'good time,' while another is experiencing a sexual assault. Under our policy, the two are distinguishable because of the requirement of verbal consent."[7] They are undoubtedly unfamiliar with Chesterton's words: "Life is serious all the time, but living cannot be. You may have all the solemnity you wish in your neckties, but in anything important (such as sex, death, and religion), you must have mirth or you will have madness."[8]

In Antioch's regulations, the moral offense of rape is lost in the tide of a small-print moralize-by-the-numbers code. So distorted is this presentation that it does not even consider a more basic issue: Is it emotionally and humanly constructive to ignore totally the question of whether sexual relationships between teenagers is morally acceptable or not? Sexual activity is thereby treated in truncated fashion because following the steps of verbal consent is the only moral commitment to be honored. Akin to making the moral issue the use of condoms rather than whether grammar school children should be having sex, it is related to the distortion of making subjective "choice" the moral issue no matter what the objective content may be.

The illusion of infusing moral integrity into incomplete moral questions is exemplified, as noted by Paul Johnson, in the reaction of the German religious leader Otto Dibelius to events occurring in 1933 Germany. In a broadcast two days after the first anti-Jewish measures, he "appeared to justify them, and claimed the boycott of Jewish businesses was conducted in conditions of complete law and order, as though that was the whole point."[9]

Interval morality features victimhood. Victimhood as a way of life is the liberating state of grace in this moral theology. One need not deny the truth of many histories of early childhood exploitation and abuse to observe that there also exists its shadowed image, a culture of imagined or hypothesized abuse that muddles the genuine moral and social issues connected with well-founded cases. In fantasied victimhood, the person is washed free of Original Sin, which is almost always some past abuse by males, by accepting a morally martyred status, the condition of suspended or vacated moral responsibility. Because such persons have been acted upon wrongly somewhere in the past, their present actions are compromised and limited and they live permanently in the limbolike state of "recovery."

Moral judgment is flattened. In the recent "recovered memory" controversy, as a result of the new lack of operational ability on the part of even the law and the courts, the distinction between what is dream and what is reality is lost. That is an inevitable outcome in a subjective moral universe in which every action is morally the same as every other action because, without reference to standards, none can be better or worse, morally superior or morally inferior. The remedies sought—renewed death penalties, life sentences, more police—are responses to the discomfort such nondiscrimination engenders. They are efforts to quell the "What are we coming to?" anxiety caused by the notion that if everything is the same, then anything can happen.

Interval morality becomes bureaucratized. Moral theorizing without moral standards issues not into action but into the establishment of bureaucracies characterized by authoritarian groping for external controls. Instead, jerry-built regulations, ill suited to any truly human activity, are classic outcomes of systems estranged from moral authority. The framers think they are being moral the way children think they look adult when they put on grown-ups' clothes. Anybody with good sense can tell the difference.

In the makeshift moralities, the punishments do not fit the crime, they fit the system instead. When moral rules are assembled by bureaucrats ignorant of the Ten Commandments and the tradition they crystallize, it is difficult to make crimes, much less sins, out of lying (as in cheating) or fornication (as in seduction). Derived from an impoverished vocabulary of offenses, the new designated-sin offenses are dependent on the social sciences for their identities. Sociology provides such sin equivalents as "racism" and "sexism" as well as such pathetic variants as "heightism" and "lookism." Psychology is the source for "inappropriate" behavior and "insensitivity." Political science provides "hate speech," "being male," and the mother of all jellied ills, "political correctness and incorrectness."

How to Rediscover the Moral Self

Morality has become so daemonic, that is, keyed to an inner divinity, that even the possibility of its being rooted outside the individual has been obscured. As a result, moral values have been trivialized, ignored, confused with ethics, or replaced by law and legal precedent so that the law, in effect, has become synonymous with morality.

The abortion debate, for example, has been argued by both sides in a legal vocabulary on legal grounds as an almost exclusively constitutional issue. The focus has not been on the moral character of the central event of abortion but on the constitutional right to privacy. The evolution and application of the latter principle to sexual matters is now celebrated by pro-choice advocates as a quasi-moral triumph.

Perhaps the most plangent confounding of legalism with morality is made by a member of the adolescent Lakewood, California, "Spur Posse," a group of twenty to thirty teenagers whose blatant sexual conquests in search of manhood attracted national attention. Some of the youths had also been accused of burglary, assault, and the intimidation of witnesses. "'We didn't do nothing wrong 'cause it's not illegal to hook up,' said Billy Shehan, 19, using the local slang for sexual intercourse, which he says he has had 66 times, making him the group's top scorer."[10]

The use of a legal decoy in place of morality is not limited to America's blue-collar neighborhoods. The financier Michael Milken was vigorously defended as a capitalist hero, an innovator in junk bond trading, through which he was compensated $500 million in one year alone. His techniques and his pay were defended by, among others, the *Wall Street Journal* as the successes of a man playing by the rules of the free market. Those "rules," by such reasoning, confer morality on his or anybody else's activities. However, according to others, the "bottom line" on Michael Milken was that he paid people off by bribing them. Nonetheless, he continues to be defended as a martyr to technicalities and governmental meddling in markets, with no apparent sense of irony, by segments of the financial press.

Morality is a function not of any part of the person but of the whole person. As such it is a vital sign of healthy and productive human socialization and growth and cannot come into existence without natural authority, any more than flight can occur without gravity. One of authority's principal goals is the development of whole human beings.

What is the work of such authority? What exactly does it do? It does not, as does authoritarianism, restrict, control, or repress human development through force, techniques of manipulation, shaming, or impersonal or whimsical regulations. Authority's whole purpose is to inhere in constructive human relationships (including, as often mentioned, those of teachers with pupils, professionals with clients, and even artists with their works) solely to promote the achievement by its subjects of their goal of full growth. Authority is a living quality, the authorship factor, that helps people to become themselves. Authority's function, therefore, is to make it possible for men and women to author their own lives.

The process includes the gradual refinement of the ability of growing persons to tell right from wrong on their own, for themselves. That means they can balance facts and circumstances against principles and tradition, distinguish the private right from the public good, and live in reasonable harmony with themselves and others. Ideally, a moral tradition assists the young in learning to form moral judgments, that is, to draw on the riches of symbols, rites, and stories to help acquire moral authority over themselves. Authority, therefore, provides intergenerational continuity, ordinarily through the conduit of institutions, including the family, that serve the community. Yves Simon comments that "within the temporal order we would feel hopeless if the virtual, immortal life of the community did not compensate for the brevity of human existence."[11]

It is also possible for a tradition, at least through its temporary representatives, to abdicate its moral authority, especially through compromises with power, justifying them as necessary for its own survival. The tradition is then co-opted and used in support of power, its influence on the young manipulated to serve the aims of the regime. The perennial task of authoritarianism is to extinguish or silence the true authority of a tradition and its capacity to enliven conscience. That took place in Germany in the 1930s, for example, when many Christian churches cooperated with Hitler.

Conscience is not an attribute of the "noble savage," something good that is spoiled by its contact with the world. Conscience is rather a capacity that depends for its development on long and intimate contact with adults, ordinarily parents, in the setting of family life.

Putting authority back into morals begins with the formation of conscience. Rearing a child takes place on that energy curve of relationship between the parents and within the families to which they give life and growth. Through the family, the child enters a specific culture whose customs and traditions give particular expression to "the basic inclinations" of men and women, their human destiny to live together and share that life with others.

The tradition is very powerful in this regard, and the role of its symbols and rites in consolidating human growth under parental authority, especially in matters of conscience, is crucial. The tradition gradually expands the safe space of freedom in which the young learn, test, and make ever finer discriminations about the moral code as they internalize it as their own, that is, accept it now not on the word of others but on their own authority. The code is thereby seamlessly joined with the other aspects of individual self we term character.

Such a developmental process includes but is not limited to the hypothetical construct known as the *superego,* a psychological term used by Freud to describe the internal receptor and self-monitoring system that is seeded by, and buds under the influence of, the specific culture's most significant values.[12] Conscience within this inchoate moral character is the gradually and more specifically differentiated sense of morality in which the example of parents and their qualities as human beings are indispensable and powerfully determinative elements.

Putting morality back into morals is, first and foremost, the work of parents, assisted and supported by the authoritative institutions, such as the schools and the churches, of their culture. When moral education struggles experimentally in the interim between the death of authoritarianism and the rebirth of natural authority, this basic commonsense approach is often scanted or dismissed as evidence of antiquated patriarchy.

To say that human beings fail their moral traditions is but another way of recognizing that, as the great religions have taught, they are sinners. Developing consciences does not mean that persons will always follow them. The fully formed conscience is not, philosophically speaking, free to choose between good and evil but only between competing goods. When the fully formed conscience chooses the evil over the good, it experiences the contravention of its ideal as guilt. Guilt is the appropriate human signal of a moral disconnect.

The antisocial personality, formerly referred to as the psychopathic personality, is marked by a lack of conscience, a numbness of the heart to ethical considerations, and an absence of any feelings of guilt about wrongdoing. Antisocial personalities are not bound by, nor do they care about, moral restraints. They break the law, exhibit little remorse, and are made anxious only by the prospect of being caught. The evidence of such psychopathy, even among the very young for whom murder has become a source of thrills, is widespread during this period.

Theories about the development of the antisocial personality provide us with the reverse image of the process by which sensible moral education is carried out. There is a lacuna in the character of the psychopath, psychiatric researchers suggest, a break or empty space that can result from parental failure.

Lapses in conscience are often related to difficulties in the socialization process through which a sense of inner moral authority is transmitted to the young. Abundant research findings testify to the difficulties in ordinary living, for example, that are the unwanted inheritance of the children of such social disruption as divorce and family breakup. These data merely underscore the sensitivity of human beings to the psychological qualities of their upbringing. Any interference with the functions of healthy authority in the process of childrearing takes its toll. The penalties manifest themselves in many ways, often in subsequent problems with weakened, troubled, or silenced voices of conscience.

Authoring a Mature Conscience

"*I* would."

That is how President Abraham Lincoln is said to have responded when urged to act "because nobody else would know."

It is a sign of our times that we seem to like stories of people with bad consciences, no consciences, or an indifference to the dictates of conscience. Few of America's leaders, including those in religion, seem to speak with moral authority, perhaps because they speak so seldom in their own voices about anything they really believe in.

Yet the voice of healthy conscience retains compelling authority. People still stop what they are doing, even in the hubbub of modern times, to listen to what its possessor has to say. Dr. Martin Luther King, Jr., spoke as a man having moral authority, and he commanded the attention of the nation in complacent midcentury. *Schindler's List,* Steven Spielberg's movie based on Thomas Keneally's novel, caused people to speculate on how such a flawed businessman could have risen above his failings to follow his conscience in saving Jews from the Holocaust.

Conscience is not a self-contained world in which persons speak only to themselves. The voice of conscience is meant to be heard and understood by others. Like a cathedral bell, conscience's voice summons others from long distances to listen and respond both to it and to themselves. The simplest test and sign of operational consciences is that people follow them, they *do something* as a result of their convictions. They take the ideals handed over to them by their parents and community (the literal meaning of tradition, from *tradere,* to hand over), internalize them as their own, and translate them into the way they live their lives.

The actions promoted by conscience, like all behavior innervated by living authority, give and enlarge life, helping others achieve what is morally best for them and for those close to them. Hierarchical authoritarianism, on the other hand, restricts growth, obliterates individual identity, and dilutes and suppresses the functions of conscience. That is why people who have lived under authoritarian regimes, such as Hitler's, claim to be guiltless, to have had no knowledge of their leaders' actions, and excuse themselves by saying that "we only did what we were told to do."

Schopenhauer was puzzled by the fact that in emergencies utter strangers could respond to the needs of others by putting their own lives at risk. He asked in his essay *On the Foundations of Morality*, "How is it possible that suffering that is neither my own nor of my concern should immediately affect me as though it were my own and with such force that it moves me to action? . . . This is something really mysterious, something for which Reason can provide no explanation, and for which no basis can be found in practical experience. It is not unknown even to the most hard-hearted and self-interested. Examples appear every day before our eyes of instant responses of the kind, without reflection, one person helping another, coming to his aid, even setting his own life in clear danger for someone whom he has seen for the first time, having nothing more in mind than that the other is in need and in peril of his life."[13]

Schopenhauer termed this uncalculated, spontaneous response "compassion" and viewed it as the basis of moral life. That is in sharp contrast to the flabby notion of "compassion" circulated in modern culture. Such compassion justifies and romanticizes itself as a vague inner reaction that makes people feel morally superior, whether they do anything as a result or not. The popular-culture "compassion" is a synthetic that can easily be distinguished from the real thing; it lacks authority because it authors nothing.

Persons of developed moral character are attuned to the moral content of what they do in private as well as in public. Such sensitivity to the moral dimensions of events frees them from the ice jam of distortions and false moral scenarios in popular culture.

The misrepresentations can be identified by their unmistakable odor of self-righteousness, which can be picked up by ordinary people at a great distance. The "whited sepulcher syndrome" is the negative image of true moral authority. Huddled within it are the confusing pseudo-moralists who crusade for the part-for-the-whole morality campaigns, such as those for animal rights, that so muddle the philosophical meaning of "rights" as to make it unrecognizable. So, too, those who place condom use as the central moral issue connected with teenage sexual activity resemble photographers who crop a picture so that its real context is, along with its meaning, transformed or denied to the viewer. Those who want to keep toy guns away from children enjoy the illusion that they are fighting violence when they are really ignoring human nature and failing to understand the way little boys play. Ordinary people sense the pressured quality of such campaigns and their lack of persuasive moral authority.

Men and women with well-ordered consciences, as Saint Paul suggests, no longer need the law or regulations to guide them, because their choices anticipate the purpose of law. Conscience places them not in conflict with but beyond the law. Alexis de Tocqueville describes the effects that follow in the life of a person of moral authority who aspires to virtue and strength. Such an individual is the "regulating force" within the community and, already fulfilling the purpose of the law, is "free" and responsible to God alone.[14]

Paranoid manipulators get the attention of others. While those with moral authority generate growth and enlarge freedom, paranoid manipulators restrict growth and shrink the free choices of others. Individuals with moral authority move men and women to take what they already feel within themselves to be the right, if difficult, course to follow; they second the voice of conscience itself. Manipulators attempt to persuade people to go against their consciences; they sow confusion and ambiguity with the skill of criminal lawyers so that people may be led away from their own convictions and act as others would have them act.

Persons who possess moral authority urge people to actions about which they have no subsequent regrets. Paranoid persuaders, on the other hand, get people into things about which they later experience what A. E. Houseman calls "endless rue." Healthy people ask: Does this speaker really free me or lessen my freedom? Those with moral authority make us feel free, while the authoritarianism of paranoid manipulators binds us to their goals, taking away the freedom essential to moral choice. The paranoids sweep us up, making us hostage to their own pathology, giving us the sensation of being used for a cause or a purpose not fully disclosed to us.

Conscience authors our sense of sin. One of the healthy distillates of a sound conscience is nonneurotic guilt, that entirely fitting personal reaction to failure in pursuing one's own moral traditions and ideals. It is human and adult to be capable of sin: We do things with real-world effects, good or evil. To settle for victim status is to opt for passivity, a life without conscience that is deprived of the humanly defining activities by which we sign our own names to the lives we author, well or ill, on our own.

Most proposals to increase self-esteem, such as birthday parties at which every child gets a present so that no attendee will feel less prized than any other, spoil sensible human traditions while not increasing self-esteem at all. Self-esteem is a by-product of a good conscience, an outcome of self-control, the sense that we are in charge of ourselves, that we author a consequential life. It does not come from the manipulative exercises that deny reality, as in not giving failing grades in order not to injure the self-esteem of poor students. As they author their character, human beings also enhance their self-esteem.

What of those who, like the all too human Schindler, risk their own lives and well-being for the sake of others, those nameless heroes who so perplexed Schopenhauer by the high character of their morality? Where do they come from, and how do they get that way?

Some answers are found in the studies of those men and women who did risk themselves to save Jews under threat by Hitler. Samuel and Pearl Oliner studied such rescuers and reported that very few of their subjects refer to abstract principles as the reasons for their responses.[15] They speak much more about the way they were brought up, or of the inspiration of their parents' lives or their religious tradition.

In contrast with those who stood by and did nothing (who were concerned about their independence and autonomy), the rescuers had internalized to a significant degree the norms of their families and their communities. They carried the *ethos,* or living spirit, of their traditions with them and authored actions imbued with its energies.

To one who hears their voices, their uncluttered moral authority is apparent. One says "It was not a question of reasoning. Let's put it this way. There were people in need and we helped them." Another speaks of his parents: "They taught me discipline, tolerance, and serving others when they needed something. It was a general feeling, if somebody was ill or in need my parents would always help." Yet another testifies: "When you see a need you have to help. Our religion was part of us. We are our brother's keeper." And another recalls that "at my grandfather's place, when they read the Bible, he invited everybody in. If a Jew happened to drop in, he would ask him to take a seat. He would sit there too. Jews and Catholics were received in our place like everybody else."

Ordinary people sound like the rescuers as they spontaneously volunteer, for example, to drive drug dealers out of their neighborhoods and to pursue the meaning of freedom, not as allowing anything and everything, but as providing "a place of safety for loved ones." They act simply and directly; they clearly, if unself-consciously, advertise the values of family and religious tradition as the energy sources of their applied moral authority.

People with moral authority, that is, men and women with sound, functioning consciences, do not stand alone in rebelling against the assembled forces of tradition but author their good from within the tradition itself. The "regime effect" in popular culture stages everything according to the scenario of revolution, as if the persons of conscience must think their way clear of the tradition that has formed them in order to author a moral decision. The hero, in the shallows of popular culture, is often the loner, the outsider, the cowboy Shane riding endlessly into town, or the hero of *High Noon* riding endlessly out. Such concepts and images belie the facts of moral authorship completely.

III

America's Institutions:
Rediscovering Authority in Education

7

The De-authorization of Education

Education is the great institution that continues the authoring work of the family in helping the young to grow, that is, literally to become themselves in life. While teachers are responsible in a special way for the intellectual growth of children, for their mastery of the tools of thought, communication, and judgment, they also share with mothers and fathers in the work of character development. They co-author moral adults.

The institution of education now flashes like cascading MTV images on our inner screens, perhaps more a fragmented collage of protest, experimentation, and silliness than the stable and confident instrument of tradition it once was. The ill-matched bouquet of efforts is classic behavior for all once hierarchically ordered institutions: the improvisation of structures and standards after natural authority was at least temporarily buried in fallen authoritarianism. Like the death of a parent in a family, the loss of stabilizing healthy authority sends shock waves through everybody who has a relationship to the institution. Suffering that loss, the institution becomes less trustworthy, less capable of leadership, and, despite its profession of liberal ideological principles, curiously less free.

As a consequence, schools are now considered as dangerous as darkened streets, and the great and small cities of the land find themselves paralyzed in their efforts to reform and renew their public school systems. Even the great colleges and universities are flailing to maintain their balance in the sea surge of problems that fill the authority vacuum. In every system the problem is associated with leadership, its nature, responsibilities, and tenure. In short, nowhere is the trial-and-error quest for authority more obvious than in education.

The Center Does Not Hold

The crisis in leadership across American education is a symptom of the underlying problem of dismantled and dispersed authority. The effective authority of presidencies, deanships, and superintendencies is now distributed to an array of factions that tend to compete rather than cooperate with each other. Men and women capable of exercising natural leadership do not want positions made frustrating by the radical subdivision of the office's authority.

No lookout can miss the flare of organizational distress that signals the prime symptom of authority failure: its fragmentation and diffusion away from the center. Throughout education authority is transferred away from nuclear educational positions and spread among other constituencies and interest groups. That is operationally what occurs when people fail to distinguish natural authority from unnatural authoritarianism. Wanting to kill Mr. Hyde, they also kill Dr. Jekyll and begin to play doctor themselves. Frank T. Read, former dean of the University of Florida's law school, says that "the most important constituency is the faculty. Tenured professors ... regard themselves as senior partners in a law firm. The dean is the managing partner they have collegially selected ... the dean is their agent."[1]

The traditional center of university authority, the presidency, has imploded under pressures from inside the institution itself. Victorious faculty revolutionaries want power rather than the obligations of sensible authority, which include unifying the university community so that it may recognize and serve common interests and purposes, a central function of authority. Benno J. Schmidt of Yale was vanquished by special interests whose concerns were not overall unity but a successful separatism. Among those Balkan war results are the overthrow of the unifying principle and the rise of duchy-like faculty senates as the power brokers of university politics.

The devolution of central university authority is rationalized as a response to legitimate complaints about programs and as the implementation of a prevalent political philosophy. A further characteristic of central authority failure is its politicization or its shrinkage into power and its subsequent manipulation in the name of causes not directly connected with education. The center is atomized. In the same spring in which Schmidt was under siege at Yale, Columbia University's five-hundred-member faculty of Arts and Sciences was summoned by its own eleven-member executive committee to challenge president Michael Sovern's leadership in a letter declaring that the faculty questioned the competence of the administration and that trust was low.

It is virtually impossible for a president to exercise authority when such groups as senates, relishing newly asserted power, make meeting their demands the condition for validating the president's authority. By those tactics, which undercut common goals and action, such groups easily dismantle the operational authority of leaders like Schmidt and Sovern. That is the great dumb show of this era, the semaphore of an authoritarian-averse culture trying everything to cure its real but poorly diagnosed problem of authority deprivation.

Such incidents occur everywhere in a culture that has lost touch with the fundamental meaning and need for healthy authority in its institutional life. We should not be surprised—indeed, we should be able to predict—that the manifestations of authority default will be found in every major institution (and every institution-like entity, such as sports and business) during the halftime after the disfranchisement of authoritarianism and before the rediscovery of authority in which we now find ourselves. In other words, those are expected outcomes that must be understood rather than merely condemned. Because the problem has not been named, people, somewhat as they seek salt and water bidden by deep, inner unchristened needs, are trying to find authority substitutes through trial-and-error experimentation.

They may call it something else, but they are haphazardly pursuing what they need in order to be human.

The spread of effective authority to other areas or departments or boards of trustees is exemplified in the extraordinary power ceded, with the collaboration of trustees, to athletic departments at certain universities. The results are the same: meltdown and rapid spread of authority, transformed into power, away from the president's office, leaving the president emasculated and impotent.

The practical spread of power away from the center of universities to supposedly subsidiary programs such as sports reveals how easily values are monetized when authority is dispersed. Manufacturers of athletic shoes have signed exclusive contracts with many basketball coaches, guaranteeing them hundreds of thousands of dollars a year if they outfit their teams with the company's brands. According to CBS's *60 Minutes,* Bobby Knight of Indiana University must, while coaching, wear a sweater emblazoned with a combination official school seal and corporate logo to push certain athletic gear.[2] Such compensation packages make coaches independent power centers in university affairs, immunizing them against regulations so they can pursue commercial goals separate from the educational aims of the university itself. Such privileges are not only denied to but considered unethical for other faculty members.

There is at present a lack of commitment to moral authority or consistent standards because, as in post–World War II Berlin before the authoritarian ruins were cleared to allow the principles of healthy government, we live in the unrelieved interim. In education, therefore, it is not surprising that practical power passes by default to students. Authority thus ceded is not easily reclaimed.

Stories such as that of the Immokalee, Florida, high school principal, Gilbert Shely, become commonplace during the post-hierarchical period. Trying to end an epidemic of tardiness in March 1994, he announced that, beginning March 21, two-hour detention would be issued to anyone late to any class. Shely said that he "was just trying to get an out-of-control situation back under control," because more than 140 of the 900 students in the school had been late for class one day that week.

The student response was direct, simple, effective, and a classic example of how authority, transformed into power, spreads away from the center, piercing concentric bureaucratic rings until it touches one, in this case the students, that absorbs and uses it. On the first day of the new policy, "around 100 Immokalee High School students put down their pencils, closed their books, and staged a '60s-style walkout." Shely capitulated, canceled the policy, and "by second period . . . was meeting with student representatives from each class, about 40 or 50 total, asking them for advice on how to handle the problem."[3]

Principal Shely's collapse was due to a weakened and scattered internal moral authority that had neither the confidence nor the cohesion to sustain a direct challenge. Like other beleaguered principals, Shely had no position, no Dunkirk from which to evacuate a semblance of authority, not even a Vichy in which to establish its façade. The humiliating surrender of all authority was made to a small group of dissident and delinquent students who had seized the free-floating power. The principal's resort to other students for a solution ironically confirmed that their power had replaced his authority. The resulting shift, all too common during this interim, both revealed and confirmed the authority default of the institution. Life goes on uneasily, much as it does in a city in which elected government has ceded pragmatic authority to some unelected constituency, be it bank presidents or gang leaders, with whom everything must be negotiated.

Experimentation Fills the Authority Void

The experimentation that has most directly undermined healthy authority in education is that inspired by the late psychologist Carl Rogers. Rogers, charismatic and obviously sincere, offered his theories, rooted in social work and related disciplines, at the right postwar moment, that is, immediately after the fall and repudiation of the hierarchical authoritarianism of Fascism and Nazism. At almost exactly the same time Great Britain allowed the sun to set on her empire, surrendering control of her colonies to native peoples. Already pitted in a chilly death struggle against authoritarian Communism, Americans were receptive to a democratized therapy radically different from the

"Herr Doktor" psychoanalytic paradigm rooted in the once firm hierarchical class distinctions of European culture. Client-Centered Therapy made the seeker and giver of help equals in the process, emphasizing the American ideal of individual self-reliance, changing patients into clients and helping them to clarify their present feelings to recapture their self-esteem through achieving a more accurate self-concept.

The rise of Client-Centered Therapy was also linked to the massive postwar interest in careers in clinical psychology, a profession that was rapidly redefining itself as one that specialized not only in testing and diagnosis but in nonmedical psychological treatment. Rogers's books and lectures, imbued with his preacher's zeal, brought democracy to therapy and made it available to all. Such an American notion was transferred quickly from the psychologist's office to the classroom.

In a series of books written, some with William Coulson, at the height of the "Human Potential" movement in the 1960s, Rogers proposed a system of student-centered education. In a famous experiment, Rogers tells teachers to appear in class but to teach nothing, that is, neither suggest, provide, or pursue any lesson plan. Theoretically, that motivates the students to question and draw out of the teacher what they need to learn. This transaction replaces the authority of the teacher with that which flows from the spontaneous, uncorrupted spirit of inquiry waiting within students to manifest itself.[4]

As Rogers's influence helped strip away the authoritarian grandeur of classic Freudian therapy, turning attention away from the archeological dig of the unconscious, his ideas also dispersed what little aura of "Herr Professor" still clung to the American teacher. Rogers, or those experimenting under his inspiration, in effect de-authorized teaching, that is, moved the teacher off the platform of expertise and into the classroom chairs on the same level with the students. As the teacher was changed, so was what was taught, from lessons for the mind into therapy for the feelings.

Replacing Authority with Ideology

Education came to focus on a new mission, the preservation and enhancement of the students' self-esteem. This is an example of how, during the interim of its default, institutional authority's function is focused on new political or ideological ends. In education, the hallmarks of substituting self-esteem for learning are easy to identify. The new virtues for the teacher are those of the Rogerian therapist: a nonjudgmental approach and, therefore, an unwillingness to impose values on the students; an "openness" to experience, that is, a willingness to allow the experience of the students, whatever it is and wherever it leads, to be the focus of attention; an "unconditional" acceptance of students as they are and a conviction that the preservation and enhancement of their self-esteem is the chief goal of the educational process.

The strong emphasis on feelings, often practiced by teachers with little, often superficial, workshop training in rudimentary counseling techniques, generates a misplaced and unearned confidence in their own therapeutic authority, that is, their ability to author genuine psychological treatment. Such false authority is used to rationalize their crossing the psychological borders between themselves and students that were once maintained by good sense, good manners, and the traditional standards of the master–pupil relationship. Such forays into the souls of students are justified as building their self-esteem.

Subjective approaches to education de-authorize teachers who are expected not to form minds and characters but to encourage students to have "good feelings" about themselves. It also destroys what is considered a great evil, a sense of elitism, a disparaging term used to refer to the simple circumstance that some students, in a mystery of genetic endowment and Providence, are more talented than others.

Lillian G. Katz, professor of early childhood education at the University of Illinois, describes "a project in an affluent Middle Western suburb . . . that showed how self-esteem and narcissism can be confused. Working from copied pages prepared by the teacher, each student produced a booklet called 'All About Me.' . . . The booklet, like thousands of others . . . around the country, had no page headings such as 'what I want to know more about,' 'what I am curious about,' 'what I want to solve' or even, 'to make.' Each page was directed toward the child's basest inner gratifications. Each topic put the child in the role of consumer—of food, entertainment, gifts and recreation. Not once was the child asked to play the role of producer, investigator, initiator, explorer, experimenter, or problem-solver." The children never author anything outside themselves and are handicapped in learning the real meaning of creative authority and the self-mastery it demands.

Assignments encourage the student to finish the sentence, "I am special because . . ." with such pedestrian accomplishments as "I can ride a bike," or "I can play with my friends," as they are encouraged to do beneath posters of clapping hands above the inscription "We Applaud Ourselves."[5] The middling air of self-celebration creates not self-esteem but a badly distorted self-image, a handicap when they are ultimately tested about what students know or can author in a real and unforgiving world.

Those are classic interval experiences, that is, the first scratchings in the dirt for a new alphabet after that of hierarchical authoritarianism has been wiped away. Such breaching of the ordinary boundaries of classroom relationships occurs when authority is flattened and standards are reduced, like Xerox copies, to a fraction of their original size. Only one dimension remains, the subjective personalized sense of what feels "good" or "comfortable" to the participant teacher. Such invasion of students' privacy may also be observed in a cluster of other booming campus practices.

Almost every day, according to informed observers writing in the *Chronicle of Higher Education,* "in college classrooms and faculty offices across the country, students receive writing assignments requiring inappropriate self-revelations."[6] Claiming that "the ethics of requiring students to write about their personal lives have largely been ignored," such educators list their ethical concerns: whether grades should ever be linked to self-revelation, the inability of many students to make judgments about how much and to whom they should confess their innermost experiences, and the danger of manipulating students into revelations that neither they nor their teachers are able to process or resolve successfully.

The true function of authority is destroyed when the ideal of mentoring students to help them to grow in healthy ways to achieve sensible goals is so mangled as to be unrecognizable. Such transactions are exercises of power through which, in the guise of educational/therapeutic intent, the needs of the mentor rather than those of the student are gratified. Even when teachers, following curricular demands rather than their own curiosity, require such "self-disclosure," they frequently lack the skills either to appreciate or to manage the emotional disruptions that can result from intrusive psychological relationships. In the most fundamental sense, such teachers do not possess the authority to function that way.

Money as the Authority Substitute

Another classic post-hierarchical effect is the monetization of authority issues. When natural authority is rendered mute, money talks. Thus, monetization has played a prominent role in "authorizing" a no-flunk policy that most Americans dislike. According to polls, "three-quarters of teachers and principals think children should be held back for not meeting specific grade objectives." Shari Iba, a coordinator of child development services in Florida, observes: "Retention is more merciful. What is more devastating, to be with my peers and know that I am failing, or to be held back one year?"

Cathy Wilkinson, who managed to get the school to hold back her third-grader, Jeffrey, after he tested at a first-grade reading level, identifies the monetization of authority that can inspire policy during the authorityless interval. The push to eliminate flunking, "she suggests, may be a money-saving move. Indeed, with fewer teachers' aides these days, and with 32 children or so per room, there is less personal attention available to kids who are behind."[7] It is cheaper to pass them on uneducated.

The "cost-effective" movement authorizes failure by keeping children in their peer group rather than at the level warranted by their performance. Monetization flows from the pseudo-feeling good about the self that provides its bizarre rationale. But failure cannot be authorized successfully on this basis any more than mediocrity can. Financially inspired no-failure plans always result from disregard for, or the outright relativization of, standards. In short, these are the shriveled crops that grow in this post-hierarchical interim.

No-flunk policies are rationalized as preservers of self-esteem, but humans author their self-esteem through achievement and mastery, howsoever modest, earning rather than claiming a right to accolades. Ignoring this truth on the basis of financial expediency—a combination of cutting costs and receiving financial incentives—is a classic example of monetization as a substitute for the lost sense of authority that promotes full growth.

Defining Mediocrity Up, Down, and In

Sharing the same defective genes of the interim "no-flunk" experimentation is the now widespread de-authorization of competition in gym class. This allows the spread of average performances to become modal and eliminates certain elements of striving, as well as the tension of self-discipline, in developing one's talents. The expansion of the middle zone of performance and achievement deprives individuals of the opportunity to learn how to lose or to grasp the meaning and inevitability of loss in life as well as to learn how to win graciously.

On the other hand, "elites," the scapegoat term branded on superior students, are thought to have no place in a democracy, and educational policies have been devised to suppress them.[8] That is a symptom of how confused education becomes when it no longer understands, values, or sensibly exercises generative authority.

As a result of ideological de-authorization, the "nation," according to a *New York Times* report, "is failing its smartest students who sit bored and unchallenged in classrooms and ultimately learn less than their counterparts around the world." A 1993 federal study, "National Excellence: A Case for Developing America's Talent," warns that many superior students "are enveloped in a 'quiet crisis' in which they are not encouraged to work hard or master rigorous and complex material." The 3–5 percent of students termed gifted, even in special programs, are sentenced to undemanding classes that, in effect, force them to bury their talents in the ground. The difficulty of their textbooks has been ratcheted down two grade levels in the last twenty years by publishers who have little incentive to create textbooks for above-average students.

It is not surprising that with only two cents out of every hundred dollars spent on K-12 education in a given school year (1990) going to support opportunities for talented children, the nation has produced a shortage of high-achieving graduates in mathematics and science. As a result, many large companies, including Texas Instruments, Bell Laboratories, and IBM, fill jobs, particularly in research, with people educated outside the United States.

Not since Alexis de Tocqueville chronicled the country's ambivalence toward intellectuals in the 1830s, the report notes, have the signs of low academic expectations been so visible. Furthermore, because of what amounts to a brutally effective, well-implemented policy to ignore, suppress, or force the gifted into the protoplasmic middle range, American students perform poorly on international tests, are offered a less rigorous curriculum, read fewer demanding books, do less homework, and are not well prepared to enter college or the workforce. A 1992 study of the top 10 percent of the students in twenty countries revealed that American nine year olds and thirteen year olds ranked near the bottom in international mathematics and science tests. Intensifying the tragedy, the most neglected were poor and minority students.[9]

Such findings correlate with score patterns on the Scholastic Aptitude Test, which, in the generation of years between 1972 and 1992, declined 35 percent in students scoring above 500 on its verbal section. Research analysis of the scores indicated that the drop could not be explained by the increase in the number of poor and minority students who took the test.

Again, such poor outcomes are artifacts of the standardless interim in which ideology acquires a spurious authority of its own. The scores were just what teachers wanted to achieve by substituting ideology for educational goals. They wanted to flatten the distinctions between students, to force them all into an undistinguished middle range. As the late Richard J. Herrnstein, professor of psychology at Harvard, observed, "The improvement to the average has been created by getting the bottom of the distribution of ability up. The price paid is that we have brought the top down."[10]

Mediocrity is thereby defined down because many teachers simply do not want an academic elite to exist and do everything they can to hammer out a one-class student on their vaguely Marxist anvil. Such interventions, however, have consequences. One of them is that, because they deny special attention or classes to high-achieving students, fewer of them do exceptionally well on standardized tests. Indeed, standardized tests have now been redesigned down—that is, their authority has been diluted—so that scores are automatically higher. In 1996, a new method of scoring the SAT guaranteed an increase in average scores, a classic manipulation of the interim.

Those common sense–defying efforts can be understood only as typical interlude behavior, the kinds of experiment people attempt when they are bereft of hierarchical standards and have yet to rediscover genuine authority. Defining mediocrity down by pulling superior students down to middle range is matched by defining mediocrity up through pulling inferior students up to the same midrange. Slower students cannot be made more intelligent or genuinely gifted. Initially, intellectual learning is debased and replaced by self-esteem therapy. Then intellectual demands are diluted, grades are inflated or omitted, tests themselves are altered, and, with failure eliminated, less talented students seem average.

Mediocrity cannot be authorized, however, because it represents a conspicuous failure to elicit full growth—to "lead out" what is within, the meaning of the root of educate, *e-ducere*—from the young. The problem with the mediocre, as Somerset Maugham is credited with observing, "is that they are always at their best." Settling for average can never be the goal of creative authority.

An educational institution abandons its intellectual and moral authority by pumping up the middle until it laps over and obscures the top and the bottom ranges like a hot-air balloon collapsing on a fairground crowd. Its best test is that applied by the common sense of ordinary men and women.

In Georgetown, Delaware, in June 1993, such de-authorization in the cause of keeping every student in the average range was achieved by the school board's firing a mathematics teacher, Adele Jones, for "incompetence and insubordination," translations of the principal's dismay at her giving what he considered "negative grades." The principal, John McCarthy, claimed that, ideologically, students should have "unanxious expectations" and that his "goal is to use positive re-inforcement to improve the self-esteem of kids."[11]

Insubordination was alleged because Ms. Jones refused to lower her standards in teaching and grading. "I just couldn't pass kids," she said, "who were failing my algebra course. I couldn't do that and still sleep at night." In fact, the commonsense jury came in quickly after her dismissal. "[V]irtually the entire student body walked out of the school in protest, wearing improvised buttons and carrying hastily scribbled signs saying 'I failed Ms. Jones's Class and It Was My Fault,' and 'Just Because a Student Is Failing Doesn't Mean the Teacher Is.'"

Seventeen-year-old Jodie Edwards indicted the principal's theories by "suggesting that self-esteem is built by challenging, not coddling, young people. I'm proud of my 92 average. Why? Because I actually earned it." The board, however, confirmed Ms. Jones's firing.

Forcing low achievers up and high achievers down to the middle range produces an abandoned academic *lumpenproletariat*. Healthy authority is not directed toward them, that is, teachers do not try to author average students by helping them grow by defining themselves either up or down. The only course is to define themselves in, to become lodged in the system.

Many observers believe that the children most neglected by public schools are those in the middle, the ones who spend their years sitting quietly in class, neither causing trouble nor drawing attention with extremely good or bad grades. Those neglected students are greater in number and more representative of American society than interim innovators care to admit. As the last ones to be treated as individuals, many of those students become intellectual dropouts. Because authority is unknown or unappreciated, there is no commitment to their growth, to their realizing their potential. Such young people suffer the bitter side effects of interim politicizing: They may manage to graduate, but they leave high school undereducated and uninspired to develop themselves further.

Inadequate teaching is an outcome of the collapse of authoritative standards and a failure to understand the nature or responsibility of healthy authority. That is an inevitable by-product of the destruction of hierarchical authoritarianism without refurbishing healthy author-

ity as the energy for the institution of education. Betrayed by interlude ideology, many teachers redefine themselves into mediocrity.
There is no other place to go in a system that has institutionalized the
middle as its one-size-fits-all goal of education. Ideologically driven,
the teachers cannot aspire to more than they allow to their students.
That is why so many poor teachers choose the barnacle-like life in the
turgid seas of what they perceive as "the system."

The *New York Times* notes: "By most estimates, 5 to 15 percent of
the nation's teaching corps operates in the zone between incompetence, which is usually defined by contract or state law, and acceptability." Don Fuhr, a Duke University professor of education, invokes
the word that symbolizes the grim reality of teachers who define
themselves into mediocrity.

"Marginal," Fuhr calls them. "It's not the ones you dismiss that
cause you problems. It's the ones still in there, just doing enough to
get by. People will say to me, 'What harm do they do?' 'I say, first of
all, they contribute to the dropout rate. They turn kids off to school.
Second, they reduce support for the schools.' Parents know where the
good teachers are."[12]

Estrangement from natural authority leads to a vast deployment of
average and mediocre teachers throughout school systems. The
swelling middle range is actually perceived as a psychological and
democratic triumph. When there is no sense of authoring, growth is
irrelevant, and education contradicts itself by choosing the average as
a common social destiny.

In Authority's Absence, Everything Breaks Down

When authority is compromised, everything it promises—expectations, standards, internal order, an atmosphere of trust, and cooperation in generating growth—breaks down within the educational
institution. So, too, the persons within it manifest a loss of the internalized standards that are the counterpart of those of the external institution. The integration authority once achieved for both the
institution and its members crumbles for both. The institution loses
wholeness, that is, its integrity.

The results are on display in the failure in every class day to acknowledge the expectations once presented by sensible authority. Educators also reject the Western cultural and moral tradition. The once clear diamond of authority is splintered, and each strewn, glittering carat is now a light unto itself. Each group demands that its rights be met with little or no reference to the common good. Multicultural studies, with their brilliant possibilities for mutual understanding, become instead the Verdun of education. To deal with the skirmishes that flare up in an environment unbound by central authority, codes and regulations are fashioned out of the heavily politicized and adversarial atmosphere. Good order breaks down as ethnic groups, men and women, students and teachers, faculty and administration, pit themselves against each other.

What happens is predictable but somehow always surprising to those in the midst of it. Cheating, scientific misconduct, administrative malfeasance, violence, sexual assault, race-baiting, and anti-Semitism increase. Mistrust and suspicion abound, as they must when the grounds for trust are undermined. A sense of being free and safe on the campus is lessened for everybody. The age of paranoia dawns as bleakly as the first day of war.

Paranoia drifts across campuses as tear gas did at militant demonstrations of the 1960s. At its root, paranoia is an attempt to make some order out of chaos, to weld the shards of surreal experience together with the solder of madness. Fear and suspicion spark off this process because in dangerous zones anybody and everybody may be your enemy. Being on guard doesn't seem paranoid.

Thus the educational institution and its campus, where in the age of randomness anything can happen, are no longer safe places. People begin to fear for their physical welfare and even for their lives. That is why, absent authority, especially moral authority, the wild and unpredictable violence of paranoia, as powerful and indiscriminate as a tornado, devastates the institution and takes away its freedom.

The disorder of the interval in which authoritarianism no longer functions and healthy authority seems as undiscovered as a cure for the rarest of diseases is sadly documented in the multiplied cases of misconduct reported in the once presumably pure and sacred laboratories of scientific research. The operational collapse of the objectivity of the scientific method has led to a deauthorization of many reported project results and severe damage to the authority of the American scientific enterprise, making it easy for critics to say science is only another way to describe reality.

Recounting a breach of scientific ethics, the *Chronicle of Higher Education* relates: "A growing number of lawmakers, scientists, and activists charge that the National Cancer Institute covered up evidence that researchers whom it supported had engaged in scientific misconduct." Part of a "huge set of clinical trials aimed at finding the best treatment for breast and bowel cancer," the project involved more than a hundred universities and five thousand physicians and researchers. Montreal's Roger Poisson "had falsified the results of some of his experiments over the last 15 years and fabricated data for others. [The] National Cancer Institute . . . had known about the 'irregularities' since early 1991."

An explosion of media attention was joined by the alarmed protests of women's health activists and the initiation of Congressional hearings by Michigan Representative John Dingell, whose aide said that officials of the National Cancer Institute "were not paying attention to what was going on with the study for years, and once they saw there were problems, they did not exercise their full authority to get the problems resolved."[13]

Fragmented healthy authority, like a tattered binding, no longer holds the pages of everyday experience securely together. They come loose and are scattered in the sudden turbulence. That has happened in public high schools, in which, in a Norman Rockwell nightmare, it is estimated that more than half a million attacks, shakedowns, and robberies occur every month. Three million crimes are committed yearly on or near schools. Every day, nearly 135,000 pupils carry guns to school, and 20 percent of all students say that they bring some kind of weapon with them to school.

More than a fifth of all secondary school students do not use the school rest rooms because they fear they will be harmed or intimidated in one way or another. Studies reveal that the chief concern children have about being in school is the disruptive behavior of their classmates. Teachers share this same concern; almost a third of public school teachers report this as a motive for seeking a different occupation.[14]

Big cities station policemen inside schools and install metal detectors at their entrances. Authority's absence manifests itself even on campuses like that of the Naval Academy, which once took pride in its self-discipline and honor code. After a 1993 cheating episode, twenty-nine midshipmen were expelled, "the latest blow," according to the *New York Times,* to an institution "which suffered a sexual harassment scandal in 1990 after eight midshipmen chained a female classmate to a urinal."[15]

New Authoritarians, Fresh Bureaucracies

When hierarchical authoritarianism died intestate, it left natural authority a disinherited orphan. When sensible authority is so far out of relationship to institutional life, power takes its place and metastasizes to the most remote organs of the system. Described as "institutional layering" or "bureaucratic bloat," the condition is observable in the recent exponential growth of nonteaching staff members at all levels of education. For example, in the New York City Public School system, the former Chancellor reported a central bureaucracy of 3,481 positions, later corrected to 7,078 individuals or 6,300 full-time equivalents. That contributes to the current ratio of 23.5 nonteachers for every 100 teachers in the system.

Such ancillary personnel, including auditors, affirmative action specialists, systems analysts, and open expression monitors, exercise real power over students, administrators, and teachers. Between 1975 and 1985 they increased 60 percent in colleges and universities, while faculty who actually teach have grown by only 5.9 percent.[16] The new functionaries at the fringes leach authority away from the central mission of teaching, binding and blocking it by their interventions.

The Flowering of Anti-intellectualism

The most glaring characteristic of the new authoritarianism in education is its profound and pervasive anti-intellectualism. When subjectivity reigns, objectivity is forced into exile. The self as the source of standards and interpretation cannot tolerate the claims made by traditions separate from it. Just as after fascistic revolutions control is immediately imposed on free inquiry, so, in the interval, the intellectual freedom demanded by traditional scholarship is quickly rescinded. The interval vocabulary of "thought police" and "intellectual censorship" is used often in the pseudo-intellectual *lingua franca.* As the goal of intellectual authorship becomes transmogrified from the pursuit of truth to the propagation of a political viewpoint, its lead academicians, according to the late Edward Shils, disregard and denigrate even the possibility of discovering truth through philosophical inquiry, the literary imagination, and the scientific or historical method.[17] Those procedures are considered merely alternate ways of describing reality and have no particular authority to persuade us one way or the other.

That perspective gratuitously denies intellectual history and scientific discovery, because they are incompatible with its own political prejudices. A radical nucleus of supposed scholars rejects outright the authority of the Western tradition of learning, not settling for a disciplined critique of its faults, and wage war against it as if it were Tsarist Russia, a huge faded kingdom of unrelieved and irredeemable evil.

They share the anti-intellectualism of the great totalitarian movements of this interim century. Nazism, Fascism, and Communism in Russia and China identified intellectuals as the enemy and vigorously attacked the scientists, the philosophers, and the poets and writers whose approaches to truth constituted a threat to their own control of that precious virtue. The burning of books, the suppression of free inquiry, the jailing of thinkers, scientists, and writers, with the destruction of the professional classes, are considered odious by most Americans. Yet tactics not very different in spirit and tone from these are not only observable but are successfully employed on university campuses throughout the nation.

The first circular issued in the Chinese Cultural Revolution in May 1966 attacked "scholar tyrants" whose "abstruse" language tended to silence the class struggle and keep politics from infiltrating academia. China's Red Guard made its first assault at Tsinghua University. "During the early summer, the entire educational system in China came to a standstill, as dons and teachers fled in terror (when they were lucky enough to escape capture and 're-education') and juvenile lynch-law took over." A few weeks before that, Lin Piao had argued before the Politburo: "Political power is an instrument by which one class oppresses another. . . . political power is the power to oppress others."[18]

Members of the Academic Left, according to well-qualified critics, are so set against science that they seem kin to the fundamentalist creationists championed by William Jennings Bryan in the celebrated 1925 trial of John T. Scopes in Dayton, Tennessee, for teaching evolution in his biology class. Science, the left insists, is a white male European way of looking at the universe, and it suppresses the views of women and minorities.

Sandra Harding, a feminist philosopher of science who describes the *Principia mathematica* as "Newton's rape manual," says that science should be "politics by other means." She agrees with her colleague Helen Longino's position that "when faced with a conflict between commitments and a particular model of brain-behavior relationships we allow political commitments to guide our choice" and that "feminist scientific practice admits political considerations as relevant constraints on reasoning."[19]

When politics dominates a field, its scholars act in classically authoritarian ways, truncating the scope of inquiry or salting it with ideologically inspired approaches. Only in the resulting surreal anti-intellectual climate is it possible to invent courses that further dilute the already repeatedly watered-down liberal arts curriculum and at the same time degrade the population whose self-esteem they are intended to bolster. Thus "Black Hair as Culture and History" was introduced as an upper-level history seminar at Stanford University in the early 1990s. Professor Kenneth Jackson explained to an overflow crowd at his initial class meeting that black hair had interacted with society, and therefore he was trying to make it into a field.

Such insubstantial offerings honor neither scholarship nor black people, whose dignity they violate far more than they elevate it. Likewise, in the field of women's studies, many scholars identify the dangers of the free application of currently popular poststructural textual analyses. "Like all postmodern theories," writes Joan Hoff, professor of history at Indiana University and co-editor of the *Journal of Women's History*, "poststructuralism casts stable meanings into doubt. It sees language as so slippery that it compromises historians' ability to identify facts and chronological narratives and it reduces to mere subjective stories the experiences of women struggling to define themselves in particular historical contexts. . . . [T]he current wave of poststructuralism could paralyze the field of women's history."[20]

Women and minorities may easily become hostages to an anti-intellectual movement that descends not from Goethe but from Goebbels, and may find themselves manipulated anew by such invention. The anti-intellectual climate debases and de-authorizes civil dialogue. It generates bitter, divisive, racist incidents, which, with their explosive charges and countercharges, threaten the hard-won achievements of improved racial equality and understanding in America.

Promoting anti-intellectualism through the manipulation of educational policy for political ends is a familiar totalitarian tactic. Crassly ignoring the real-world needs of children, it becomes both cruel and tragic. Employing the classroom to achieve the egalitarian ideological rather than educational policy is exemplified in the law-driven and court-driven movement of "full inclusion" of the disabled into classrooms with their age-mates. Despite truly disabling physical and psychological differences, these students are forced into equality for political reasons. Everybody is the same and everybody must be treated the same, no matter what distortions, frustrations, or tragedies may result. The human costs in this program are raised exponentially because the students involved are truly disabled, some of them with extensive psychological or physical impairments. While everyone wants such students to be educated or trained to the maximum their severely limited possibilities will allow, denying their problems cannot lead to that goal. Lawyers, however, do not necessarily look at matters from the commonsense viewpoint.

Whittier, California, offers us an example of the new and potentially tragic egalitarianism in action. A ninth-grade scene is described in the *Wall Street Journal:*

> "Write down four things you learned today," teacher Amy Walkup tells her fifth-period algebra class. Fourteen of the 16 high school freshmen

comply. Of the other two boys, Joey repeatedly jingles a set of keys, and Philip says he wants to eat and starts crying. Joey is autistic, and Philip has Down's syndrome. Both 14-year-olds go to regular classes at Whittier High School under a new policy placing all 469 ninth-graders in regular classes full time, regardless of their mental, physical or emotional characteristics. Whittier High School plans to institute this change in succeeding ninth-grade classes until the entire school is under the same policy.[21]

What is the engine of this drastic integration of all students, irrespective of abilities? Whittier's principal, Fred Zimmerman, explains: "With recent court cases, this will be the direction of all schools." The legal leverage through which the massive experiment is imposed usurps the authority of educators and coerces them into decisions that are rooted in social rather than academic convictions. "More and more severely disabled children around the country," the *Journal* article continues, "are being taught in regular classrooms on the theory that they benefit more here than in segregated, special education classes and that their nondisabled classmates *will learn tolerance*." (Emphasis added.)

Anti-intellectualism, the counterfeit money of contemporary education, buys only falsehood and is a product of authoritarianism, not authority. When false "truths" are forced on people by pragmatic authoritarians, it is called indoctrination. But truth, and the genuine ecstasy that is a by-product of its pursuit and discovery, are generated only by healthy authority.

Whatever is anti-intellectual is also anticreative and destructive of the climate in which disinterested—that is, depoliticized—scholarship can seek truth. George Will notes: "Academics who blithely insist that 'everything is political'—for example, whether, or how, to read Emily Dickinson—are postulating that all decisions are motivated by the desire to acquire power over others . . . emotional impoverishment is inevitable because love is impossible, selflessness being unimaginable."[22]

The range of freedom narrows, and other concomitant values of free inquiry also suffer. The most salient of these is trust, a virtue difficult to find in this authoritarian environment. When authority is degraded, standards collapse, and trust loses its meaning. Anything goes: falsified data, cheating, and dishonest and exploitative relationships.

That also explains why the word "honor" may now be used more often in crossword puzzles than in public discourse. Honor is a public and social virtue. While it depends on inner qualities, it necessarily manifests itself in the outer relationships and circumstances in which it is tested. Honor cannot exist without healthy authority and the sensible human standards of aspiration and expectation into which it infuses its energy and life.

Many academicians, however, appear puzzled at the rash of cheating, at the dishonor and lack of trust found in higher education. Misperceiving the problem, they offer misbegotten solutions, such as the abandonment of final exams or programs to improve students' self-esteem as the cure for cheating. These are wildly off the mark, but one can hardly expect honor-bearing standards to be invoked when they have, on philosophical principle, been sent into an exile as cold and scattered as that of the Gulag. Neither can we expect students, professors, or researchers to be trustworthy when, in effect, that virtue has been deconstructed into oblivion. How can the academy be other than in disarray in such circumstances?

Making Law Do the Work of Authority

The depth of anti-intellectual politicizing on campuses may be observed in its impacted relativism, with its denial that moral or intellectual truth is attainable, which leaves its proponents without a foundation for their crusades against what they perceive as the greatest evils of the age: racism, sexism, gender inequality, and homophobia. Having eliminated or demonized the authority of the Western moral and religious tradition, advocates for morallike positions are forced, as were the biblical pharisees after the destruction of Jerusalem's unifying temple or canon lawyers after Catholicism's weakened grip on its sacramental essence, to construct in their place endless, obsessive codes of conduct.

What is striking, however, is the fascistic flavor of the enforcement processes used in conjunction with codes on sexual behavior, alleged racism, ethnic prejudice, or hate speech. The penalties often include, in the classic communist style, political or emotional reeducation programs. Charges are often accepted as valid merely because they are made; the civil rights of those who are accused are suspended, and often extremely punitive measures, such as firing, suspension, or expulsion, are prescribed. Freedom is always the first casualty of de-authorized morality.

Americans, however, have grown accustomed to some degree to having the courts take over basic educational decisions, such as the conditions of enrollment and the design of the curriculum. While that has often been criticized as unwarranted interference on the part of the courts, its relationship to the collapsed authority of educational institutions has seldom been acknowledged. The courts often act only because educational institutions have become too enfeebled to act for themselves in matters that are their concern.

The very notion that ethical codes might reflect the traditions and ideals of different institutions seems, in a world in which so much has been yielded to law, an alien and improper thought. Indeed, ethical hearings in higher education, especially under the pressures generated by rootless ideology-driven codes of campus behavior, are now thick with lawyers who have changed their procedures utterly. Some private universities—but very few—have withstood the development of such codes and the restructuring of their ethical inquiries into judicial-like hearings.

Kill common sense and you always kill freedom at the same time. Freedom in education implies the provision of an environment in which learning can be safely authored and law is meant to support rather than supplant such healthy exercise of authority. The Detroit Board of Education provided an illustration of this process when it forsook a carefully thought-out plan to improve retention of black males in the 170,000-pupil school system. A coalition of national and local minority leaders, education officials, and civil rights advocates had argued the merits of establishing all-male, Afrocentric schools and appropriate courses, such as those that had been developed successfully in Baltimore, Washington, San Diego, Milwaukee, New Orleans, Miami, and New York.

Opponents challenged that educational plan, however, on legal grounds, contending that single-sex public education violated the Constitution's equal protection clause forbidding gender discrimination in federally funded programs. Federal Judge George E. Woods ruled in August 1991 that the plan was unconstitutional and that a new program allowing girls into the schools would have to be drawn up. This indeed occurred, destroying the progressive program by obliterating its commonsense human purpose and transforming it into a legal issue.

Although Valparaiso University in Indiana was founded as a Lutheran institution, its administrators became embroiled in the problems that follow when, detached from that tradition, a code for sexual harassment hesitates to speak the language of the law whose effects it nonetheless desires to have. After a highly emotional "Take Back The Night" anti–date rape rally in the spring of 1993, the school's president, Alan Harre, convened an eight-hour meeting of administrators to hear testimony from thirteen women recruited by Kirsten Lee, a campus activist who had helped organize the earlier rally.

One of the outcomes of the session was the development of "a 'victim-friendly' procedure for handling charges of sexual assault brought by one student against another. As with similar procedures at other campuses—including Northwestern University—students can bring allegations directly to administrators without involving law-enforcement officials, and the disciplinary hearings are conducted in secret." This policy was invoked that September against a male student accused of rape by a female student.

The student "was told that his guilt or innocence would be decided at a hearing to be held in only four days. . . . On the morning of the hearing, the lawyer for the accused rapist submitted the names of eight witnesses" who would have testified in the young man's behalf. "But his lawyer was not allowed to call any of the witnesses. It was ruled that the accused's witness list had not been presented enough in advance. Nor did the accused man get to confront his accuser. The woman remained out of view in another room. She gave her testimony and responses to questions on audio tape.

"The hearing . . . lasted 11 hours, until 3:30 a.m. . . . only the victim, her three witnesses, and the accused were allowed to testify during the hearing. The young man from Chicago was found guilty as charged. His lawyer's request for an appeal was rejected. *Because this was not a court of law but rather a disciplinary hearing before adminis-*

tration officials on the private university's campus, the sentence was not incarceration."[23]

The defendant was expelled from the campus for as long as his alleged victim continued to go to school there. In response to this hybrid procedure, which aped the authority of the law while eschewing its safeguards and consequences, he has filed a $12 million lawsuit. Defending the disciplinary process, akin to that at many other schools, including Swarthmore, Williams, Brown, and Yale, a Valparaiso spokesperson suggested that the procedures have nothing to do with whether a student is guilty or not guilty at civil or criminal levels.

Confused about its authority, driven in a good cause by ideology rather than its moral tradition, and adopting authoritarian procedures, Valparaiso finds itself in the web of litigation while trying to avoid the substance and consequences of law itself. So the circle closes in a hundred environments in which natural authority could be exercised in a responsibly human way. The last state of any country is worse than the first when, instead of rediscovering and supporting natural authority, that country allows lawyers to become the gatekeepers of every endeavor. Then you no longer have life but only the devouring law, not freedom that seeks safety but only legalism that makes everything dangerous.

Killing Parents and Bringing Them Back as Law

In loco parentis, the school's former understanding of its role in furthering the parenting process, was cast aside a generation and more ago. Students were presumed to be fully socialized and responsible adults.

The presumption is not and never has been the case, but that cannot be blamed on the students themselves. It was rather a function of the era in which throwing authoritarianism overboard carried healthy authority into the deep with it. With authoritarianism dead at last, there was no longer any need to feed it with either expectations on, or restrictions of, student behavior. So dawned the mottled era in which all were to be allowed "to do their own thing," even if that meant failing, dropping out, or burning one's best gifts away with the lime of drug and alcohol abuse.

New models arose at the dawn of the Space/Information Age as, for example, in the early 1970s, when the consumer movement gained influence as the gradations that separated purchasers from product makers and vendors were erased. As the monetization of all relationships continued in the post-hierarchical interlude, the consumer model was easily transferred to education. The institution of learning had lost its sense of authoring as, indeed, had many confused parents. It looked like progress to many to cast these relationships afresh in the bright, depersonalized egalitarian mold of consumerism.

That supplanted the traditional parental model, in which care for civility, ethics, and morals had been central. Those were irrelevant for students presumed able to regulate themselves. Perceived as "consumers," they were to be treated as such, vested with their "rights" and provided with "consumer information" about the "services" they wished to purchase in the college marketplace. Indeed, federal and state governments quickly bought into that model, adopting legislation protecting students' privacy and requiring that "consumer information" on such things as financial aid and related matters be provided to them as they were to shoppers in grocery stores and automobile showrooms. In parallel fashion during this period, medical and nonmedical therapists came to be termed health care providers, and their patients became consumers.

The ironic denouement of the colleges' disavowal of the parental role, and the introduction of the consumer service provider model, has been the massive intervention of the law to re-create, for all practical purposes, a new set of parentlike responsibilities for colleges based on consumer protection legislation and relevant judicial precedents. Having abdicated their authority out of what they thought was a spirit of progress, they found it quickly replaced by regulation.

The market conceptualization was appropriated and expanded on by federal and state legislatures across the country. Bills were passed endorsing "consumer rights" that required colleges to provide information about all aspects of the educational universe, including the extent of campus crime and the scope of state and federal laws against alcohol and drug abuse. In the absence of natural authority, authoritarianism in the name of reform was reinvented. Statutes often went well beyond setting guidelines for reporting information to students and frequently contained explicit or implicit requirements that specific disciplinary policies, such as restrictions against underage drinking, be adopted, enforced, and monitored by colleges to protect students and members of the public.

The new tree of regulation, rooted in the colleges' ownership of property and the obligations thereunto attached, is a telling example of how, when a vacuum is created by the abandonment of commonsense authority, some other force, usually the law, eventually seeks to fill it. Such a contentious outcome results from failing to understand how healthy authority melds structure and independence so that students may complete their intellectual preparation and moral socialization.

The young cannot be blamed for their virtual abandonment, by a generation intent in a hundred ways on overturning the demands of authority, to an educational institution that had lost its own sense of moral authority as well. The process of rediscovering such authority has already begun. James Reed, Dean of the College at Rutgers, describes why colleges are involving themselves once more: "Tragedies began taking place, and we couldn't claim any more that students are adults and are not our responsibility. . . . We have a moral imperative to reassert authority."[24]

All the problems of despoiled authority—its spread and transformation into domination by the power of law and politics, change of purpose from educational to therapeutic, political, and social reform, proliferating institutional ineffectiveness, growing public distress with and distrust of the public school system, the self-defeating collapse of all distinctions for the sake of an expanded but degraded average-range education and achievement, the betrayal of the advantaged and the disadvantaged—are upon us already. America only lacks a Dickens to dramatize the subtle but pervasive cruelty of an educational system whose presumed leaders, like French aristocrats applauding the revolution while the tumbrels rolled toward their doors to take them to the guillotine, have de-authorized themselves.

8

Rediscovering Authority in Education: Recommendations

Recognize that change has already begun. It is highly significant to observe the first moves away from the empty radicalism that provided temporary housing for such things as values clarification, teachers as therapists, and speech and sexual harassment codes as virtual morality. Those small restylings indicate that education, largely because of its readiness to make and withdraw investments in trendiness, is telling itself that the party is over. Life without sensible authority is only life-style. Living and working as adaptations to formless interval conditions can no longer be sustained. The experimenters have lived in what they thought was the future and discovered that it does not work. Their efforts to find new modes of existence and function tell us that the rediscovery of healthy authority is under way.

Many of the signs are as small as the bromeliads that bloom on the Florida Keys in what still seems winter, as spring's first flag of return to North America. The culture itself is advertising its new discovery of an old truth: Men and women cannot comfortably live in the protoplasmic, decentered condition that characterizes the modern interval, especially in education. Many of the responses to the contemporary chaos revalidate authority even as they attempt to rediscover it.

For example, the first movement away from the radical rejection of all but subjective authority is found in the decision by *Social Text,* a left-wing journal of cultural politics, to abandon its editorship by a collective, along with the impoverishment in which it once gloried, and to be published by Duke University Press in a thoroughly traditional manner. The *Chronicle of Higher Education* notes: "The journal's . . . move to a university press is an admission that the journal needed professional help and will, despite its activist leanings, remain ensconced in academic culture."[1]

Use tradition to strengthen authority. The flight to tradition as a stabilizing center is a symbolic acceptance of a larger authority than a collectivist diffusion provides. "There hasn't been a rethinking of mission in years," one editor of *Social Text* observes in the same article. "It's an identity crisis." In a different context, *USA TODAY,* which originally set out to break with the traditional forms of newspapers, has decided to send its personnel through mandatory courses to help them acquire the formal manners and social customs that many of them lack. That includes how to dress, how not to be offensive, and how to modulate one's feelings to enable social discourse to flourish. That is but one of the almost unnoticed indications that the powerful currents of the standardless culture are turning at last.

The creative gestation period for the birth of these lesser and greater cultural entities is located at the beginning of the 1990s. The cost of interval living in every field had become too high. On a wide front people asserted that they could no longer tolerate disorder, danger, soaring crime rates, or the tragedies of generations being born into a world that had abandoned the institutions essential for their growth as truly human beings. The flames of the burning hulk of a dying interval culture are brightest just before its end. Some of the most dramatic outrages of education's wandering experimentation, for example, have been acted out during this period. The most outrageous examples of political correctness were the final surges of flame through the empty vaults of the post-hierarchical time. The impulses to reexamine and perhaps to recapture or reinvent some of the discipline of tradition leap from a newly kindled fire of the human spirit that attracts us as powerfully as the lights of a great city turning on at dusk. For example, in an "appreciation" of the late critic Clement Greenberg in the *New York Times,* Michael Kimmelman observes that "at a time when the art world is as fragmented as ever, there is a longing for someone to establish order in the way Greenberg seemed to do. . . . A nostalgia for those days . . . is strong. This nostalgia also involves an intellectual community that spoke not in the often arcane jargon of today's academy but in a language aimed at an audience broader than one in university campuses."[2]

The true meaning of authority and tradition now must be restated because their very names surprise and startle the sensibility of "modern" people like obituaries of once famous people thought long dead. But authority, banished by relativism and subjectivity from its role as an organizing nucleus of human learning, must, even according to some of the most radical of contemporary scholars, be respected and restored if the pursuit of knowledge and wisdom is to be saved from the transformation by politicization.

Thus Richard Rorty, an American philosopher whose questioning of the nature of truth and merit is invoked by many to disassemble the heritage of Western culture, indicts transformed educational methods to which this has given rise. "It strikes me as a terrible idea," he responds when an interviewer presses him to denounce the traditional college approach to freshman composition. "I think the idea of freshman English, mostly, is just to get students to write complete sentences, get the comma in the right place and stuff like that—the stuff that we would like to think the high schools do and, in fact, they don't."

Rorty endorses E. D. Hirsch's notion of "cultural literacy," according to which American high school students should master and share a common vocabulary and body of knowledge. A shared historical perspective is imperative if students are "to have a sense of citizenship in a country. . . . I think of America as a spectacular success story of the growth of democratic freedom, whereas my opponents on the left think of it as a racist, sexist, imperialist society. Having admitted that. . . , it seems to me it's still the best thing one can offer, whereas my opponents tend to think that having said that you can sort of set it aside."[3] Americans can take heart from these observations from a man who speaks with authority because he has never lost his feeling for its true meaning or its true demands on thinkers and educators.

Do not be afraid to assert the claims of natural authority. Education is so depleted of true authority that those who understand its nature must exercise it confidently. Good sense, like the first fine day of spring, draws people automatically toward it. Positive authority consolidates its strength around the person or group using it.

In the universe of education, leaders with a sense of natural authority and common sense need not tilt at the disintegrating windmills of values clarification, speech codes, bureaucratic regulation, and the forced illusion of self-esteem. Those lack centralized, compelling authority and are dying by breathing their own air. Let the dead, as the Bible suggests, bury the dead.

The scriptures are, in fact, enlightening on this matter. People have wondered at such stories as the fortress walls collapsing at the sound of a trumpet. That is just a way of describing how falsehood crumbles at the first sound of truth. The first premise for the rediscovery of authority is that in education it is an enormously attractive substance. The only successful strategy is to make yourself the center around which healthy authority can be reconvened.

So profound have been the fragmenting and estranging effects of the authority crisis in some schools that parents have given up all hope of successful collaboration with the system itself. "We're mad as hell, and we aren't taking it any more," Lisa Spillane, mother of three, told the *New York Times* regarding the plans of West Pikelands, Pennsylvania, parents to take their high school out of the Downingtown Area School District by asking the state Education Department's permission to secede.[4]

The distrust surfaced after the U.S. Education Department's 1983 report "A Nation at Risk" described widespread deficiencies in public education. Attempts to involve parents in changing the schools have been "disappointedly mixed." Parents who do not want to secede from school districts are establishing their own public schools, setting up charter schools outside of local districts, and sometimes teaching their children at home. That is a clear example of parents' attempt to rediscover and to reestablish their natural authority over the healthy overall development of their children.

Authority in education can be successfully rediscovered only if parents and teachers understand the nature of their respective authority and, despite the overlap, acknowledge the distinction in their obligations and goals. They are playing the same game but at different positions. Success flows from teamwork in a process that depends not on the faddish and superficial notion of empowerment but on the mature collaboration of these distinctive sources of natural authority.

Parents and teachers must understand their respective fields of authorship with the young. A test offered by the late Seward Hiltner of the Princeton Theological Seminary has helped clergy to distinguish between what they author as pastors and as counselors. If the service they provide demands that those to whom they deliver it be called "clients" or "patients," they are exceeding their pastoral authority. If they can still comfortably refer to them as "parishioners" or "church members," they are offering help that falls within their pastoral authority.

If teachers act in a manner that enables them to call their charges "students" or "pupils," they are safely within, and therefore free to exercise, their proper authority. If, however, what they are doing forces them to describe their charges as "patients" or "clients," they are trying to exercise a therapist's authority that is beyond them. If they view them as "consumers" and themselves purely as "providers," they have literally bought into a monetized substitute for their natural authority. In the same way, if they regard those they serve as "family members" or "children," they are exercising parental authority, that is, attempting to author what is better authored by parents in the home than by teachers in the classroom.

Do parents often teach, or assist their children in mastering, their school subjects? Of course they do, as anybody with common sense would agree. Many teachers also assist in the tasks of parenting through their example, advice, and capacity for healthy relationships with those they instruct. Nonetheless, the fundamental focus of the authority of each, like separate spotlights that sometimes merge as they rove across the players on stage, is distinct and, lest they be confounded, should remain so.

Recognize that research confirms your good instincts. The family's crucial role in the child's success in school—the parents' continuing to author their childrens' growth—is emphasized in the research results that have issued from an ongoing comprehensive national survey of students, parents, teachers and school principals.[5] There is a commonsense ring, for example, to the finding that students do best in school when their parents view themselves rather than administrators as being in charge of their child's educational career.

So, too, children whose parents talk to them about school events or what they learned in class do better on achievement tests. Children whose parents restrict television during the week, provide music lessons outside school, and offer some form of adult supervision after school also do better on achievement tests. In addition, children who spend less than three hours a day without adult supervision have higher test scores than those who are unsupervised for longer periods.

Teachers who understand their authority also produce better students. Children whose teachers expect them to achieve at a higher than average level do better on math and reading tests. The more homework teachers assign, the higher their students' achievement level. Parents should not hesitate to request a teacher who will expect the child to succeed and to learn more than a minimum, and one who also assigns a fair amount of homework.

Researchers and educational experts also advise that parents who want to exercise their authority wisely should not expect a painless transition. Just as parents cannot cry for their children, neither can they learn for them. Children must struggle somewhat to grow into their responsibilities in every new year of school and, unless they have prolonged academic difficulties that may need assessment, it is their task to make school work.

Recent studies have shown remarkable improvements in black school achievement. The National Assessment of Educational Progress, conducted by the U.S. Department of Education's National Center for Educational Statistics, points to an unexpected but significant factor in these increases. As described in the *Wall Street Journal,* "Black achievement on the K-12 level has been rising for the past two decades. But evidence suggests that credit for this appears to lie not, for the most part, with desegregation or compensatory education. It appears to lie instead in the increasing *amount* of education attained by black parents."[6]

Black parents rediscover their generative authority through their own educational achievement. The research reveals substantial gains in black parents' education between 1971 and 1990. The data "also confirm that blacks from more highly educated families have higher achievement. . . . The increased education of black parents is not necessarily the direct cause of the achievement gains. Rather, the family's educational status probably stands for specific family behaviors and attitudes—such as motivation, educational aspiration, child-rearing practices, enforcement of help with homework, and so forth—that translate into actual academic improvement for children."

Stimulating families possess authority of a very special kind. The crucial role of such intrafamilial stimulation is underscored by recent research on brain development. Summarizing a report by the Carnegie Foundation, the *Wall Street Journal* observes: "Scientists have known for decades that environment affects behavior, but only in recent years have they started to understand that the brain is literally shaped by experience. They now believe an infant's brain develops more quickly in the first year than they had expected and that sensory experiences can affect which brain cells and cell connections live or die."[7]

This research seconds what common sense and good parents have appreciated for generations, as noted by Edward Zigler, director of the Yale University Bush Center in Child Development and Social Policy and a founder of Head Start. Stimulating a child is simple, he says, "but it does take time: putting children on your lap, letting them turn pages when you read to them—normal everyday interactions. 'Drop the nonsense about quality time,' he says, 'It's quantity time that children need.'"

Parents should not hesitate to impose structure on their children's lives. They should arrange the household so that there is a time and a place free of distraction, such as television, for study and homework. Parents give their children a message about their values and their high estimation of the value of school when they are willing to alter their own schedules and lives to provide good educational conditions at home.

These commonsense policies allow natural authority to flow freely in the family, the school, the neighborhood, and eventually in the wider culture. Like all human enterprises, this will always be imperfectly accomplished, but that is also its remarkable strength. It matches the healthy needs and longings of human beings and does not distort or disserve them by categorizing them as purely commercial units. That, as in the consumer model, diminishes rather than enhances their natural growth possibilities.

Parents should anticipate mistakes. They may help children to buy school supplies, but the children are responsible for taking their books and pencils to school every day. If a child gets a bad mark for forgetting a notebook, that's a mistake from which he or she can learn an important life lesson. It is not the parents' job to take all responsibility or to try to obviate such mistakes or misplays. They are as inevitable as they are invaluable, if properly managed, to the overall growth of the children.

To despair of finding self-discipline among the young is to abdicate authority and ignore the situations where it is found even in contemporary culture. McDonald's, the fast food chain, creates a restaurant environment in which self-discipline is expected and where, even when crowded with students, it is generally found. Franchise restaurants may be the last outposts of civility in which people behave in an orderly manner, stand in line, and clean up after themselves, which suggests that the expectation of good behavior, made by both parents and teachers, can replicate such good order in classrooms.

The 1996 presidential campaign highlighted the rise in drug use among adolescents. A survey reported in *USA Today* blames parents, "who have the greatest influence on whether a child avoids drug use. . . . [M]any baby boomer parents expect their teenage children to experiment with illegal drugs and do not consider that a problem." That represents an abandonment of their authoring relationship, a rejection of their own healthy authority. Joseph Califano, director of the National Center on Addiction and Substance Abuse, suggests that parents can express that authority and make drug use less likely by having their children (1) attend a drug-free school; (2) eat dinner with their families six or seven times a week; (3) be concerned about doing well in school; (4) feel that using drugs is morally wrong; (5) not have friends who smoke cigarettes or marijuana, or use alcohol; and (6) attend church regularly with their parents.[8]

Teaching manners in the home is a foundation for moral development but other institutions also have a role to play in this area. Schools, for example, should have sensible regulations for meals that build on, rather than undermine, what parents have already achieved. The importance of such activity is noted in Roger Scruton's review of Leon Kass's *The Hungry Soul,* "Animals feed, while people eat. This distinction (between *fressen* and *essen*) is one of which we are in danger of losing sight, as the purely utilitarian attitude to eating requires no manners, least of all a table. We should not, Kass argues, look complacently on the change. For fast food and TV dinners express a 'spiritual anorexia,' an inability to swallow the food of the soul. The rational being is nourished on conversation, taste, manners and hospitality."[9]

The simplest example of a healthy partnership between parents and teachers may be in the area of homework. The teacher has the authority to assign it and the obligation to correct and return it in a manner that will help students achieve their goals. Parents have the obligation to see that the homework is done in a timely and satisfactory manner. Each exercise of authority reinforces the other and strengthens itself at the same time.

Catholic schools, the object over the last generation of satires beyond numbering about their standards, the strictness of their professional religious teachers, and their insistence on such human values as fidelity and chastity, turn out, in the 1990s, to be the institutions that, by the judgments of research and market choice, have retained their educational authority. More than half a generation ago, the late sociologist James Coleman concluded that inner-city Catholic schools, although recipients of less funding, not only outperformed their counterpart public schools but, through their moral authority, generated an environment in which students behaved better and declared themselves happier than public school students.

Parents, most of whom are not Catholic in the inner cities, where many of these schools survived while every other institution made pilgrimage to the suburbs, endorse them in a way that even those American analysts whose only measure is monetization can understand. According to the *New York Times,* they "scrape together the money for the Roman Catholic school around the corner" instead of going to the "public schools that they feel are too large, too dangerous, and too lax."[10]

The reasons for the success of Catholic schools are summarized by Sister Jeanette Salbert, a co-principal of East Catholic High in Detroit, Michigan: "We know each student personally, we teach a value system, and we work very hard to get students into a college-bound curriculum. They're not dumb—they've never been given the opportunity to realize how intelligent they are. Our teachers won't take a 'can't do it.'" This is the voice of healthy authority speaking.

Research done by the Rand Corporation, seconded by studies from the University of Michigan and the University of Chicago, offers an explanation of the success of Catholic schools that validates Sister Jeanette's judgment. The decisive elements flow from the headwaters of natural authority and include personal attention from teachers who view their work not as just producing a paycheck but as fulfilling a mission. There is a traditional emphasis on shaping the character as well as the mind of the student. An academic curriculum is in place for everybody, and no vocational program is a backup for poor performers. Perhaps the richest adornment of this confidently authoritative approach is its freedom from strangling bureaucracy.

Researchers also observed that de-authorized public school systems rob teachers of confidence in, or hope for success with, such traditional approaches. They seem as wary as inexperienced hunters in an unexplored jungle of imposing rigorous standards on pupils who might respond by devouring them. They are not at all sure that they could really expect poor students to succeed in the classroom when they have chaotic lives at home. Among the qualities that Catholic schools were found to hold in common are a sense of intimacy, an emphasis on values, an insistence on high standards, and a practice of consistent discipline.

Because the universe created by such sensible authority is safe, it is also free. Students can pursue their own intellectual and personal development encouraged by teachers who hold up to them the highest standards and values. Authority does not need to be rediscovered in such schools because it has never been misplaced or degraded.

The rediscovery of natural authority is not, however, a monopoly. Harvard's Richard F. Elmore observes: "You don't have to make invidious comparisons between public and private schools to say we ought to think about these ideas. They are all public property. They can be in any school. They are in a lot of public schools, and there's no reason they can't be in more."

Recognize that rediscovering authority is a spiritual challenge. The moral authority of Catholic education, arising partly from dedication, partly from reality, has not been replaced by the monetized version found in some other systems. With little extra money, they are immune to the highly selective bureaucrats who thrive best when they are well funded. Catholic educators constitute a community whose members have never wavered from their vision that the mission of education is essentially spiritual.

"We're not social workers," Brother Paul Beaudin, Principal of St. Francis de Sales and St. Lucy Academy in New York City, explains, "We empathize with the plight of the kids, but we don't waste class time. We don't have encounter groups and we don't say, 'It's a shame, these poor Hispanic and black kids from the inner city' because in the end, we'd be ignoring their education and give them nothing."[11]

Contemporary educators who want to rediscover their authority must first distinguish sound spirituality from shallow psychologizing. A rule of thumb may be employed to distinguish spiritual meaning from superficial psychological explanation: The more you draw on spirituality, the deeper, richer, and more compelling its authority becomes. Such authority can never be exhausted. The more you draw on oversimplified psychology, however, the more quickly are its reserves emptied and the pseudo-quality of its authority becomes evident. Spirituality can survive every human experience and illuminate even the most tragic. Shallow psychologizing disappears in the presence of anything but unexamined and untested optimism.

Extrainstitutional initiatives include the movement on the part of many parents to teach their children at home. While in some circumstances that may be an eccentric choice, such a movement can also provide a clear opportunity for parents to rediscover and implement their generative authority. As such, home schooling may be understood as a purposive experiment in reaction to the multiple trial-and-error efforts of the interim period. It also signals that diverse groups are striving to bring an end to the trackless interval by bringing authority back into education.

Those who see its healthy possibilities are described by the *Wall Street Journal* as a "new breed of home schoolers—families who eschew traditional education not for religious reasons, not to thumb their noses at the establishment, but simply because they think they can do a better job teaching their children themselves. Sophisticated and well-educated, these parents are bringing home schooling out of the underground and into the mainstream." The number of children being educated at home is approximately 500,000, or about 1 percent of the school age population, and is growing at the rate of 15 percent a year. Although the phenomenon was pioneered in the 1980s by Christian fundamentalists, "the fastest growing segment of home schoolers, education experts say, is this new breed of parents."[12]

Although home schooling is vulnerable to potential social isolation and intrafamilial criticism, such as objections by grandparents, the students "appear to be keeping up with, and sometimes surpassing, peers in traditional schools. In Washington State between 1986 and 1990, 3,634 home-school students scored, on average, in the top third of all students tested nationwide, slightly better than state public school students. In Oregon 67 percent of home schoolers who took national achievement tests during the current school year scored at or above the national public-school average." A telling validation of this experimental effort is found in the fact that, although a decade ago many jurisdictions considered those schooled at home to be truants, the practice is now authorized by law in every state.

Reintroducing good sense through the cooperation of parents and teachers in restoring natural authority to the education of the young is like finding the cure to an illness that society had long passively accepted as fatal. The mothers and fathers and the teachers who have worked together have, like the pioneer bacteriologist Robert Koch when scoffed at for forwarding his germ theory, experienced widespread intimidation from a passing interim environment hostile to common sense. They have succeeded by conveying an unambiguous vision of common purpose and vigorously reasserting their convictions about what schools are supposed to do. That shared sense of direction generates of and for itself enormous moral authority because it is based on the considered experience of good people rather than on the vague notions of mediocre theorists.

The revival of confidence in convictions held in common allows parents and teachers to summon educational experts back to their original calling so that they may rediscover the constituent elements of authority: a positive energy transmitted through human relationships to another person to generate growth toward worthy goals. That authority is present in the parochial schools and in experimental schools that achieve academic success despite such obstacles as low budgets and locations in difficult neighborhoods, and it can be present in public schools as well.

Commonsense suggestions on creating a climate of healthy authority are offered by Edward Wynne and Kevin Ryan.[13] They suggest that sensible authorities need not be authoritarian to structure healthy expectations, such as making and enforcing rules in a consistent manner, giving and correcting challenging homework assignments, keeping in contact with parents as well as with other teachers, and enforcing regulations by policing playgrounds, hallways, lunchrooms, and bathrooms to make them safe and therefore places where freedom rather than intimidation reigns. Enormous energy—the energy of healthy authority itself—is needed in order to carry all that out and to elicit respect from students as well as between members of the staff.

In education, professors and teachers must take themselves, the work they author, and the students in relationship to whom they author it as the subjects and objects of their moral authority. The atmosphere need not be Dickensian, but it should make it possible for those involved to accomplish their tasks without distraction or impediment. A morally authoritative education depends on clarity regarding rules, attendance, assignments, rewards and punishments, dress, behavior, and the achievement of goals. Such a morally authoritative education creates a special ethos in a school, a sense of belonging, pride, and loyalty that, because serious hard work is involved, generates enormous self-respect and self-esteem.

There is a connection between the acquisition of virtue and the ability to perform well in school and to succeed in life. "Long on facts but short on the qualities that so often produce success in life, including dependability, honesty, and perseverance, many children do not realize their potential," Professor Kevin Walsh of the University of Alabama says. "In extreme cases," he adds, "the absence in schools of an emphasis on a child's character contributes to classroom discipline problems, truancy and juvenile delinquency."[14]

Walsh emphasizes garden variety virtues, each with the common denominator of the self-discipline that produces a sense of self-mastery and self-esteem. Simple rules requiring students to ask a teacher's permission to leave the classroom or not to speak until one's turn show students how to respect authority as well as how to practice patience and courtesy.

Restoring those constituent elements of sensible authority to education does not depend on larger budgets, new textbooks, or enlarged facilities. Because they are essentially spiritual, these qualities depend on the insight and character of the faculty and administration and their willingness to invest themselves in the task of restoring the opportunity for their development to the curriculum. That effort cannot be interpreted as some undemocratic crusade to impose alien values on pupils. They are, in fact, basic democratic virtues.

Health is the best response to the intimidation suffered by parents, teachers, and administrators trying to rediscover their healthy authority in education. Sensible parents are not the crazy ones, and their soundness of instinct and judgment constitutes their most powerful gift to their children and to the teachers who want to educate them as complete moral persons.

Parents can make many mistakes in raising their children, just as teachers may in educating them, but, if they are fundamentally healthy, the outcome will also be healthy. Authority is not complete control with zero tolerance for error. That is authoritarianism, as evidenced in many of the bizarre educational movements that allow no deviation from their fascistic imperatives.

Teachers are strongly helped when mothers, fathers, and other interested community members stand by the restoration of demanding academic programs. These reforms threaten bureaucracy and administrators only if they can rely on the strength of the healthy community around them. Parents should support common sense and healthy authority—easily distinguished from unhealthy authoritarianism by the nature of their respective methods and their goals—in every instance and on every issue of significance in education.

The restoration of authority to education is indispensable for children who will live in the Knowledge Society. The Space/Information Age places a premium on specialized knowledge. We already live, as Peter Drucker terms it, in the "Knowledge Society," at the center of which stands education and the schools. Society will see its future intimately connected to the performance of the schools and will insist that the authorityless interim be brought to a close and that the vague and unproductive experimentation that flourished falsely within it be ended. Thus the institution of education will be not only revivified but transformed by its product—knowledge—and by the pressures of history that make it the nucleus of a new social dispensation. Thus, the acquisition and distribution of formal knowledge will, according to Drucker, occupy the place in the politics of the Knowledge Society that the acquisition and distribution of property and income have occupied in the two or three centuries known as the Age of Capitalism.[15]

The proclamation of the advent of the age of generalists, in medicine or in any other profession, will be understood as the last mistaken notion of the authorityless interim. That great flattening will be rejected because it belongs to a past authority default rather than on a future profoundly rooted in the rediscovered authority of ever more specialized learning. The future is a function of specialization, not generalization. The time for the rediscovery and reimplementation of authoritative education, purged of its long interval siege of self-induced illnesses, is at hand.

Knowledge workers will dominate and reconfigure society, and education will break clear of the wreckage of its authoritarian structures to become an integral lifelong experience. Specialized, continuing education offers the institution every opportunity to recover its healthy authority. At the center of society, education will purify itself and shed the burdens that weighed it down during the latter half of this century. The schools will be free to be schools and, indeed, will experience market pressures to provide superior education instead of acting as agents of ideological reform and social service.

IV

America's Institutions:
Rediscovering Authority at Work

9

The De-authorization of Work

Sigmund Freud famously responded to the question about our purpose in life by saying, "To love and to work." Men and women may never become fully perfect, but they do make purchase of what is elusively termed "meaning" by experiencing the truth of themselves and their lives—author who they are—through loving and working. Loving and working are principal functions, therefore, of healthy or natural authority. Meaning is not delivered through an intellectual answer, a rational solution laid out for the assembled guests at the end of the mystery; it is a function of the totally absorbing work of authoring. As such, authoring resembles the slow process of becoming mature and being wise more than the quick fireworks of being clever and giving the right answer.

Widespread confusion now exists in the parallel universes of intimacy and work. Such alienation leaves the human spirit, like a string-severed Stradivarius, mute about its own deepest purpose. That describes the interval human condition, that is, how men and women suffer when their connections with natural authority are so damaged that they can no longer bring the music of love and work out of their own depths. The interim has offered a Rolodex of experimentation in these most significant and sensitive areas of human activity. When hierarchical authoritarianism disintegrated, so, too, did the forms and expectations connected with love and labor, which had vanished in its dust cloud. Indeed, consultants on love and work—how to organize relationships and businesses—predominate over all others, providing us with a veritable encyclopedia of the trial-and-error searches under way in the post-hierarchical authority vacuum. The woes of love—and their cures—are legion, but they are outnumbered by the complaints about and remedies for de-authorized work.

The differing resonances of a fine and a fake violin reveal themselves to us immediately. So, too, do the differences between authoritative love and work and nonauthoritative "as if" love and work. Work characterized by "clock-watching," for example, may copy but cannot create. No man or woman can or will say of such drudgery what they do about the work they genuinely author. "I love it," they profess of the latter or, as if anticipating a meeting with the beloved, "I can't wait to get there."

Reverse images of love and work are found in many contemporary offices and factories. Government task force reports have noted that millions of American workers feel bored, blocked, and economically trapped in their jobs. Job dissatisfaction often leads to a high rate of job changes, absenteeism, mistakes at work, and accident proneness. As in a lobotomy in which a dulled personality results when the connective tissue between the frontal lobes of the brain are cut, apathy sets in after the psychological and spiritual fibers linking the author-worker with the work authored are severed.

When it fails, work, like love, comes apart, for both supervisor and the supervised, at the center. Each is essentially involved in authoring, the executive ordered to the satisfying and profitable growth and productivity of the workers, and the latter, in turn, to the prideful and fulfilling authorship that expresses their human need to do work that creates something new and whole in the real world. Like symphony conductors and orchestra players, they author something individually and co-author something together that requires the best that is in them. When they author a great performance, they create something beyond themselves that enlarges those who hear it as well. Authorship in any work, therefore, concerns the achievement of the transcendent. Sometimes that is as familiar as a truly driven nail or as lofty as Beethoven's

Ninth Symphony. Authority in work means creativity, a dynamic that cannot be simulated, that issues into growth. There is more to everybody when it is done than before it began. At the unifying authoring center, of course, stands the conductor through whom all the other freshly authored sound must pass. The conductor's task is to be an authority, not an authoritarian.

Whether called leadership, headship, managing, mentoring, or supervising, the problem is that of authority. Studies of leadership and leaders yield the personality factors that are also at the core of authority. The test of leaders is, as with teachers, whether they can use their own inner resources to help others grow, or be productive, in pursuit of a positive goal that stands outside both of them. Theories, parallel to those about nature and nurture, abound about whether leadership is a natural gift or a technique that can be learned.

Leaders as Authorities

Research confirms common sense about effective leaders. They share crucial attributes.[1] The first, termed *surgency*, contrasts dynamic agents of authority as sociable, gregarious, assertive, and leaderlike against less competent ones who are quiet, reserved, mannerly, and withdrawn. Potent leaders also manifest emotional stability in their calm self-confidence. Their opposites are possessed by their emotions and show it in their anxiety, insecurity, and worrisomeness. Furthermore, people who exercise authority well are well organized, work hard, and act responsibly. Their conscientiousness makes them the polar opposite of people who are impulsive, irresponsible, undependable, and lazy.

Good leaders are not hard or tyrannical but rather sympathetic, cooperative, good-natured, and warm. Their agreeableness contrasts with the grumpy, unpleasant, and cold traits of persons who do not lead well. Persons who sit easily in the saddle of authority are found to have a healthy sense of curiosity and to be imaginative, cultured, and broadminded. Those who experience and give little comfort in work, on the other hand, approach their narrow interests in a concrete-minded and practical manner.

The observation that a leader at ease with authority gets the most out of others is reinforced by the research conducted on commercial airline flight crews and cited in Hogan's research. Breakdowns in team performance are the primary cause of air transport accidents. Flight crew performance—defined in terms of the number and severity of the errors made by the crew—is significantly correlated with the personality of the captain. Crews with captains who are warm, friendly, self-confident, and able to stand up to pressure, that is, those who possess the characteristics previously listed, make the fewest errors. Conversely, crews with captains who are arrogant, hostile, boastful, egotistical, passive-aggressive, or dictatorial make the most errors.

Yet identifying and promoting people who can lead well remains a largely neglected aspect of the larger unnamed national problem of authority. The fact that the center of authority in America is not holding—that it is, in fact, diffuse and shifting—is reflected in the estimates that, despite the apparently enormous commitment to the cultivation of leadership through executive and other search committees as well as extensive screening procedures, the rate of leadership failure in American business is 50 to 60 percent. In short, those chosen and prepared explicitly for leadership fail more than half of the time.

Newspaper stories about the retirement or replacement of chief executives gleam with high-gloss public relations phrases: "to pursue other opportunities," "for personal reasons," "to prepare for an orderly succession." The subtext is that executives depart chiefly because they cannot exercise authority effectively.

Sometimes product lines change or a business downturn is overpowering but many business leaders fail for personal rather than structural or economic reasons. Indeed, people fated to fail in the executive suite are often very good in one particular area, such as accounting, engineering, or sales. They falter precisely because of the expertise that gained them their reputations. Perhaps promoted because of their narrow virtuosity, they find themselves in positions that demand the broader gifts of working with and through others if they are to succeed. In short, they are expected to be authorities rather than experts, to give the speech to move others rather than take it down in flawless shorthand to gratify themselves. Unable to build a team, they fail as leaders and their management careers stall out.

Those faltering executives who suddenly "leave to pursue other interests" fail, according to both commonsense appraisal—nobody in the firm is ever surprised—and the results of research, because of overriding personality defects or character flaws. They kill authority's generative possibilities because they neither possess or understand them. Their alienation of their subordinates prevents them from building any kind of team. They cannot get an orchestra together and cannot help it to play harmoniously. Hogan and his group describe research on managerial incompetence at the Center for Creative Leadership and Personnel Decisions, Inc., which has found that many bright managers who are also hard-working, ambitious, and technically competent fail, or run the risk of failing, because of their personalities. They are perceived as "arrogant, vindictive, untrustworthy, selfish, emotional, compulsive, overcontrolling, insensitive, abrasive, aloof, too ambitious, or unable to delegate or make decisions."

Authority defaults, in both selection and execution, are at least as common as successes in American enterprise. The investigative focus has expanded recently to explore whether it is leaders themselves or the context of their leadership that is crucial to its effectiveness. Other speculation concerns the role of followership and teamwork, or whether groups should have any leader at all.[2] Those radar echoes play off authority or leadership as protean entities, decentered and diffuse, their relationship to power as unclear as the popular strategy of empowerment. The theoretical analyses exemplify the problem rather than solutions. This research is itself trial-and-error experimentation in the world of management. Knowing that something is wrong, but lacking an understanding of natural authority, the investigators focus on distraction and shape their advice to its vague outlines. As a result, their counsel often misses the real point of authority default and seems faddish and superficial. Here, as in other spheres, the one-size-fits-all recommendation of "empowerment" reveals classic interval confusion about the nature and function of authority.

Work in general has become one vast laboratory for such pragmatic experimentation. From time and motion analyses through the scientific study of leadership to a library of popular books on management techniques, an astonishing array of experiments has been undertaken, less out of scientific curiosity than from practical economic motivation.

This intense focus on profit is characterized, for example, by an emphasis on process rather than on persons. Such heavily monetized intermission behavior is marked by bottom-line rationalized reconfigurations of many businesses and industries, not all the effects of which have been positive. Indeed, the human costs, both in individual tragedy and in loss of morale and productivity, have yet to be fully calculated.

Monetization drives out other values that are crucial to an understanding of work as a human activity. Jude Wanniski writes in the *Wall Street Journal* that macroeconomics relies on the "manipulations of aggregate demand or money supply [that] can homogenize the behavior of millions of individuals. . . . All the variables necessary to a productive economy, such as 'risk taking' and 'innovation,' however, cannot be reduced to a mathematical formula."[3] Cost-cutting and downsizing lead to an abandonment of the model of the company as a familylike, career-long source of employment and affiliation. The hiring of temporary employees in many fields cuts the expense of benefits but transforms the corporation from a reliable and credible agent of relationship and security to one of impersonal, profit-driven indifference. That, in turn, eats away at worker loyalty and morale.

In the disordering circumstances of such trial-and-error efforts, constantly shifting goals and provisional definitions of what leadership is and does wreak havoc in the domain of work itself. As a result, the workplace has become less a site of fulfillment than a place of danger, barely a notch above urban streets as a setting for possible injury. Warning labels and orange stickers abound as they do at crime scenes. Existential anxiety is invoked, because anything can happen at any moment. The experience of the workplace resembles that of the family after the death of a parent or of a school when the symptoms of authority default and deprivation begin to appear. The loss of natural authority leads inevitably to discontent and danger. That is exactly what happens in those work environments in which the need to search for authority advertises its profound absence.

Even though enormous advances have been made in reducing risks in plants and offices, workers' compensation claims for job-related injuries have escalated in almost every business and industry in recent years, adding sizable unanticipated costs to their balance sheets. Workers and employers have come to regard each other with suspicion. Workers claim that bosses are trying to keep from them what is rightfully theirs (compensation), while the executives charge that the employees are virtually stealing what they do not deserve through carelessness or fakery. Credibility and loyalty, functions of healthy authority relationships, are casualties in such an atmosphere.

Research suggests that increased occupational stress is related to the conditions that emerge when authority is exercised poorly. Job-related stress occurs when workers are pressured by conflicting demands, when they have too much or too little to do, when they are responsible for the professional development of others, and when they have little control over the decisions that affect them.

Authority defaults generate unmistakable physical and psychological symptoms. These may show up in impaired cognitive functioning, in a restriction of the range of perception or "tunnel vision," or in a diminished ability to concentrate, to be creative, or to make decisions. Combined, those deficits lessen the ability of workers to grasp and master their job requirements and challenges. They cannot readily or confidently author their work.

The symptoms may also be emotional. Workers can experience feelings of anxiety, depression, alienation, mental fatigue, apathy, and hypochondria. They may also abuse alcohol, tobacco, or drugs. Workers may begin taking unnecessary risks in their working life or in traffic on their commute to work. They may express unprovoked aggressive and violent behavior toward other workers, strangers, or themselves.

Many persons now enter their workplaces in a guarded and suspicious manner, while many others fear that their actions may easily be misinterpreted. Such suspiciousness and paranoia breed victimization and scapegoating. Those are intensified by the electric, ill-modulated, and nonintegrated sexuality, acted out seductively or through offensive overtures, that arises in this atmosphere as the doppelgänger of missing generative authority.

That shadow side of work, bearing so much of the afflicted person's frustrations in relationships and self-expression, is the ideal medium for the explosions of rage that occur at so many worksites across the nation. The de-authorized plant, store, or office, the shadowland that harbors the unhealthy opposites of true authority, becomes the stage on which pent-up anger is unleashed in random assaults and shootings. The *New York Times* reports, for example, that thirty-four postal workers have been killed by colleagues at work since 1983.[4]

Another sign of compromised authority is evident in the new bureaucracies that swarm like clouds of bees above every place in which Americans work. These include risk-management specialists and insurers who perceive an office or store filled with youthful secretaries and clerks as an undertaker might: Everyone is a sure candidate for doom and for their costly ministrations.

Transformed by the heavy emphasis on the bottom line, the psychological conditions and satisfactions of work have also been seriously degraded. Noël Coward once described work as "much more fun than fun." Today's shadow refrain is that "work isn't fun any more." Far from perceiving work as creative and enlarging, many people, from laborers to professionals, now experience their work as oppressive. They look forward not to going to work but to getting away from it.

People author their existence through love and work that tap into and flow from the deepest levels of their personality as expressions of their individual character. If the real personality is not engaged, nothing as weighty as love or work comes into being. The mistaken identities of love and work include the sexual deliriums and obsessions and the generally doomed, immensely distracting flypaper emotional involvements in which people's flailing escape movements entangle them further, the Herculean labor despised because it is done only for money, and the heart-isn't-in-it work that leaves tombstone inscriptions on computer screens across the country.

De-authorized or corrupted work areas are now problematic from almost every viewpoint. Whether people should be allowed to smoke at work, for example, has become a more significant issue than the work they actually do. Work and the place in which it is performed are confounded, as in an art gallery in which the paintings and statues are kept in storage while frames and pedestals are elaborately discussed and displayed.

When the authority natural to fulfilling work fails, the substitute authority of the law and the courts is increasingly invoked. As a result, the troubled arena of work now seeks legal refereeing of the shadowy counterfeits of generative human and work relationships that now fill it. Such nongenerative behavior is obvious in the accusations of sexual harassment and the ambiguous and disconcerting mood to which even their possibility gives rise. The response, as in other settings such as colleges, is often a set of guidelines or regulations that attempt to reinvent common sense or the Ten Commandments.

Ideologically driven, such regulations are insubstantial measuring tapes of human intention and behavior and lack the compelling moral authority of sensible human argument or of deeply rooted law. They quickly become the subject of endless interpretation and disputes and, as the vagueness of their own authority base becomes obvious, are turned over to a different standard of authority, that of the law and the courts, for resolution.

10

Rediscovering Authority at Work:
Recommendations

Restoring the authorship of work revives the individual's creativity or capacity for generative or productive authority and is also good for business. Forging again the link between the worker-author and the authored work frees internal motivation and decreases the need for extrinsic threats or sanctions.

Both healthy authority and nonexploitative capitalism are ordered to real-world growth. The human growth of workers in relation to what they produce is, when commonsense analysis is applied to a library of business studies, intimately related to the productivity and growth that constitute the goal of management. The basic elements of the authority of a business leader are the same as those in the natural authority of parents, teachers, pastors, and artists. Such authority is not power aimed at control but the energy that fosters the growth of another in the achievement of a worthy goal that is a distinct accomplishment separate from both the manager and the worker. Healthy authority in work fosters human productivity.

To reestablish the link of authorship in the world of work, executives must examine those conditions, practices, or practical values that interfere with it in the first place. Laying off workers, according to the *Wall Street Jour-*

nal, supposedly improves profits and cuts costs, but many companies slash furiously only to be puzzled by subsequent poor performance. A Wyatt Company study of more than five hundred big companies describes downsizing's frequent failure as a "persistent paradox" and offers "some of the first concrete evidence that management behavior during cutbacks—such as the way employees are treated—can affect the company's financial performance."[1]

When authority is poorly exercised, workers view and perform their work differently, their loyalty is lessened, their willingness to make extra efforts is diminished, and, in the long run, these human reactions adversely affect the success of the enterprise.

One of the best examples of reestablishing the authorship franchise to individual workers is found at the Cooper Tire & Rubber Company of Findlay, Ohio, as part of the strategy that led to a decade of 20 percent annual gains. The company's restoration of authority, according to *Barron's,* is "in part, fostered by its longstanding practice of having the person who builds a tire sign it. This helps foster pride in workmanship . . . and . . . creates a bond with the consumers buying them."[2] Business leaders speak the language of creativity and growth more confidently when they appreciate that these are the elements of healthy authority.

Noting the undesirable effects of paternalistic and command-and-control models of relationship between managers and workers, the management consultant Diane Riggan notes: "Building a competitive, flexible, talented work force can be accomplished only by treating all employees, regardless of age, like adults."[3] To restore the authoring capacity of workers, employers should ensure the right fit between employees and job content. Commonsense authority sees to it that employees lacking needed job skills are given training to perform the necessary tasks. If they are not trainable, the authority default lies in the hiring process and must be addressed at that point.

As in studying, or even in athletic competition, sensible authoring begins with setting up realistically high work performance expectations for everybody and raising them incrementally as performance improves. Leaders who wish to author their workers to author their own tasks better will allow them enough freedom to make decisions about the shape, content and context of what they do. Productivity improves when bosses encourage employees to author their jobs, that is, develop them fully or, in the language of consultants, "grow the job." As market needs change, employees can then modify themselves and their work to achieve transformed goals. That is generative authority in the workplace.

When workers are treated as adults, they act in adult fashion. This, too, is commonsense authority, well known to parents, teachers, coaches, and many others committed to the growth of others. Healthy authority generates responsibility or it is not healthy authority in the first place. The worker free of paternalistic infantalization must accept the full responsibilities of being an adult. One of the hallmarks of generative relationships is their reciprocity: The authority giver—parent, teacher, supervisor, or mentor—is an adult helping somebody else to become an adult.

Business Week notes, "There is still a robust need for relationships between employer and employed that rely on stability, security, and shared economic interests . . . the new compact between company and worker dismisses paternalism and embraces self-reliance. 'That [unconditional lifetime employment] is no longer the name of the game,' says Kevin Becraft, director of employee relations and resources at IBM, which has cut 171,000 jobs since 1986. 'Instead, it's life-long employability.' The key difference: shared responsibility. Employers have an obligation to provide opportunity for self-improvement; employees have to take charge of their own careers."[4]

The emerging condition of employability in this fashion may also be understood as a Space/Information Age effect. Its inexorability is dictated by the Space Age's uprooting of all the directional signs that were once firmly planted in the earth and the Communications Age's setting side by side places for employer and employee at the information feast. The result is that the role of intermediaries is disappearing. What Gertrude Stein said of her California hometown, "There is no there there," can now be spoken in bittersweet tones of the middle of business organizations. As at the birth of the Industrial Revolution, a tragically high human price is paid in midlevel layoffs. Restoration of the in-between positions will not occur, however, and other jobs for the now vanishing hierarchies that supported the mid-managerial class will be authored. They will not be in the middle, because that is the territory washed away by the currents of Space/Information Age change.

The benefits of these developments cannot be written off as regrettable side effects of history. *Business Week* suggests that at "companies that are flattening hierarchies, and, bit by bit, decentralizing decision-making, workers are gaining greater control over what they do; self-direction has superseded that workers do only what they're told." The rewards of accepting greater responsibility are identified as higher pay and greater flexibility in developing more fulfilling combinations of varied work and family life.

For example, at the European Collision Center, a tiny auto body shop in Cambridge, Massachusetts, the workers' sense of their relationship to their work has been successfully altered to accommodate the loss of the model of hierarchy. Bodymen take what they term "ownership," and what we might term "authorship," of a car while it is in the shop, staying with it from start to finish. No one looks over their shoulders: "There are a set of parameters, then they have to be responsible," *Business Week* quotes the owner, Wayne Stevenson, noting that workers are cross-trained to take on new tasks and sent back to school yearly to keep skills up to date. Customers love what they get, and Stevenson's traffic has doubled every year for five years.

The willingness to take on self-direction and personal responsibility with very little or no input from "above" is also found in the increasing numbers of contingent workers who perform part time, undertake contract work, or are self-employed. This workforce may be more flexible, more willing to change and implement new ideas and new technology. That development raises questions however, about the place of what *Business Week*'s former editorial page editor, Jack Patterson, terms the "intangible but indispensable values" long associated with work—a sense of loyalty, shared goals, a sense of community, a forum for the exchange of ideas, and feelings of loyalty and being part of a team.

Such evolution sets the stage for what Peter Drucker calls the "knowledge workers," those persons who have a knowledge base and associated skills rooted in a lifetime of training and learning. The emergence of such workers underscores an increasingly crucial distinction between them, the ones who can author sophisticated work, and those who lack the interest in, aptitude for, or educational advantages necessary to fill, this role. Already, the Bureau of Labor Statistics' occupational forecast for the year 2005 predicts that the gains will be in high skills–high wages jobs while losses will continue in low-skill union jobs. In addition, low-pay service workers who support knowledge workers will increase.[5]

Common sense and healthy instincts are basic qualities of sound authority; they are never associated with authoritarianism or overcontrol. Healthy leaders can, for example, use themselves as sounding boards in judging what factors influence the relationship of the workers to their work. The capacity for everyday observation is a vital asset during the interval period on which experimentation with authority wears a thousand faces: Total Quality Management, reengineering, business-process redesign, benchmarking, the virtual corporation, relationship marketing, ISO 9000, and others. Sensible managers make their own judgments on what they can use to implement their own healthy authority in their particular circumstances. As the *Wall Street Journal* notes, they readily scrap textbook models and the wisdom of management gurus to select what fits their situation.

In the long run, the good judgment of leaders—the way they employ their natural authority—is critical to making decisions about new business methodologies. Commonsense questions, according to *Business Week's* Russell Mitchell and Michael Omeal, include: Does this approach strengthen workers' direct relationship to the product or does it remove them farther from it? Does this technique reinforce their sense of being persons or diminish them and make them feel more like objects, impersonal pieces of a machine, or disposable parts?

Furthermore, is this method compatible with the scale, central function, and values of this enterprise? Does this approach force employees to violate their integrity in any way so that they cannot be true to themselves in implementing its techniques? Is this an option open to discussion and modification by participant workers or is it a procedure that is being forced from the top down onto those who must apply it? Is this innovation depersonalized in its very nature, that is, does it discount human factors and conceptualize everything in terms of numbers and profits?

The crucial question for leaders is simple: Does this help the business and the workers to grow in relationship to each other, or will it bring pseudo-growth to the business by denying real growth to the workers? An effective business demands the same kind of authorship that is necessary in a great symphony orchestra. Authority is essentially the management of creativity, the harnessing of this indispensable human energy source artfully so that everybody, from the president to the newest employee, reaps the unique and enlarging rewards of being creative in what they do in the workplace. The music that issues finally from a symphony is the product of an enormous, risky, cooperative human adventure. It requires concentration and self-discipline to guarantee the application of everybody's highest level of talent. Nor is it born without practice, sour notes, mistakes, and misunderstandings. It needs players ready to author their music and a central conductor ready to author the players. The latter's intuitive understanding of authorship links them in authoring themselves and something beyond themselves at the same time.

11

The De-authorization of the Professions

D*aedalus,* the journal of the American Academy of Arts and Sciences, devoted its Fall 1963 issue to "The Professions." The guest editor, Kenneth S. Lynn, celebrated the sense of the age: "America has become more cognizant of the professions, and more dependent upon their services, than at any previous time in our history."[1] A generation and a half later, America's professions are in disarray, their authority appropriated by others, their members demoralized, and their once crisp identity rapidly blurring. Their decline is accompanied by a renewed faith in magic, a development that some suggest occurs when institutional authority fails. Indeed, a cohort of New Age magic-driven substitute professions has arisen in medicine, religion, and other fields. What the editors of *Daedalus* perceived to be the fulfillment of a vision and the beginning of an era was in reality its climax. Indeed, the patient seemed fine just before he took a turn for the worse.

This journal appeared in the same seemingly placid autumn in which the President of the United States was killed in Dallas. All this occurred against the background of the initiation of one of the nation's greatest professional achievements, the first journey of human beings to the moon. The assassination of John F. Kennedy is a blood-red bookmark dividing an apparently well-ordered past from the turbulent present. The murder in the streets of the country's highest authority figure, in Shakespeare's phrase, "set loose the dogs of war." This horrific incident can be understood as the symbolic ignition of the nation's mounting internal conflict over the traditional hierarchical power display and control of American life of which professionalism regnant was a prominent feature.

The first real adventure into space was a matching event of comparable impact on the human psyche. Those first steps across the threshold of the Space/Information Age were dynamite charges rigged to the Eiffel Tower hierarchy used by every profession to symbolize and structure its specific authority. The professions did not, and perhaps could not, distinguish the pure water of their earned authority from the seamburst casks of another age in which it was carried. The essence of their authority was so intermingled with its hierarchical social class accidents that professionals became extremely vulnerable in all aspects of their lives when hierarchical institutions became dysfunctional.

The decades since have witnessed a decline in all the aspects of professional authority: their presumed social privilege and even their claims to unique knowledge and skills have been challenged by alternate approaches, as in medicine, law, and religion; their methodology, as in the physical sciences, has been read as a "text" and its aspirations and rights deconstructed. Other manifestations include the recourse to magic, pseudo-spirituality, and fraudulence not seen since men in checked suits hawked elixirs from the backs of wagons.

Paralleling their lack of instruction about the difference between authority and authoritarianism, most Americans have had little education about the traditional ideal of professionalism or of how it contains and expresses the essential concept of responsible generative authority. Nor can they see how professionalism's present unsung exile symbolizes America's larger problem with authority. They cannot see that professionalism cannot be banished any more than religion could be banished by the Soviet Union.

The story of the growth of the professions is, however, the chronicle of a long, disciplined, apolitical effort to authorize, or root in healthy authority, the claims to particular knowledge and practical arts made by medicine, law, and the other developing specialties. The idea of authority as a positive energy transmitted through the relationships of masters to novices for their growth toward an external ideal of wisdom and practice is critical to any appreciation of the professions and what is currently happening in and to them. For professionalism demands, even in the face of its degradation and dilution, that authority vindicate its claims in any field, that it reexamine them conscientiously, guarantee their educational transmission and the supervised mentoring of candidates, and guard them ethically. The claims of the traditional professions to authority rest on the functioning of their members as authors in the fundamental sense, that is, agents of real-world truth and growth.

Authority over the well-marked field of their expertise was once central to the self-concept of professionals. Physicians, for example, now find that others, including insurers and government agencies, have co-opted them, using the levers of money and regulation to force decisions on them that they, left to the traditions of their calling, might not make in this way or perhaps at all.

A clerk working for an insurance company in Denver, for example, now tells a doctor in Cleveland that his medical decision to keep the patient in the hospital for a few more days does not conform to the insurer's guidelines for that condition, that no further coverage for the hospitalization is available, and that it is time for the patient to be discharged. A fulfilling achievement in which physicians had pursued their ideals by investing themselves totally and which they felt to be under their control is suddenly under siege by unseen strangers who want to run their affairs according to an entirely new set of assumptions.

Imposed guidelines affect not only hospitalization but also medication, surgery, and other treatment options. The Federal Trade Commission has ordered the professions to abrogate their traditional ban of advertising for clients and to permit it on the market theory that it will increase competition and lower prices. That has forced many professionals, including physicians, psychologists, and lawyers, to rewrite their ethical codes, which ruptures the relationship of professionals to the authorship of their own ethical guidelines, thereby imposing external control on matters that by their nature depend for their validity on intrinsic authority.

As the hierarchical gradations of professionalism disintegrated, so, too, did the once precisely drawn lines within which they held the exclusive franchise. Among other identifiable Space/Information Age effects, new occupations of paraprofessionals have developed in medicine, law, and many other fields. As the title "Health Care Provider" blurs distinctions between and within professions, psychologists, for example, have begun to expand their territorial claims, seeking hospital privileges and the right to prescribe drugs for their patients. Social workers and others have made claims on the field of psychotherapy and now practice independently. Indeed, psychotherapy has become the Bosnia on the map of professional life: Many groups want a piece of contested territory, most of them think they could govern it better, and the result is classic interim trench warfare. Persons of very different backgrounds and training now claim the right to treat emotional problems. That has led, as confusion about authority typically does, to a diffusion away from the center so that the once highly prized claim to be a professional is now so diluted as to be applied, with no sense of irony, even to fast food employees and temporary workers.

A prime effect of the authority diffusion that has followed the end of hierarchical authoritarianism is the degradation of the idea of professionalism. Once a designation of pride, something to which mothers urged their children to aspire, being a professional is coming to mean anything in general, so it becomes increasingly difficult for it to mean something specific.

Professionals trained in one era find themselves very uncomfortable in this new world in which their authority, gushing out of the splintered barrels of authoritarianism, has been diffused, co-opted, politicized, and thoroughly monetized. In many settings, for example, professions no longer seem to be callings but more like jobs for highly skilled technicians who do the bidding of others. As a result, many professionals would like to escape from their universe, once the object of their ambition, but now in which their authority has been so compromised.

Some physicians, for example, seek to retire early or to move into corporate rather than individual practice. Others retrain for what they perceive to be less stressful specialties within their fields. Many feel alienated and depressed at this massive cultural metamorphosis. Such men and women, however, are not easily replaced. Their years of training and experience cannot be reproduced or transferred readily to others. Serious questions present themselves about whether future doctors, lawyers, and other candidates for the professions can, in present cultural circumstances, aspire to, achieve, or practice according to traditional professional ideals or standards.

Medicine, psychology, and education, for example, have been awkwardly fitted to the consumer–provider model, with its pronounced monetary market orientation. Few persons, including legislators, social scientists, and members of the media observe or understand the implications of this transition. Indeed, in the development of health care legislation, professionals from the field are often consulted less than economists and social planners. Those who practice medicine are regarded as fixed assets, "givens," to a large extent depersonalized in the calculations that actuaries, dull as grindstones to their professional values, make about their distribution, mode of practice, and reimbursement.

Such reactions exemplify the time lag that exists in general culture before the predictable effects of large-scale movements—such as that of the baby boomers approaching the thresholds of marriage, parenthood, and retirement—fully manifest themselves. As yet even sophisticated individuals have not experienced the total impact of the evolution/revolution in professional life. Americans still expect the kind of service and confidentiality that went with the bygone era of professional authority. Their characteristic ambivalence about authority survives but it is in soft focus beyond themselves on reforms that will not dilute but improve what they already have in health care. Poll data indicate that Americans want things to change and want them to stay the same. Many analysts suggest that the 1994 Clinton Health Care Plan failed because it represented a scale of bureaucratic buildup the public could not fathom and was not ready to accept.

The public expects professionals to be available, to be highly specialized, to be personally interested in their concerns, and to serve them as they always have. They do not fully understand the de-authorization of professional function that is taking place all around them or how the ultimate impact of this will touch them in their everyday lives. Although Kenneth Lynn wrote in *Daedalus* that the professional tradition was an "institutional inheritance" that "no one in his right mind would suggest dismantling," that is exactly what is happening.

When the authority of a profession is transformed without making careful distinctions between what it professes (to know medicine and how to practice it) and how it professes it (the social structure through which it practices), the two can become seriously and irretrievably confounded. Hammering down outmoded hierarchical forms is like tearing down the rollercoaster. You remove an unsightly structure but you also remove even the chance of an exhilarating ride. The equivalent of that for medicine, and analogously for other professions, is that you remove the capacity to author health care in an unselfish and dedicated manner.

The core of the traditional professional commitment is spiritual and necessarily includes such virtues as care and good counsel, knowledge, wisdom, and artistic insight, as well as honor and honesty.[2] Those are experiences that must be authored humanly; they cannot be downloaded from the Internet. Such constitutive elements are found in professions as diverse as medicine, psychology, law, architecture, ministry, and accounting. The pursuit and expression of these characteristics cannot be successfully monetized any more than love can in friendship and marriage. Despite the turmoil surrounding the professions in America, these spiritual qualities alone can stabilize and revivify their natural authority.

When *Daedalus* decided, in the early 1960s, to review the professions in America, they were still incarnated largely in the still prevalent authoritarian structures, and they spoke with an authoritarian vocabulary. Hierarchical authoritarianism's collapse, its *coup de grace* delivered by the Space/Information era, leaves professionals without the temporary social shelter they once enjoyed. For all the dislocation, however, the plight of many sincere professionals receives little understanding and practically no sympathy. Professionals are thought to be living well, driving big cars, and enjoying good fortune on a plane of privilege.

The public deals with its professionals the way family and friends deal with prized members who are ill. They want them to be the way they always have been; they do not want them to be convalescents with needs of their own. They want them to be vigorous and available whenever they are needed. Beleaguered, assaulted, the subject of everybody's reform or experiment, yet pressed to serve consistently, contemporary professionals have difficulty maintaining the soul of their ideal and their sense of commitment. Because they feel that they no longer have control over what they author, they have trouble being authorities, the heart of their self-understanding and work. The same problem faces all professional institutions: How can they rediscover their essential natural authority now that authoritarian forms and vocabularies have become obsolete?

Members of the traditional professions profess to have authority in their respective fields. But to make claims to superior knowledge or arts, even if it concerns neurosurgery, smacks of "elitism" and that is the Vichy of America, a capital thought to be built on suspect loyalties to which the slightest pledge of allegiance constitutes a betrayal of democracy.[3] By virtue of their preparation, experience, and credentials, professionals stand as elites who do, in fact, know more, in theory and practice, than the average citizen about the substance of what they perceive as their calling. And Americans want them to be that way. When the shadow of illness or any other problem falls over them, they want the best professionals available to take care of them, not the charlatans with whom, with their elixirs and varieties of magic, they are sometimes infatuated when they are well.

Being a professional is not an easy claim, although it may seem so in America where the word "professional" has been appropriated by almost anybody who gets paid for what they do, from waiters to athletes to stunt men and hit men. The true professions are not effortlessly democratized. Entrance to them is difficult and requires candidates to vault successfully across progressively higher hurdles of achievement and examination. Citizenship is not qualification enough.

Professional services may be provided by action or through advice. Their common denominator, as the sociologist Everett Hughes wrote in *Daedalus*, is "knowledge systematically formulated and applied to problems of a client." But that foundational "knowledge, on which the advice and action are based, is not always clear; it is often a mixture of several kinds of practical and theoretical knowledge." Professionals' basic claim to authority flows from having acquired this authoritative knowledge.

Professionals profess, in a commitment like that of novices professing themselves to a religious state of life, "to know better than others the nature of certain matters, and to know better than their clients what ails them or their affairs. This is the essence of the professional idea and the professional claim."[4]

Such a claim also includes, as noted, a mass of learning rooted in, and ever associated with, a spirit of and a commitment to continuing research and discovery. The professional is expected to be a lifelong student. Also required is the acquisition and constant honing of practical knowledge, that is, of the art demanded by the service that is to be performed. Surgery is an obvious example in medicine, but so too is the skilled giving of counsel in law or in care of the soul. These are not mechanical or merely technical in nature. They require a subtlety of learning and depend for their success on developing a healthy professional–client relationship.

Traditionally, professionals meeting the stringent criteria for admission to and credentialing by their particular professional bodies have claimed to have the exclusive right to practice, as a vocation, the arts they profess to know. This is the basis for *licensure,* a term from the Latin *licere,* "to permit," which indicates that, on the basis of recognized knowledge and practice, professionals are permitted by the public to do things, such as perform surgery, write prescriptions for drugs, or draw up contractual agreements, that are not allowed to people in general.

License, therefore, depends not only on fulfilling certain legal requirements but on the judgment of the larger and more sensible majority of the public. This latter conviction is, in fact, the sentiment on which laws and regulations are based. The functioning of the professions is accepted and thereby validated by ordinary people who understand that such an action does not violate democracy but implements its processes. Common sense knows what contributes to the common good. Professionals are expected to treat those they serve according to their dignity as human persons.[5] Self-interest, therefore, must yield to the concern for others in the exercise of professional authority.

The late Talcott Parsons, the distinguished Harvard sociologist, regarded "professions as carriers of the central values of contemporary western civilization." Those who enter them are responsible for "the rational, even-handed application of advanced knowledge and skill to the solution of human problems in order to advance the common good."[6] In other words, when professionals are true to their calling they author more than just their specialized services. They author as well a climate or *ethos* of high expectations, purpose, and standards in improving the growth of the human family.

Professionals are therefore "expected to think objectively and inquiringly," that is, with professional distance that keeps emotional involvement from flooding their field of judgment. For that reason, such professionals as physicians do not practice on themselves or on relatives or close friends. Maintaining objectivity—standing far enough away to see things accurately—undergirds professional detachment, a function of freedom from conflicts of interest in any set of circumstances related to the fulfillment of traditional professional obligations.

The profession cannot, in other words, be separated from the professionals who practice in its name, that is, those who author its services. Lowering standards of admission or practice for political or ideological reasons, as has happened in various ways in recent decades to allow unqualified candidates admission to graduate programs, ultimately betrays the profession, the public, and those whose lack of qualities is overlooked in order to grant them a place they may not be able to fill in professional life. The lowering of standards for ideological reasons is the kind of trial-and-error behavior that occurs after hierarchical authoritarianism has been flattened and before the nature and need of natural authority have been rediscovered.

There is therefore no such thing as a right to professional status. The standards involving judgment on and selection of candidates at every level are not in place to preserve the power of an elite inner circle, although critics such as Sidney Wolfe and Ivan Illich so allege. The quality control safeguards concerning acceptance by and functioning within a profession are in place not to defend its fort on the frontier of culture but to guarantee the high quality of the services delivered to the public.

Traditional professions claimed autonomy as a prime and defining characteristic. Professionals themselves created the solidarity of feeling and values that brought into being the ethos of their respective callings and served as the foundation for their specific codes of ethics. They also organized learned societies, established appropriate journals, and set the standards for membership in their ranks as well as for acceptance in, along with the criteria for, programs of training in medical, legal, and other professional schools.[7]

Self-governance dictates that professionals author the acceptable conditions of their existence and function as highly trained ethical individuals, holding their own disciplinary hearings and making judgments according to their own standards and codes. So, too, professionals traditionally presented themselves as people who were "retained" or "engaged" rather than "hired," distinguishing their fee for service in a calling from a paycheck for a job.

The concept of self-control as a condition for true authorship seems as quaint as candlelight, yet it remains at the very core of the professional claim as it is at the center of healthy authority wherever it is manifested. Professionals present themselves as *trustworthy*. They do not say "Let the buyer beware" but "Let the buyer believe."

Autonomy and trust are essentially spiritual qualities. "Spiritual" does not refer to explicitly religious thoughts or behavior. It connotes instead the mass of nonmeasurable, noneconomic values, such as honor and truthfulness, that are considered in ordinary life to define the highest human aspirations and conduct. These values express the human spirit at its least selfish and in its most creative and generative mode.

Such a spiritual quality is trust, perhaps the most highly prized of all human attributes, an absolutely necessary condition for authoring professional services, indeed, for authoring any worthy human exchange. When people say they have confidence in their doctor or their lawyer, they are saying that they believe in them, that they are in a sound relationship to them as sources of authority. They feel as people spontaneously do when they are the subjects of natural authority: that they have grown, that they are safe, unused, and unmanipulated, that they are trusted by an agent of authority and trust that agent in return.

Trust cannot be manufactured; it must be authored, that is, it is a function of the way a person relates to others. So vital is it and so sorely has it been missed during the long post-hierarchical period that how to develop it has become the subject of trial-and-error experimentation. Such "trust exercises," often found at management seminars, as letting oneself be blindfolded and led around by others, or allowing oneself to fall freely into the arms of others, are contemporary charades, games played to mimic but not to replace life. Trust is not a trick but a demanding and undefended gift of the self to another fallible human being. No trust exists except that authored and reciprocally nourished in personal relationships.

The rediscovery of professional authority depends on reestablishing trust and autonomy as essential, nonnegotiable conditions for professional function. Otherwise, professional life will continue to be degraded until it attracts only the uninspired and the timeservers while it repels men and women whose intelligence, curiosity, and inventiveness make them ideal candidates for lives of authority as professionals serving others in a trustworthy fashion.

Knowledge Workers: The New Professionals

Professionals seem now to stand culturally de-authorized, their days of glory apparently at an end. Their shadow counterparts seem, on the other hand, to prosper. This, like a poll sampling, is a snapshot revealing an instant in time, the moment near the end of the post-hierarchical era, just before professionals' rediscovery of their authority in what Peter Drucker terms the Knowledge Age.

The Knowledge Age may be understood as the age now emerging, in which job demands will increasingly transcend the formerly dominant blue-collar skills. These new jobs, which will constitute over one-third of the workforce by the year 2000, require what Drucker describes as "a good deal more formal education . . . the ability to acquire and apply theoretical knowledge [and] a different approach to work and a different mind set." Unlike the work of farmers and machine operators, for example, which requires relatively brief apprenticeships, knowledge workers need to learn throughout their work life.[8]

While the preferred social structures that were once almost inextricably identified with the professional class are gone with other hierarchies, the idea and the ideals of professionalism are reemerging as yet another sign that the post-hierarchical period may be drawing to a close. Those who make the traditional claims to authority based on superior knowledge and highly developed skills are already becoming central figures in a society whose reconfiguration is a result of our entrance into the Space/Information Age.

The Space/Information Age dismantled the hierarchical systems through which the professions operated and with whose social ranks and styles they had been identified. That left professionals naked to their enemies during the tumultuous interlude in which, because authority was forgotten or disowned, the world experimented with operating without it. Professionals were bound to go into decline precisely because they built their lives and work on claims to the very authority that had been repudiated. The very same Space/Information Age that swept professionals out of the ruins of pre-Copernican towers now makes them the first citizens of the Knowledge Age. It may, some years hence, also be called the Age of Authority, because that is what, of necessity, is being rediscovered within it. New forms will replace hierarchical ones but they will now express healthy authority rather than authoritarianism.

Freed of the social class baggage that almost carried them under the torrent of change, fully qualified professionals now have responsibility for authoring the dynamic quest for knowledge and its application that characterize the extraordinary time in which we are already living. America will increasingly depend on those whose professional commitment to the disinterested search for theoretical and practical knowledge depends on and increases their healthy authority. The current superficial prejudice against the specialization of knowledge is a last gurgling cry from the postauthoritarian interim. Natural authority is being rediscovered by the specialists of the Knowledge Age. The age of the "generalist," as in general practitioner in medicine or law, despite political and populist forces, is not the wave of the future but the last lapping of a retreating tide.

Drucker identifies the need for specialists as the impulse for repro-fessionalization. "The central work force in the knowledge society will therefore consist of highly specialized people. In fact, it is a mistake to speak of 'generalists.' But 'generalists' in the sense in which we used to talk of them are coming to be seen as dilettantes rather than educated people. . . . But knowledge workers, whether their knowledge is primitive or advanced, whether there is a little of it or a great deal, will by definition be specialized."[9] The calling of professionals is to unearth and apply knowledge. The art or skill of professionals is indivisible from their search for knowledge. In the rapidly developing Space/Information Age they are the critical authoritative agents of discovery and application. The explosion of knowledge in every field requires ever finer specialization—ever more competent professionalism—if what is learned is to be applied successfully to our lives. Specialization is indispensable, as Drucker observes, to effectiveness in the discovery and transmission of knowledge and in bringing it to bear in real-world conditions and time.

Distinctions are crucial in this context. Specialization may refer to that flowing from and expressing generative authority, as in medicine, in which ever finer and deeper probes into the unknown about human functioning yield new knowledge and more sophisticated treatment techniques. That is the increased specialization found in knowledge workers. It differs greatly from the so-called specialization associated with certain academic hybridization, such as professors of literature applying deconstructionist techniques to science and law, that is not generative and is often politically authoritarian.

These essential specialist professionals will necessarily design fresh Space/Information Age organizations to succeed the flattened spires of hierarchy. This new age requires these designs to serve as the fora for an exchange and application of ideas that, instead of being controlled from the top, will now be broadcast instantly on networks that are among the most potent of the Space/Information Age's effects.

Beyond that, however, the patterns of organization will provide structures through which the great institutions can reestablish themselves and renew their natural authority. If old hierarchical social systems left room for only one person exercising authoritarianism at its apex, the postinterim structures provide space for collegial teams exercising authority together.

Drucker observes: "With knowledge work growing increasingly specialized, teams become the work unit rather than the individual himself. . . . Equally important is the . . . implication of the fact that knowledge workers are of necessity specialists: the need for them to work as members of an organization. Only the organization can provide the basic continuity that knowledge workers need to be effective. Only the organization can convert the specialized knowledge of the knowledge worker into performance."[10]

This affects all the settings of knowledge workers, including hospitals and universities and the professional societies through which they identify themselves and communicate their ideals and their ethical codes. These structures cannot resemble the ones established along hierarchical lines. Their function is not the preservation of authoritarian ranks and privileges but the rediscovery and rehabilitation of the seminal authority of the professional and the traditional ideals and standards of professions in the new age. This dawning epoch places more responsibilities on professionals than they had in any previous era. They can be shouldered only by increasingly specialized knowledge workers, the new professionals, who embrace and express generative authority rescued at last from the ruins of authoritarianism.

12

Rediscovering Authority in the Professions: Recommendations

The Military: A Profession in Particular

The military provides a recent example of a profession's active rediscovery of authority. Perhaps because they had been so powerfully deauthorized in the popular culture, those who led the reform of the military after the Vietnam War, including Senator Barry Goldwater and the late Representative Bill Nichols, were strongly motivated to examine the traditional control–command structure along which authority flowed in the services.

They understood, for example, that the military institution had become a classic example of decentered and diffuse authority. Interservice rivalry was a poisoned fruit of this disarray. In Vietnam, according to the *Wall Street Journal,* "getting a shipment of gear from the U.S. to the war zone often meant that commanders had to file three separate transportation orders with three separate military bureaucracies: the Army bureaucracy that handled rail transport, the Air Force bureaucracy that handled air transport and the Navy that handled ship transport."[1]

Authoritative decision-making had also been corrupted, as noted, by the referral of so many decisions back to the White House. Lyndon

170

Johnson, boasting to visitors of his control of Vietnam War operations, would claim that U.S. planes "can't even bomb an outhouse without my approval."

The reforms made possible by the Goldwater–Nichols bill of 1987 removed authority from Pentagon service chiefs and transferred it to one unified field commander. To clarify the line of command, it vested more authority in the Chairman of the Joint Chiefs to deal directly with the President. That remarkable transformation occurred because men of tested military experience and personal moral authority realized that the services had suffered the consequences of authority breakdown. The diffusion of command had sent them, much like the Light Brigade a century before, into a valley of death, that is, into an interval of floundering, demoralization, and defeat in the field. Offering a model for our larger culture, these men understood that genuine authority needed to be restored. They drew on their own authority as the basis for the legislation they designed to accomplish that mission. In this case, the law was not used as a substitute authority but as a proper instrument for the refurbishing and reinstatement of the natural authority of the country's military professionals.

The professional soldiers were permitted by President George Bush to exercise their authority in the field without referring everything back for his decision. No longer were there two centers, one in the military and one in the civilian commander; now the President authorized the military to exercise uncompromised control over operations. At the same time the rival authority centers of the branches of the service were harmonized into unprecedented cooperation.

Beyond that, the commanders and other officers and officials who had been influential in reforming the military also emerged in the consciousness of the people as men of moral as well as professional authority. America recognized immediately what they had long been missing: the heroes who had been exiled at least in part by the same spirit that had degraded the armed services.

The moral authority of such figures, including former Defense Secretary Dick Cheney, has endured not because of the stars on their shoulders or the titles on their office doors but because it flowed fundamentally from their personalities. Men like Colin Powell and H. Norman Schwarzkopf embodied natural authority; in them one could recognize authority as a moral human energy rather than a legal title or a function of manipulation.

In reviews of the successful hundred-hours land war, much credit was given to the new deployment of authority. The victory was as much over bureaucracy as over Iraq. According to Marine Lieutenant General Walter E. Boomer, what General Schwarzkopf did "was give his field commanders a mission and say go do it, and you didn't hear from him after that. That's all a commander can ask for. He knew we were evolving a plan and he didn't second-guess us."[2] The ability to make decisions in the field and to revise them in the light of new information was critical to the allies' achievement of surprise, which shortened the war and reduced casualties to a minimum.

Benefits of the recovery of authority included the increased morale of the professional soldiers and the concomitant elevation in the esteem with which they were regarded in popular culture. Soldiers were soon voted one of the most trusted of all the professional groups, well ahead of members of Congress and lawyers. A further significant aspect of this re-authorization of the professional military was a fresh attitude at the Pentagon, where highly qualified young officers began to seek once-spurned assignments with the joint staffs.

Recommendations: For Professions in General

Although the circumstances of other professions are different, the contemporary military illustrates basic principles for rediscovering and restoring their natural authority, for the common good as well as their own, can be identified and, with appropriate adjustments, be applied in other settings. The successful rehabilitation of healthy authority, for example, is always a function of the sensible moral authority of those professional leaders who appreciate that they are not victims but molders of history.[3] Authority *authors*. It does not wait to be authored.

Professional leaders must live in the utterly changed present conditions rather than attempt to restore the past. The conditions of American professional life have been irrevocably transformed, and nothing—no movement, lobbying effort, or legislation—will restore them to the way they were when *Daedalus* celebrated their illusory triumph more than thirty years ago.

This, of course, demands something that cosmetic public relations or fantasies of restoring the past cannot deliver, the hard but liberating truth about the present: The conditions of professional life are far from ideal; indeed, they are so bad that they threaten the survival of the professions in any way that recognizes or embodies their natural authority. That insight, like necessary surgery, frees leaders from preoccupation with secondary symptoms and arguments so they can marshal their strength to cure the central problem.

The hierarchies in which the professions had been embedded for so long have already been smashed into kindling by historical forces beyond the control of even the most concerned professionals. The latter can live, and indeed thrive, without, for example, the godlike enthronement that, before the revolutions of the last century and the impact of the Space/Information Age, was granted to them as a divine right. The small remnant of professionals who expect respect for such extrinsic reasons brings down wearying criticism on those professionals who unself-consciously earn a spontaneous response to their intrinsic authority. The former are living, like Civil War reenactors, in a stage-set past.

The shriveled vines of authoritarianism need not even be hauled away and burned. They are dead and will decay fully if left in the open air. Professionals only frustrate themselves when they pay much attention to hierarchical structures or attempt to revive or otherwise reestablish them. To rediscover their own authority, they must kick aside the dead husks of authoritarian style and prepare the gardens, that is, new models of function, in which natural, creative authority can be rooted.

Identify and develop new models to replace hierarchies. This is a slow and evolutionary process requiring reflection, self-observation, and some capacity to understand cultural change. Letting go of hierarchies does not mean that professionals should embrace too eagerly some of the notions that are based on the equalization of "power" relationships. Neither should they commit themselves prematurely to management models that involve them in, for example, extensive consensual decision-making.

The recovery of essential generative authority within the professions hinges on a willingness on the part of professionals and their societies to jettison much that is accidental, unnecessary, and therefore irrelevant to the authority that is integral to carrying out their commitments of service to others. They save themselves by reestablishing their nuclear commitment to aiding society, pursuing knowledge, and serving others in accordance with the disinterested tradition of their callings.

In establishing new models, professionals cannot realign themselves in their relationships to others by sacrificing their claim to know more about their special field than others. Their knowledge and skill cannot be disowned or masked in pursuit of some falsely modest egalitarianism. Indeed, their mature claims should speak for themselves in a manner that attracts confidence and respect.

Professionals can live with or recover from losing superficial status accoutrements and still retain their basic authority. Far more important than social preferment for doctors and other professionals is their scientific curiosity and dedication, marked by their being lifelong students who keep abreast of the latest advances in their field.

In the medical profession, for example, dedication to knowledge finds its center in the *doctor–patient relationship*. Doctors sheath their autonomy by authoring themselves a demanding schedule of ongoing self-development, self-monitoring, and self-control in the service of others. Such intrinsic self-discipline generates and expands their moral authority.

Autonomy and self-control are the lining of the mantle of professionalism. In the ongoing process of historical change, that garment has been greatly modified, as have all authority systems during this period. There has been, for example, widespread pragmatic experimentation in efforts to replace hierarchically based authority, leading to its widespread decentering, diffusion, and monetization.

Physicians, for example, have found new contenders for a share of their once undisputed authority. Physician extenders and nurse practitioners offer many medical services once reserved to doctors. Psychologists, who not many years ago could work in a hospital setting only under the supervision of a physician, even one with no psychological training, have now successfully lobbied the legislatures of many states for the right to gain hospital privileges and, in certain circumstances, to prescribe drugs.

Paralegals carry out many functions that in a previous era were the exclusive province of those admitted to the bar. Lawyers find it problematic but nonetheless true that many people now choose to represent themselves before the court or in other legal matters. In the Roman Catholic Church, priests have discovered that many of the tasks that once defined their professional activities—distributing the Eucharist to the sick, preaching, and administering parishes—are now done routinely by married deacons and nonordained laypersons. Prerogatives once acknowledged to be exclusive territorial rights in every profession have been subdivided by related professionals or by paraprofessionals who have acquired at least some of the knowledge and skills of the relevant profession.

That development, although many-sided, may be considered an example of the rediscovery and redeployment of authority in ways that, because they are nonhierarchical, bear, as a slender stem supports and feeds while a rigid wire only holds in place, the natural growth and flowering of the relevant professional authority. Here we have new forms that successfully transmit various flows of natural authority. The prefix *para* is the first witness to testify to this postinterval development. It means "alongside," not "beneath." So paraprofessionals stand *alongside* rather than *beneath* traditional professionals. *Para* is significant because, as in the Space/Information Age, it eliminates *above* and *below* as reference points in matters of authority. A new general metaphor must reflect these "alongside" relationships while still recognizing the great difference in training and experience among members of these fresh professional arrays.

It is essential but difficult for professionals, immersed in their daily concerns, to achieve and maintain perspective on what looks more like a violent revolution than the rough surface of inevitable sociological changes. The paradox of these developments lies in the fact that while others have come to share in many of their functions, the professionals often retain the ultimate legal responsibility for the consequences of those activities, no matter who actually carries them out.

For physicians the new situation means that people with less train-ing than they, or perhaps none at all, monitor their decisions, fre-quently by telephone from distant cities. For disconcerted physicians, these estranging long-distance procedures are a function of the mone-tization of authority in health care. They arise from the insurance company protocols that govern reimbursement for procedures and treatment. Not only do they extend our contemporary sense of dis-connectedness but they also modify the authority of the professional on the scene, bringing home how medical authority has been decen-tered and vaguely dispersed. Such people operate not *alongside* but *outside* the physician. Their goal is not healing the patient but the increase of the bottom line. They provide an example of the post-hierarchical diffusion and decentering of authority, not an effort to rediscover genuine medical authority.

At the same time, however, physicians must author clear judgments about what is in the best interests of their patients. That is the irre-ducible core of their professional authority. In cases in which their judg-ment clashes with that of reviewers', they cannot passively accept the insurer's demands. In such instances, even though it is frustrating and time-consuming, physicians must make the case for their clinical judg-ment. In those circumstances the professionals either author or are de-authorized. Otherwise, they may experience ethical conflicts, increased demoralization, and a permanent compromise of their healthy authority.

Here we detect a hint about the kind of metaphor that will sym-bolize authority relationships better in the future. Doctors standing in their place in the long chain of actors in the universe of health care, each called a "health care provider," retain a vestige of hierarchical pri-macy when some mishap occurs at any point along the line. Legally, they are still perceived as the most significant, the most knowledge-able, and therefore the most responsible of those actors. Although that may not sound fair to them, it is nonetheless a true condition of the post-hierarchical health care world. It also suggests the foundation on which they can rediscover and rehabilitate their healthy authority.

The transformation of professional autonomy and self-monitoring compel
professionals to perform well one central task: to refine and perfect their

exercise of clinical judgment. The valence of such "alongside" recommendations is, and will ultimately be recognized as, far weaker than that of the clinical judgments of physicians on the scene. In such circumstances, the best response for all professionals is careful self-control and self-monitoring at that fine point of clinical decision-making through which they author the principal work of their calling.

Professionals must keep well honed the skills on which they draw in those moments when they most fully profess their calling, in which they author the work that defines them. What is it about their knowledge and skill, that is, what they can author as nobody else can, in these concrete circumstances? The points at which they are most fully and exclusively themselves as professionals cannot be surrendered to others. Paraprofessionals refuse to accept the responsibility of those moments, thus defining even more sharply the unique interventions of the primary professional. Those are the areas in which the professionals' hard-earned authority, that is, what they have acquired through long study and extensive experience, commands the attentive response of others.

The healthy, generative authority of professionals flows not from the social structures in which they live at any given time but from the knowledge base and specific skills they have acquired in the classical manner. Everything else is accidental.

Their highly personal competency is the only foundation sturdy enough to bear their public profession that they know better than the untrained or the less fully trained about medicine, law, theology, military matters, or any other discipline. The critical mediation occurs not between the individual and some licensing board but in the fusion of knowledge, skill, and judgment by individuals within themselves. Licensing boards recognize but cannot create that personal accomplishment by granting it public credentials.

Professionals must renew their understanding that authority does not exist except as a function of personality. It cannot be made up for by inflated claims, testimonials, regulations, or flow charts. Professional authority is fundamentally natural authority, rooted in human experience and transmitted through human relationships. Simply put, recapturing sensible authority that will prove reliable in the real world of their work depends, as in the example of the military, on the ability of highly trained professionals to reestablish moral authority within themselves. Professionals, like Vietnam generals, now find that they are saddled with full responsibility while their authority is diminished. It is essential to recall that authority inheres naturally and ultimately in the fully trained professionals on the scene, whether it is a battlefield, an operating theater, or a courtroom. No living thing can thrive without a dynamic organizing nucleus.

Recognizing the personal character of natural authority implies that we know the difference between this free, nonmanipulative dynamic and its authoritarian, manipulative shadow self, power. Seeking power for the sake of the self, as in prestige, influence, celebrity or preferment, is a world apart from seeking authority for the sake of serving others. The latter embodies the professional ideal of authority. It transcends politics, ideology, or personal ambition. Those who mistake power for authority, as in vain efforts to restore hierarchical social structures to the professions, are in themselves symptoms of the problem.

Moral authority precedes the public acknowledgment of the professional claim in any and every field. The internal work of the professional is defined as that which cannot be delegated to or done by anybody else. Despite the romantic egalitarianism of the Critical Legal Scholars, law professors and janitors are not equals and cannot, as the critical scholars suggest, exchange tasks or compensation. The janitors know that as well as the law professors. So, too, does the greater public, which needs the service of each but experiences no difficulty, or sense of unfairness, about distinguishing between them as to knowledge, experience, and skills.

The rediscovery of professional authority begins whenever professionals, in whatever field, choose to be thoroughly professional even if society does not appreciate or fully acknowledge it. By recapturing their own moral authority they write a signature that does not wash away. Culture will sooner or later read and respect it as valid.

Such professionals constitute the kind of elite of the intellect that Thomas Jefferson foresaw as the healthy flowering of a democracy. Such a vigorous grouping supplanted the unearned elitism of royalty and the privileged classes against which the colonies had taken up arms. Although the new nation chose to call its leader Mister President, emphasizing its rejection of hierarchy, it recognized the authority of individual achievement and, until very recent years, could differentiate the true equality of human personhood from the individual differences that arose from genius and education.

Validating the notion that some persons know more than others demands the self-discipline characteristic of professionals bound by the ideals that constitute the ethos or spirit of their calling. That remains true even after, as with medicine, psychology, law, and other fields, ethical codes were changed by actions of the Federal Trade Commission's forcing those professions to sign consent decrees to allow advertising. No evidence suggests that it has increased competition or lowered costs. People pay tribute to the professions by their practical testimony that what is of primary importance in selecting professionals is not whether they offer bargains but whether they possess competence.

So, too, professionals must support the highest professional standards through periods, such as the present one, in which they are ignored or thought irrelevant. They must resist the monetization of professional authority, that, in an era in which professionals are increasingly treated as paid employees, weakens rather than assists in the rediscovery of healthy professional authority.[4]

Conscientious professionals must be actively concerned about the long-term effects of such monetization. The most obvious is that a younger generation of doctors and lawyers will perceive their work not as a calling but as "just a job." That outlook is reflected in young professionals who choose their specialty, for example, not because it matches their internal interests or gifts but because of its proposed salary and benefits. Men or women who choose a profession for "lifestyle" factors—eight-hour days, time off, the "best" offer—effectively bargain away the authority they have by emphasizing the external factors that define authentic professionalism.

V

America's Institutions:
Rediscovering Authority in Government,
Business, and Religion

13

The De-authorization of the Institutions of Government and Business

Government

As the millennium approached, no hierarchical structure creaked more from historical distress than the British monarchy. Pocked by the dry rot of highly publicized scandals, the House of Windsor's residual usefulness as a unifying royal symbol and as an integral aspect of Great Britain's constitutional government is being seriously reexamined. The splintering of the royal family by divorce and other disengagements is, in fact, a predictable outcome for an institution that had lost its intrinsic authority. Melancholy emphasis on that loss was provided by the heavily monetized argument offered for preservation of the royal family: that it remains central to Britain's tourism business. It now seems natural for the English press to employ commercial images—the "mismanagement of the royal firm," "lack of strategic thinking in top management," for example—in analyzing the monarchy. The last of the hierarchical royal houses that had entered the century vested in authoritarian power departs with barely a memory of it.

Things were no better in America, where millionaires once married their daughters to European royalty and transported Graustarkian castles back to the United States. In a country established through revolt against a king, the idea of royalty pertained only to the Kennedys and movie stars.

America's Founding Fathers devised a system of separated powers in which, ideally, natural authority could thrive. The equal forum provided for the voice of the people in Congress depended on the common good rather than divine right. The democratic experiment aimed not to restrict growth but to offer opportunities for the flourishing of its people in safe and therefore genuinely free conditions.

Nonetheless, more than two centuries into America's history, a strong ambivalence toward authority still tingles in the air. Authority is suspect in every office from that of the lawyer and the doctor to the Oval Office of the President. Meg Greenfield, a *Newsweek* columnist, notes the "fundamental ambivalence of voters . . . concerning the way we want our elected officials to be. Carter was a political victim of this ambivalence . . . the luggage toting and other gestures of apparent self-denial and humility seemed both fitting and smart. But there remained—and always does—a counter impulse: people wanted from him at the same time, as they do from all presidents, some emanation of power and authority, even some aura (though the word may give them fits) of the *majesty* of the office."[1]

Many modern leaders take office with a handicap peculiar to the times: Seldom, if ever, hearing authority spoken of positively, they may not understand what generative authority really is. Power, despite its inlay of authoritarianism, has always been described to them as the prize. President Bill Clinton's often criticized management style may be a function of his generation's having been raised in a thoroughly anti-authoritarian atmosphere.

President Clinton's formative political experiences occurred when traditional political authority was being ravaged by the Vietnam War and traditional moral authority was being undercut by the Sexual Revolution. It would have been unusual had he entered the White House in January 1993 with the attitudes toward authority that Dwight Eisenhower brought to his presidency forty years before. President Clinton's antihierarchical style was presented as a fresh if vaguely problematic virtue. "Throw out the pyramid chart," *Business Week* suggested. "Purge the word 'hierarchy' from government manuals. Bill Clinton is moving into the White House and bringing with him a management system that could turn the place into a New Age vortex of collaboration, creative tension—and, maybe, chaos."[2]

That seemed prophetic as the shifting center of Clinton's administration became apparent, even to those sympathetic to him. A year later the free-form approach, according to the *Wall Street Journal,* had aggressively diffused traditional lines of authority: "Clinton's cabinet grows increasingly irrelevant to policy making," some of its members "being whacked" and others "routinely steamrollered" by "the young White House Staff."[3]

Even one of his closest advisers, James Carville, wondered out loud about whether the President himself had any well-defined center of authority or political conviction: "Where is the hallowed ground?" As the country stood on the brink of an armed invasion of Haiti late in September 1994, *Newsweek*'s cover story asked "Who's in Charge Here?" and went on to observe that "Clinton's policymaking has always zigzagged, especially in foreign areas, but last week it seemed to spin in circles. At times it was not entirely clear who was running the show: President Clinton? or his ambassador plenipotentiary, former President Carter?"[4]

The Clinton White House manifested the signals of the post-hierarchical age: Authority was diffuse, moved away from the center, separated itself from Democratic party leaders, and even revealed reflexive authoritarianism in its troubled and unclear role in such matters as the suicide of Deputy Counsel Vincent Foster, the firing of Travel Office employees and associated problems occasioned by underlings who arrogated unwarranted authority to themselves in assembling files on former administration staff members.

The principal symptom of divided authority was exemplified in the President's installing his wife, Hillary Rodham Clinton, an unelected official with no public accountability, as "the first presidential spouse," according to the *New York Times,* "with her own power base in the White House and her own set of top officials throughout the government who owe their jobs, and loyalty, to her as much as to her husband." The appearance of a copresidency "created confusion especially in a White House that has a quotidian struggle with tangled lines of authority, and the tendency to trip on them. 'It's hard to run a White House with nobody in charge,' said an influential friend of the Clintons. 'It's especially hard with nobody in charge and two presidents.'"[5]

Mrs. Clinton immediately prepared to develop a national health care plan within one hundred days, to be signed into law by her husband the following Christmas Eve. The standard tactics of authoritarianism were not hard to observe in the establishment of a five-hundred-member consultant group, whose names and affiliations were to be kept secret, as were their deliberations. That planning group was presided over by Ira Magaziner, who, as later analysis revealed, determined beforehand the policy changes that would be implemented from the top down, or hierarchically, on the American people.

That huge, covert, and unparalleled hierarchical intervention developed *in camera* a 1,342-page legislative product filled with what can only be described as authoritarian prescriptions, mandating penalties such as fines and imprisonment for participants. "Require" was used 903 times, "penalty," 111. It also established an elaborate control structure: From atop a hierarchy, seven overseers would hand down the principal decisions about the universe of health care. When President Clinton formally proposed it in September 1993, before these and other specifics became widely disseminated—an uncontrollable and inevitable occurrence in the Information Age—the proposal enjoyed the support of 60 percent of the American public. A year later the legislation had failed and was withdrawn from the congressional agenda.

The neo-authoritarian health care overture cratered for the same reasons hierarchy has failed in other institutions in the Space/Information Age. Writing in the *Wall Street Journal*, Michael Rothschild explains that the Clinton proposal died from internal rather than external causes: It reflected "Machine Age thinking and metaphor ('The health care system is badly broken and we're going to fix it') that could not work in the Information Age: Centralize decisions through monopoly power, ensure stability through tight controls, insist on a 'one size fits all' standard, and allow no room for local innovation. Plan everything out in advance. . . . Hillary and Ira only feigned interest in proposals offered by the public, Congress, and even administration officials. They had already made the crucial design decisions. . . . But the era of the social engineer ended with the demise of the Machine Age. Ira [Magaziner] is a mainframe in the age of networked PCs."[6]

Those problems were compounded by the loss of the center in the presidency itself and the consequent drift of authority, transformed into power, to other centers, such as Congress. Joseph A. Califano, Jr., former Secretary of Health, Education and Welfare, charts this shift: "Congress has become the King Cong [*sic*] of Washington's political jungle, dominating an executive branch that can no longer claim the coequal status that the Founding Fathers saw as crucial. By the 1990s, Congress had ... legislated itself into a position of independent power, shedding its reliance on the White House."[7]

The transfer of authority to other power centers had been accomplished, according to a former White House chief of staff, Donald Rumsfeld, by successful gerrymandering of districts, guaranteeing re-election; the rise of political action committees (PACS) that made members independent of the president for their campaign funds; and the enormous growth of their staffs and perquisites.[8] A 1992 *Business Week* survey of Capitol Hill insiders identified the most influential person in shaping legislation as not House Speaker Thomas Foley but his wife and chief of staff, Heather Foley.

Voters dismissed this bloated, power-absorbed Congress in 1994. The new Republican majority openly declared war on its most flagrant defects, passing a number of bills revolutionizing the way the Congress functions and the government does business. Because of the uncertain exercise of authority in the Clinton White House, the President's executive authority shifted piecemeal toward a new center in the Congressional leadership of House Speaker Newt Gingrich and Majority Leader Dick Armey. As the election year 1996 began, Congress spent much of its authority in a power struggle with the President about passing a new budget. Neither the executive nor the legislative branch could define or exercise its authority effectively. Authority seemed broadly diffused, its function transformed almost beyond recognition in a battle over political and ideological positions. The ongoing contest over the size and role of the federal government was, in reality, a struggle over the nature and function of authority. The new Republican majority found its own authority destabilized by its spread away from the sharply defined center carved out by the new Speaker. It passed quickly to the satellite location of the freshman Republican legislators. Along with senatorial colleagues, they declared their independence from their leader on several crucial questions, including the balanced budget amendment that they had once enthusiastically supported.

The Gingrich Devolution: Rehearsing the Future or Repeating the Past

De-vo-lu-tion, *n.*, . . . 3. A delegating of authority or duties to a subordinate or a substitute.— *The American Heritage Dictionary*

Because authority and its exercise are the real issues behind the confused and confusing struggle about the nature and frustration of authority in our institutions, it is important to examine the position of the President's chief intellectual adversary, House Speaker Newt Gingrich. Gingrich made "devolution" his theme, arguing that the central authority had taken maximum power to itself with minimal public consent, thereby abusing the rights of citizens and becoming unresponsive to their needs. His solution was to take away from the government many of its functions and to hand them over to smaller political entities—the states, cities, towns, and ultimately the citizens themselves. That kind of devolution rejects both liberalism and the modern model of government.[9]

Riding a wave of popular dissatisfaction, Gingrich proposed symptomatic relief, forcing action on many issues whose common denominator was authority and its exercise. But the new Speaker also advertised the problem of his own unresolved view of authority. He experienced constant difficulty in locating himself or the country in time or place. He advertised his problem of dual age citizenship in the very title of one of his talks, "From Virtuality to Reality," and exemplified it when he said, "The thing that I find fascinating is that we are not in a new place; it is just becoming harder and harder and harder to avoid the place where we are."[10]

Gingrich led the passage of much legislation that addressed authority default symptoms during the first months of the new Congress. On the first day, for example, he oversaw "eight rule changes—cutting congressional committees, reducing the number of committees and subcommittees, imposing a six-year term limit on committee chairs and an eight-year term limit on the Speaker, requiring a three-fifths super-majority for any income-tax rate increase, banning the practice of voting by proxy . . . and a bill requiring that the laws passed by Congress apply to Congress. All were designed to limit the power of Congress to act as the guiding force of a powerful central government."[11]

A review of the Gingrich innovations and frustrations allows us to understand their intuitive, embryonic character and to recognize their family resemblances to other institutional attempts to deal with the overall crisis of authority.

The proponents of devolution make no distinction between authority and authoritarianism. Power and authority are used as synonyms and "empowerment" is the unexamined solution for what is wrong. Power is perceived ambivalently. It is a medicine for the illness it causes. "Empowerment" is good but power must be removed or limited because it lends itself to easy abuse.

The failure to distinguish between authority and power makes it difficult for leaders to interpret the central problem of government correctly. Gingrich's long-range goals, according to Michael Kelly, are to hollow out central federal authority. The devolution crusade does not acknowledge the already compromised nature of that central federal authority. The result may weaken further the very authority whose healthiest elements need to be acknowledged and strengthened.

While devolution deals with some of the symptoms, such as the power that has spread to individual legislators and committee staff members, it envisions little if any role for healthy generative authority at the center. This mirrors Omahe's notion of "decomposing the center," that gained brief popularity as a management technique. Central headquarters were done away with, only to have their positive characteristics discovered again later.

The "future" that Gingrich finds in the work of Alvin and Heidi Toffler is actually a well-observed description of the familiar landscape of the post-hierarchical interval. "The new civilization," they write, "brings with it new family styles, changed ways of working, loving, and living; a new economy; new political conflicts; and beyond all this an altered consciousness as well."[12] In fact, that is not the future but the effects the nation has experienced since the authoritarian-bearing hierarchical structures began to collapse because of the first ground tremors of the Space/Information Age. Those include the sexual revolution, the fracturing of family life, and enormous changes in the conditions of work in the professions, business, and industry.

Furthermore, the Toffler proposals to replace what they view as the increasingly obsolete principle of majoritarian rule with a minority-based twenty-first-century democracy and to replace representative democracy with semidirect democracy reflect not new but questionable post-hierarchical proposals from sources as different as Lani Guinier and H. Ross Perot. Such thinking, limited because of its inability to factor in the role of healthy central authority, paves the way for the dissolution of central government. The logical outcome of such thinking would be for California, Texas, and Florida to authorize themselves one day soon as the Hispanic States of America. Such a development in effect would de-authorize the republic by shattering and diffusing its central stabilizing and identifying authority. Should that occur, it would be a function not so much of successful Hispanic rebellion as of the natural consequence of the failure of federal authority.

Gingrich also places more emphasis on the pure technique of transmitting information than on its content. In one of his asides, for example, the Speaker of the House has mentioned empowering the people through the Internet: "We can wire the world." That begs the most fundamental of questions about authority: Who authors the information in such a vaguely conceived Internet? What are its character and its purpose, and in whose hands will its authorization, or potential regulation, lie?

Gingrich alludes very little to space or to its equal position with information in defining the era in which we live. Entering space has changed everything about our sense of place and has shaken the universe and human personality free of the hierarchical templates in which they were once so firmly encased.

Evidence of the increasing experience of a decentered world accumulates every day. It may be found, for example, in Chicago's Michigan Avenue Nike store, designed so that it has no central reference point. The familiar staples of spatial orientation have been deliberately removed and it is difficult for people to know where they are. That reflects our present state in a universe shorn of hierarchical gradients. In other words, design has adapted itself to reflect our decentered condition in which the plate of reality is broken so badly and its pieces scattered so widely that nobody thinks it worthwhile to pick them up and nobody remembers how to put them together again.

This condition is very disordering to people who grew up in a well-ordered world and expect life to be organized centrally and to possess reliable standards. Those who have matured during the post-hierarchical period are not uncomfortable with chaos because they lack a well-developed sense of standards or of centrality in either their day or their year. For example, many young people never eat meals at regular times, preferring to "graze," as it is termed, throughout the day. The Nike store reproduces the formless, consumer-grounded, phenomenological surge of their lives. That advertises their authority deprivation, the longing that expresses itself obliquely, for example, in Baby Boomers' surprise at reaching menopause or their fiftieth birthday, events they often treat as if they were explorers entering never discovered lands rather than as humans encountering universally recognized life experiences.

It is fascinating that one of the most articulate defenders of traditional values, the radio commentator Rush Limbaugh, sponsors a line of popular neckwear, "No Boundary Ties," whose design symbolizes the free field of contemporary experience. Football coaches wear athletic gear whose off-center, jagged lines challenge those that define the field and, therefore, the game over which they are supposed to be authorities. All such large and small signals tell us how immersed we are in this interim-like state.

The political story of 1996 was the budget-inspired impasse between the President and the Speaker and the sharp diminution of the latter's power and authority. Neither man fully understood the nature of generative authority and its centrality for effective leadership or governance. Clinton settled in many ways for the manipulation of power while Gingrich offered an incomplete version of rediscovered authority.

Yet the Speaker and others of both parties are trying to find their way out of this period in which Bill Clinton's ever changing presidency remains a remarkable but understandable function. Governors such as Tommy Thompson of Wisconsin and John Engler of Michigan have taken bold steps to reestablish effective generative governmental authority in programs that have challenged and tamed the shapeless monster of a huge federal bureaucracy that has dissipated its claims to effective authority. The 1996 election year reflected how profound and unresolved is the nation's problem with authority, dramatized in its longing for a leader who might match the challenge of the age and its frustration at not finding one. The rival candidates were startling symbols of the unsettled post-hierarchical period: Bill Clinton, the quintessential interval figure, the politician who survives because his easily transformed and transferred center mirrors the age; Bob Dole, a man from the other side of the century, a war hero candidate who represented a vanished and perhaps unrecoverable age of order of national life. The Nike store versus the Second World War.

Business: Why the Dinosaurs Died

Lee Iacocca was hailed in the 1980s as the entrepreneurial savior of the Chrysler Corporation. Businessmen searched his bestselling autobiography for clues to his imperial style. By the early 1990s, he and his monarchical aura had gradually faded to black in the corporate and public consciousness. Iacocca and other business leaders came to be regarded not as something new but as something outdated, classic tycoons who could not adapt to the Space/Information Age's leveling of their authoritarian hierarchies. As it may have been with the original gigantic reptiles, a new, radically altered climate killed those dinosaurs.

The dinosaurs did not die alone. In addition to the ousting of Robert Stempel as head of General Motors and Kenneth Olson of Digital Equipment, George Bush's election loss in 1992 was bracketed by the resignations of James D. Robinson III from American Express, John F. Akers from IBM, and Paul E. Lego from Westinghouse Electric. *Business Week* noted that "Taps is being played in corporate corridors for the whole way of doing business that was modeled on the command-and-control procedures of the military. Organization men to the end, these postwar executives created largely self-sufficient hierarchies with explicit chains of command. . . . Rapid change, not devotion to some internal order, is now the imperative. [The] successor will be younger—and far more comfortable with a flatter power structure where alacrity and agility are prized over rigid, almost military, obedience."13

Later that year, the same magazine ran a cover story, "The Horizontal Corporation: It's About Managing Across, Not Up and Down."14 One of its summary subheads reveals how hierarchy has passed from a revered and comfortable homeland into a Carthage-like bastion to be destroyed: "Smash the hierarchy, break the company into its key processes."

Long-established hierarchies hold out like bombarded cities, a fact emphasized by Lotus Development's former CEO, Jim Manzi, in a talk on the meaning and use of the information superhighway: "There are also barriers . . . from the persistence of old organizational forms and structures—forms largely based on hierarchy and command and control that people have become comfortable with and are reluctant to change. But to take full advantage of the information superhighway new organizational forms are required—forms that are anti-hierarchical, anti-power, and even post-structural and anti-organizational."15

All this is described in the vocabulary of the Space/Information Age. Thus a *Business Week* cover story claimed that the horizontal corporation "largely eliminates both hierarchy and functional or departmental *boundaries*. . . . The organization might have only three or four layers of management between the chairman and the staffers in a given process."16

General Electric's Chairman, John F. Welch, described by *Fortune* as "the leading master of corporate change in our time," uses the same Space Age notion in endorsing the thorough cultural change he has emphasized in his huge company. "What we value most," he says, "is *boundarylessness*. It's the ability to work up and down the hierarchy, across functions and geographies, and with suppliers and customers. We have gotten rid of the Not Invented Here syndrome. We'll go anywhere for an idea. When there are no limits to whom you'll go, where you'll go, what you'll touch, the results are remarkable."17

The Information Age, as noted by Manzi, transcends hierarchies because information is now perceived in a different manner. It is ceasing to be a function of power and is becoming a function of generative authority. "Information," Manzi observes in his address, "is really more animist than physical, more a flow than a stock, it is meant to be communicated, which means it is lively, collaborative, and purposive. . . . The information superhighway is not being built to carry information, it is being built so that people can communicate and do things."[18]

By this understanding, information possesses the same DNA as dynamic authority which is not a static possession but always a function of human relationships, not a stock good but a flow good. The dinosaur generation of CEOs located authority spatially at the top of the hierarchical pyramid, from which they issued orders downward and up whose slopes all supplicants laboriously climbed toward them. Power was their main idea of authority. In turn, information was power, something to be held tightly, cinched in a sack like a miser's gold pieces rather than invested in others. Such attitudes have been thrust aside, less on theoretical grounds than for the pragmatic reason that they do not apply where there are no longer any pyramids.

In this new age information and authority are living entities, found not in the dead weight of the uninvested gold but in the spirit of the person who knows how to spend it. As such they overlap and interpenetrate each other. Healthy authority craves transmission to others. Information craves a sensible authority that understands how to use it. Information and authority share a spiritual rather than a material nature.

The Space Age, in which boundaries no longer exist, and the Information Age, in which the sophisticated transmission of information makes it available to everyone in the organization (or the population) at the same time, are the powerful dynamisms of contemporary change, as witness the fall of the Soviet Union, in part because it could no longer control information flow. Business leaders have rediscovered a value they cannot easily name. Manzi describes it negatively as "anti-hierarchy, anti-power, and even post-structural and anti-organizational." He can, however, list the expansive human virtues associated with generative authority. "Perhaps paradoxically," Manzi concludes, "these new organizational forms will not work without the reaffirmation of some timeless values—such as trust, openness and even humility."[19]

That hard-to-name substance is, in fact, generative authority. Unable to name it, executives experiment broadly, not understanding that they are trying to make room in their organizational planning for healthy or natural human authority. This energy is, as Manzi senses, antipower and therefore undermines the models, such as the imperial boss and the Coolidge-era corporation, into which it is introduced.

Examples of the irresistible dynamic of the Information Age can be found throughout the contemporary workplace. Computer networks, according to the *Wall Street Journal*, have popped up everywhere, generating new and sometimes uncomfortable management problems. When desktop computerization first started, workers generally used their machines in isolation. Now, however, office computers are increasingly yoked together in networks using cable or phone lines, "servers" as they are called, that store data, direct traffic, and employ new software called groupware, thereby transforming personal computing and office life into a collegial instead of an individual experience.[20]

The workplace revolution dissolves the authoritarian power that was always tightly held inside hierarchies and communicated to as few people as possible. "Because they enable hundreds of workers to share information simultaneously," the writer continues, "groupware networks can give lowly office workers intelligence previously available only to their bosses. Networks can also give the rank-and-file new access: the ability to join in on-line discussions with senior executives. In these interactions, people are judged more by what they say than by their rank on the corporate ladder." That is another transformation dooming old-fashioned one-way authoritarianism and setting the scene for the rediscovery and implementation of healthy authority. It resembles the discovery that, after trying numerous exercise and diet "regimens," walking in the fresh air and eating unadulterated food are the best things for our health. They possess natural and compelling authority. Why, we ask, have we tried all those other things when this is so much easier for humans to use?

The author describes how at Wright-Patterson Air Force Base near

Dayton, Ohio, this new software has brought about a transformation in communication and the exercise of authority. "'[R]ank doesn't really matter when you're on-line,' says Lt. Col. Donald Potter. 'An enlisted man could send a message to a colonel.' Five years ago, he says, 'there wouldn't have been an easy way for a sergeant to share an idea with a colonel short of making a formal appointment to see him in his office.'"

No easy magic is available in these new times of very difficult transition for executives who do not fully appreciate that pumping fresh authority throughout the business depletes the stuffy power they inhaled and exhaled in older systems. Not surprisingly, they adjust to the new age gradually and uncertainly, dealing first with the symptoms that the transformations cause them to experience.

Many business leaders find themselves computer illiterates, strangers inside the Information Age, unable to read the signposts or talk readily to anybody. That is a definition of alienation, the symptom they experience and attempt to address. The *New York Times* reports that "50 chairmen, chief executive officers, presidents, and other business leaders attend a retreat sponsored by Computer Associates International, Inc., to learn how to work computers in the Information Age. The 5th in recent years for business people who had never worked them but knew that 'computers and information networks have become crucial to virtually all types of business.'"[21]

Flattened hierarchies unexpectedly occasion reverse performance reviews. With no up and down, and with information radiating to everyone equally, evaluations no longer come only from the top down. This unmistakable symbol and result of the passing of hierarchies was chronicled in the *Wall Street Journal:* "In 1992, subordinates criticized their superiors at 12% of 897 U.S. companies surveyed by consultant Wyatt Co. The figure 'is a lot higher than that now' and may reach 30% in five years, says David Campbell, a senior fellow at the non-profit Center for Creative Leadership in Greensboro, N.C."[22]

In the new age, such reviews are also becoming lateral. "Once limited mostly to a few manufacturing operations," according to the *Wall Street Journal,* "peer appraisals are spreading to white-collar employees at hundreds of companies. Driven by the movement to leaner, less hierarchical organizations, some employers are including peers in efforts to collect '360-degree feedback.'"23

Celebrating multisource performance reviews as ways of defining values in an organization, Welch says: "To embed our values, we give our people 360-degree evaluations, with input from superiors, peers, and subordinates. These are the roughest evaluations you can get, because people hear things about themselves they've never heard before. But they get the input they need, and then the chance to improve. If they don't improve, they have to go."24 Welch enthusiastically mixes authority and authoritarianism, one of the headiest and most confusing mixtures of the age of experimentation.

One need not hire a teacher with the skills of Daniel Boone to follow the trail of developments in business that lead into a future in which, if only for pragmatic reasons, the cleared land is already being seeded with authority. Although hardly a perfect process, it is a clear transition away from the progressively nonfunctional hierarchical-authoritarian style to new forms of leadership. There will of course be compromises, as when consultants speak of "empowerment" but are really striving to express "authorization," or in the development of alternative models to hierarchy, such as pizza, randomly spiced, as suggested by some consultants. The latter will one day be compared to the bizarre flying machines of the early twentieth century, some of which flapped like giant bird wings. While hardly workable they symbolized the medium of the new age of transportation as the air rather than the ground, its essence as not locomotion but flight. The medium of this new age of business leadership is that of collegial human relationships rather than autocracy, and its essence is not power but natural authority.

14

The De-authorization of
Religious Institutions

The major religions share with Big Business in the ongoing partly re-actionary, partly enlightened struggle to transform themselves into twenty-first-century institutions. The vocabulary of the one may be sacred and that of the other secular, but their challenge is exactly the same: How do major institutions restructure themselves without los-ing themselves in the process? At its root, the problem is to rediscover and reframe the way they exercise authority. In fact, this constitutes a spiritual dilemma for both entities.

The Roman Catholic Church grasped the problem of the age early in the century, perhaps in reaction to Pope Pius X's (1901–9) exces-sively authoritarian rejection of the modern world through the en-cyclicals and other measures he initiated to suppress the influence of "Modernism" on church life. In Vatican Council II (1962–65), the Church responded by reorganizing itself, restoring the fundamentally nonhierarchical collegial pattern established by Jesus Christ in his re-lationship with his apostles.

This effort to replace hierarchy as an outdated setting in which au-thoritarianism flourished resulted in a period of experimentation and turmoil in world Catholicism. As noted by David Remnick, Pope John

Paul II (1978–) is "determined to reverse what he sees as the multiple crises of the Church—principally, an erosion of moral purpose and obedience to hierarchical authority."[1] Many Catholics, feeling themselves still loyal believers, trust the Vatican II emphasis on the perennial Catholic theological teaching on the primacy of their own educated consciences not only as a return to tradition but as a recognition that only they can author their moral lives from within themselves.

Operationally, collegiality has in fact succeeded hierarchy at the basic parish level of Catholicism throughout the world. The priest is no longer a hierarch but a figure in a very different relationship to his people. The new model of collegiality, that is, of people associated in cooperative lateral relationships, is to some extent a function of the age's expanded information and the theological sophistication shared by millions of lay Catholics because of the widespread impact of Catholic education. Ordinary parishioners now know as much as or more than their pastors about the teachings of their Church and take seriously their obligation to form their own moral consciences. They are also deeply involved in running parishes and in carrying out ministerial duties once restricted solely to priests. One could argue that the transition to the positive authority of collegiality is irreversible; indeed, evidence abounds that the long "baroque" era marked by the exaltation of papal and religious figures has already ended. History, however, fashions such endings from its roughest and most uneven material. Although Pope John Paul II dazzles the world with his dramatic spiritual leadership, it is his centrality in the process of collegiality, not his royal prerogatives at the top of a hierarchy, that is determinative in the effectiveness of his leadership.[2]

Catholicism does not struggle alone with the transformation of its authority forms. Subtle yet unmistakable signs of conflicted central authority and identity are obvious in other religious denominations. The *New York Times* reports that for "many of the nation's major Protestant denominations . . . [d]ollars that once flowed readily up from the pews—helping to build seminaries and start missionary corps—are no longer reaching church headquarters the way they once did."[3] That trend has affected Presbyterians, Lutherans, and even Southern Baptists, leading to budget shortfalls, downsizing, and layoffs much like those experienced by business entities.

A study of thirty-one evangelical and mainline denominations conducted by the Empty Tomb, a nonprofit Christian research organization, confirmed the centrifugal dynamic at work. Money that once went to the center is now spread among local congregations. Some view this change, according to Gustav Niebuhr, as generational, with those under forty-five less likely to share the denominational loyalties of their elders.

The fragmenting center is even more dramatically exemplified by the Episcopal Church in the United States, in which inner divisions over such changes in tradition as allowing the ordination of women have led individuals and congregations to depart and to become Roman Catholic. A parish that moves *en masse* to a not untroubled Roman Catholicism to find a more secure identity and stable authority is indicative of how "blurred denominational lines" are in "America's fluid religious landscape."[4]

As in the world of government and business, the Space/Information Age has affected organized religion, obviating the need for hierarchical structures and making less available the ground in which authoritarianism roots itself. This has brought a severe and devastating challenge to the authority of institutional religion, largely because it had so identified its essential authority to teach with an incidental but controlling authoritarian style. The response of Vatican II, reviving collegiality and a commitment to theology and scripture, may be understood as overdue and yet ahead of its time. Pope John Paul II's reaction—to reestablish hierarchy vigorously and uncompromisingly—is destined to fail precisely because of the nonhierarchical environment created not by heresy but by the Space/Information Age. The effort to restore hierarchical forms has, in fact, failed because it has diminished the attention of believers, that is, their readiness to listen to what hierarchs say. Where there is no obedience ("to listen to") there can be no authority. Increasingly, bishops appointed to be unquestioning supporters of traditional hierarchical forms turn out to be proper but unimaginative and largely unimpressive leaders. Their position in the Church has been reworked so that they no longer stand out *above*, although they are readily accepted *within* the ranks of believers. That is the most significant natural dynamic shaping Roman Catholicism as the millennium approaches. Despite the effort to restore hierarchy, the Pope and the bishops will eventually make a transition away from the obsolete hierarchical model into the center of a collegial church.

Intimately related to the destabilization of central authority and identity for the Catholic and other churches is the problem of expressing traditional truths in a sharply changed universe. Can they, as it was said of their founder, "speak as one having authority?" The Space/Information Age has stripped away the template that served as the justification for terming bishops everywhere as "the hierarchy." The disintegration of hierarchy does not, of course, mean that the bishops lack a genuine foundation for their teaching authority. What it does signify is the enormous problem faced by all religious institutions that mistake metaphors for facts.

Any church that insists on the concrete historical meaning of essentially poetic language or metaphor thereby roots its authority in the denotations rather than in the connotations of spiritual language. In effect, they fail to read or employ correctly, or de-authorize, the mythopoetic language of the Bible. That gives them a deceptive sense of control over how and what they teach. This works as long as no other developments, such as advanced and widely disseminated scholarship on biblical texts, occur to threaten the presumptions on which control or power is based. That is to say, such authority functions as long as most people accept the Bible as a source of historical fact rather than spiritual truth.

For example, such familiar metaphors as the Virgin Birth and the Promised Land are still regarded by religious institutions as historical occurrences or places whose latitude and longitude can be plotted exactly. Those essentially spiritual concepts are taught as if they represented concrete events and locales—as if the scriptures were a news account—and men have often shed blood over such ideas.

Such images are, however, neither historical or geographical but spiritual in nature. The metaphor of the Virgin Birth, for example, tells us that every man and woman can be unburdened of their sins and faults and be born into a new spiritual life at any time. The Virgin Birth refers to a profound religious and mystical truth, not to a physical reality. In the same way, the Promised Land is a metaphoric evocation of our ever available opportunity to enter that territory of the spirit that is within us. It does not refer to any geographical location outside of the human heart.

The connotations of those metaphoric expressions of religious truth tell of conversion and renewal of heart. Accepted in that fashion, they possess a commanding authority. Insisted on as facts about biology or territory, they are de-authorized by the advances in theology, scripture study, and knowledge that can no longer be controlled by ecclesiastical bureaucracies. That control fails when everybody shares the same access to learning that the once all-powerful religious bureaucracy, such as that Roman Congregation formerly known as the Holy Office, professed to control. Those who treat religious metaphors as hard facts miss their spiritual significance and thereby diminish their own authority. Such literalists, as Joseph Campbell once observed, order lunch and then eat the menu.[5]

Viewed from the perspective of these new times, such old teachings lose nothing of their essence if their accidents are allowed to drop away. They gain rather than lose authority by being understood as metaphors of the spiritual life. That, it must be noted, is a crisis of *organized* or institutional religion, not of religion in general or its capacity for moral enlightenment and the growth of the soul. It is a crisis of the casing rather than the contents of religious teaching.

Many persons wonder, for example, whatever happened to right and wrong, once seemingly so firmly in place and now floating so freely about us. If the Space Age takes away our capacity to speak of *up* and *down,* the whole vocabulary once employed by organized religion to describe *right* and *wrong* also changes. That does not mean right and wrong have no meaning. The central challenge for institutional religion is to learn to speak spiritually about those abiding truths again, that is, to author spiritual truth in its own language.

Speaking spiritually includes being at ease and fluent with the mythopoetic tongue in which spiritual truth is ordinarily expressed. When religious leaders, including the Pope, can do that, they recover the authority they are supposed to have as spiritual leaders but which today is confounded and confused with the authoritarian claims of hierarchy. Authority's healthy exercise depends on authoring metaphors that evoke and accommodate the destratified universe in which we now live together. That is the spiritual counterpart of what other institutions are doing in trying to rediscover and reexpress their authority in ways that match the human experience of this Space/Information Age.

The End of the World is an appropriate spiritual metaphor for our consideration. When religious leaders understand that the End of the World does not mean the physical end of the world in disaster movie fashion, they may better appreciate their challenge. The End of the World is metaphorical in character, not a linear historical prophecy of some imminent day whose evocation scares people to death. It describes a change in our perception occasioned by spiritual insight. The End of the World occurs whenever we see into the world's true nature. Then the superficial world in which we have been living dissolves, and we begin living in a deeper realm of the spirit. That is what the poet William Blake meant when he wrote of our ability, once "the doors of perception are cleansed to see the world as it is, infinite."

15

Rediscovering Institutional Authority: Recommendations

But let us not destroy the scaffold until we have raised the building
—Sir Joshua Reynolds[1]

Authority is located in and is inseparable from the center of the individual. Authority's rediscovery depends on our being able to see it in the way a great photographer captures an often-seen subject as it has never been seen before. Yosuf Karsh photographed Winston Churchill in a pressured instant after having given a major address early in World War II. Pausing rather than posing, his text jutting from the side pocket of his open jacket, Churchill stands timelessly and truly, leader and leadership, man and moral authority all in one. So, too, healthy authority is inseparable from the human beings who generate it and transmit it as the energy of growth to others.

If authority may be seen in Churchill, authoritarianism is inseparable from Adolf Hitler as he mesmerizes a torchlit crowd of Nazi party members. Defining authority for us, the Prime Minister worked for freedom and growth. Embodying authoritarianism, Hitler strove for control and conformity. If those at the center of an institution lack moral authority, so, too, do the institutions, whether they are churches, schools, or governments. Nazi Germany's institutions were thoroughly corrupted by authoritarianism that jolted them fiercely and briefly into explosive and destructive action for a dozen years. Their heritage was enslavement, death, and ruin. Overcontrolling authoritarianism, of course, can be observed on lesser scales. The results, however, are similar in the denied, stunted, or distorted growth of those shaped by its restrictive character.

To be perceived accurately, authority must be located at the center of the individual rather than in the machinations of power or the structural elements of a political machine. The human personality alone is the source and the sustaining environment of moral authority. Therefore the moral authority of any institution is always a function of the moral authority of those human beings who stand at its center. That is the organizing point, as the nucleus is for the cell, of authority's capacity to create and enlarge life.

There is no substitute for what a man or woman who possesses intuitive natural or generative authority can accomplish, no matter the institution in which they function. Neither is there a manual or course that can successfully teach this pivotal characteristic of leadership. Knowledge is so critical that it defines the present age. It is, however, the knower, the possessor capable of integration and vision—the Prime Minister, the executive, the pastor—who remains the source of authority.

Ordinary persons need not be Churchillian to believe in and trust themselves and thus to rediscover their natural authority. Indeed, it is important to remember that authority is not larger than life. It fits any really human life exactly. This kingdom of God lies within all healthy persons. Their lack of fame may be more an asset than a hindrance to their exercise of sensible authority. Such persons may seem outnumbered and beleaguered in a nondiscriminating popular culture where good and bad, right and wrong, sense and nonsense, have been granted equal citizenship rights. Even so, the natural authority of ordinary people generates an effective, if not culturally celebrated, set of sensible standards.

Leaders who want to get a look at how authority functions in their own lives need ask only a simple question: What is the central purpose of this institution? Identifying that, they immediately discover how or if they are exercising their authority to honor that purpose.

Long-term generative leadership depends on its spiritual component. Moral authority needs regular rediscovery and reinforcement, especially during this post-hierarchical period, marked in every institution by a chaotic and piecemeal experimentation with no-fault and no-moral living. The leaderless era has not done away with the need for people who grasp the fact that healthy authority is essentially spiritual rather than economic or structural. It is not accidental that in books on business and government the vocabulary normally reserved for churches is used to describe the function of central authority.

While it has been observed that sales conferences sometimes borrow evangelical techniques and that a new fad for business associates is to "go on retreat" together, the spiritual nature of authority's challenge is the subject of highly public but seldom accurately interpreted revelation.

Authority's indispensable function is, unlike the superficial pieties often invoked by politicians or at company dinners in its name, intrinsically religious. Nowhere afloat on the cataract of management literature do bottled messages require leaders to be "controllers" or "numbers crunchers." They insist, however, that they be spiritual. Many of them may protest, as Saint Peter did when chosen by Jesus to head his apostles, "I do not understand spiritual things." Yet the work of leaders is described unambiguously as spiritual.

The leader is responsible for "vision," for being a "seer" in its traditional sense of "one who sees." If a government agency is to run or a business to flourish, the person with central authority is responsible for the clear enunciation of its "sense of mission." Thus David Osborne suggests that in "reinventing government" the first question to be asked is, "What's our mission?" Agencies must be then "converted" to the "vision" that comes from the answer. Conversation about vision and mission must, Osborne insists, "start at the very top."[2]

Because the Information Age culture necessarily focuses the aim of the institution, individuals need to rediscover their own authority in relationship to it. Identifying and living according to traditional standards resembles finding high ground in a flood. Its gift to ordinary people is a place of safety and perspective from which they can view the pounding torrent. Through such an escape in the company of like-minded and supportive people we experience for ourselves the biblical myth, what we might term the "Noah effect," contemporary Noahs climbing together onto a saving ark. The intimidating and briefly powerful waters will subside, leaving only faded marks where they had once prevailed.

The explosive and sudden arrival of an array of communications tools has magnified the Noah effect, that is, the availability of effective dams, reservoirs, diversions and other controls on the flood plain of popular culture. Expanding capacities for access to and reception of information under their own control enlarge the opportunities for Everyman and Everywoman to rediscover and express their own generative authority.

They can therefore challenge the advertising–public relations complex, which, in the vacuum of true authority, has exercised such dominant and highly monetized power over what people learn, watch, or buy. That complex's capacity to condition people's behavior depends on exclusivity of control. That was secure when only three networks dominated television, just as one company did phone service, or, in government and other businesses, when information could be tightly controlled at the top. But these conditions no longer exist and cannot be restored in the Space/Information Age.

The present fledgling historical period is still so novel that, as with all invention, its wonders will be spectacularly trivialized at first. But play, as technology consultant Casey Dworkin observes, is an important aspect of learning a technology and is to be expected as people begin to learn the rudiments of authorship, the exercise of creative authority, in a startlingly new age. This expanded authorship potential for ordinary citizens in more serious matters has been evident in recent congressional and state elections. When ordinary citizens can have direct access to a variety of background and other materials related to candidates and issues, the advertising–public relations specialists cannot so easily spin those materials to their own purposes. What they had once received in predigested form and secondhand, many Americans tapped into firsthand via C-Span and other networks outside the once exclusive broadcast chains. That constituted a very small but sure first step in their rediscovering and exercising their own authority.

This development reflects the Heisenberg Principle of Indeterminacy, the intrinsic impossibility of measuring both the speed and the position of an electron at the same instant. In like manner, it is impossible to maximize the possibilities of communication and to manipulate or to control them at the same time. One cannot successfully darken something whose nature is light itself. Nor can one place a boundary on a dynamic entity that cannot, of its nature, be effectively measured, much less bound. That is why authoritarian governments, such as China's, are doomed in their efforts to control the flow of information across or within their borders. Not only is the Jinni of communication out of the bottle but the bottle itself is smashed. That reality presents dilemmas that, ironically, make the nourishing of natural authority and its attendant virtue of trust the pragmatic choice for the sensible management of this still infant but fast-growing and little-comprehended phenomenon.

Given the ever expanding nature of and access to information through technology, "New Media" are creating an environment far more favorable to authority than to the subtle authoritarianism of the advertising–public relations complex. The technical advances that support the rediscovery and reapplication of personal authority have appeared in the last decade of this century. In the twenty-first century they will be regarded as mere foreshadowings of the immense cultural changes that will have flowed from them.[3]

This represents a transfer of authority from those who perceive information as a static entity—in the words of Jim Manzi, Lotus's former CEO, a "stock" good—to those who understand information as a dynamic entity—a "flow" good. This transformation ends permanently the monopoly control over information that had previously been in the hands of those who were tellingly vested with such hierarchical titles as Press Lords and Media Barons. This slowly accelerating transformation not only offers new opportunities for average persons to recover their authority but also portends a bewildering revolution for the "Spinmeisters," as they are called, in every field in which their effectiveness depends on their capacity to control and "manage" information and news.

As the suitability of hierarchy as a model for human institutions continues to decline, institutions must restructure their authority in models that truly reflect human experience. We suggest that the solar system offers a good transitional pattern for restructuring generative authority. This matches our current experience of a unified universe.

Leaders in every field are looking for models to take the place of the hierarchies that no longer work well. Much of their energy has gone into flattening and discarding the latter. Although they see that hierarchies have collapsed, they do not understand why and, therefore, lack an organizing principle on which to pattern new forms for their natural authority. Once they understand this goal they will look for structures to accommodate its healthy energies. Appropriate models do not precede but follow the recognition of natural authority as a spiritual reality.

As hierarchical structures were once modeled on a false perception of the heavens, so fresh human structures may now be found in a more accurate perception of the cosmos. The solar system, in which the separate planets, each in its own orbit, circle the central nourishing sun, offers a suitable model for renewed structures. The planets have different compositions of minerals, riches, and climate. Their journey around the sun varies greatly. Some have moons of their own circling them in turn. It has recently been suggested that our moon is powerfully functional, stabilizing the earth's spin on its axis and preserving it from tilts that would lead to wild climate changes.[4]

These extraordinary relationships may well mirror the structures in which persons, although functioning in separate orbits, may maintain a tense but optimal balance with each other around the nourishing center, that is, the sunlike font of knowledge, wisdom, understanding, and integrated purpose.

One might suppose that institutions whose hierarchies have faltered could reimagine themselves better as solar systems than as the pizza pies or upside-down pyramids suggested by business consultants. In the age to which Peter Drucker gives its name, knowledge is the source of authority, the sun whose strength radiates out to everything in orbit around it. The application of this model will become second nature as we enter more deeply into Drucker's view of an economic order in which knowledge, not labor or raw material or capital, is the key resource.

As noted, the urgent questions for professionals and the leaders of institutions and businesses is: What is the essential human activity at the center of what we do? What at that center is the source of its natural authority, and therefore the sun for each particular solar system? In medicine, for example, Dr. Edmund Pellegrino suggests that, despite enormous changes that have emphasized economics, the center remains the doctor–patient relationship, the focus and inspiration for all the rest of medicine's creative energies. Once agreed upon, the development of a model energized by this authoritative center becomes possible. Finding the sun in the solar system of any institution immediately locates the source of its natural authority.

This principle applies to every institution and, while little grasped yet, suggests the order of change that will require a rediscovery and redeployment of natural authority as the energy of the structures, longed for today, that will be demanded tomorrow.

VI

The Law:
America's Authority of Last Resort

16

The De-authorization of the
Legal Profession

The law necessarily suffers the same authority crisis that has shaken every profession in what we term the post-hierarchical age. As court-houses have generally been built along classical lines, so, too, has the law presumed that its traditional vocabulary and structures would guarantee it similar magisterial stability. The accelerating collapse of hierarchies operates like a neutron bomb, leaving the shells of institutions standing apparently unharmed while making life progressively more difficult for people within them. The courthouses still stand in marbled elegance, but the judges and lawyers inside find their standards challenged and their authority questioned, diffused, and monetized. As Mary Ann Glendon, a Harvard law professor, observes, "The concepts of professionalism promoted by bar leaders were remarkably stable and consistent from the 1920s to the mid-1960s. . . . Today's lawyers are wandering amidst the ruins of those understandings."[1]

The law, following its word origin, "that which is laid down," first sank its foundations in the deceptively stable earth of the pre-Copernican universe. But the earth has moved for the law exactly as it has for other institutions. As a result, law in America finds itself severely pressured from without and from within. From without, almost every other institution including religion and many quasi-institutions, such as sports, turn to the law to give support to or supplant their own authority, thus making the law packhorse and scapegoat for the woes of other institutions. Within the universe of the law itself, largely unsuspected by the average citizen, the law agonizes with self-doubt and scouring self-examination about its own identity and authority. The quiet but profound crisis of the law is just coming to term in our consciousness as does an illness that has not yet made us feel sick enough to do anything about it.

The problem surfaces in social criticism and the arts, in the monologues of Jay Leno and in the acerbic stream of everyday jokes. In *A Frolic of His Own,* the novelist William Gaddis, who had previously explored forgery in the contemporary world, selects plagiarism as the principal metaphor for the authority crisis of the law. Like storytelling, the law is supposed to serve as a tool for imposing or rescuing order from the demeaning chaos of everyday life, but his characters quickly discover that the law tends to be a poor substitute for justice, that it forces people into adversarial relationships of mistrust, promoting a sense of disintegration instead of order.

In describing the state of the law in America since 1960, Glendon writes of the "remarkable rise in the influence of legal innovators and iconoclasts with shallow roots in legal traditions and poor grounding in normal legal science. Over the past thirty years, a heady New Age spirit has wafted from high courts, celebrated practitioners, and elite law schools into every nook and cranny of the profession."[2]

She is, in fact, describing the distress of the profession of the law in this post-hierarchical period, an interval condition in which the law claws itself as does an unrelieved patient crazed by his symptoms. For the legal institution the symptoms are those chronic in this post-hierarchical period: a loss of stability at the center, the shift to new foci of power away from that decaying center, a decline and dilution of standards, pragmatic experimentation, increased work dissatisfaction and intraprofession turbulence, thorough monetization as a replacement for traditional motivation, and an unrelieved swelling caused by bureaucratization.

Authority Failure in Post-hierarchical Law

Pragmatic, ideologically driven changes in the law's identity arose in the 1970s. The Law and Economics Movement, for example, fully applies economic ideas concerning incentives and efficient behavior to legal situations. The Critical legal theorists challenged the law's claims to represent abiding human truths, contending that it reflects instead the dominant political and social moods of successive historical eras.

The formerly tightly bound nucleus of institutional law—the confidence that came from its unquestioned place in society and its educational, practical, and ethical traditions—has been cracked, and its authority diffused. Like cobwebs sprouting in courthouse rafters, small but profound developments signal the law's identity diffusion. Not only have entirely new theories challenged the law's stable sense of identity and historical continuity, but the pursuit of justice has also been replaced by a search for economic fairness. In lesser ways, one can observe the dispersal of the law's function in the rise of mediators as substitutes for litigators and the drop in affordable services for many people, resulting in their going outside the system to make their own wills and contracts, to avoid probate, or to represent themselves in court. The explosion of improvisation is to be expected in the post-hierarchical interim.

The inconstant star of legal authority is visible in the profession's shifting attitude toward its own ethical obligations. As Stuart Taylor, a former president of the American Bar Association, observes, the organization's actions say that preserving confidential relationships with their clients is more important than lawyers' preventing themselves from being used as shields for ongoing crime and fraud. In 1983 the ABA's House of Delegates voted to prohibit lawyers from disclosing their clients' illegal plans even when silence could implicate the lawyers in civil or criminal liability as accomplices. In contemporary America the distinction between clever lawyers, the law, and justice is increasingly difficult to make. Murder trials, such as those of the Menendez brothers and O. J. Simpson, have promoted widespread skepticism about the ethical obligations and actions of lawyers in general and trial lawyers in particular.

Americans who follow trials on television are watching a theatrical presentation, the first model for the court, but if people see the movie they do not have to read the book, that is, they may well take this klieg-lighted but strangely bedimmed façade for the whole institution of the law. Nonetheless, televised trials are powerful and persuasive experiences in which the emphasis on star lawyers doing star turns does not necessarily enhance the authority of the law. Many Americans now accept, as an appropriate summation of what takes place in courtrooms, the comment of Justice Oliver Wendell Holmes when refusing relief for Sacco and Vanzetti. When his secretary once asked, "But has justice been done, sir?" Justice Holmes replied, "Don't be foolish, boy. We practice law, not 'justice.'"[3]

The law, according to David Trubeck, a University of Wisconsin law professor, has been searching for an alternative foundation, for some way to ground a legal vision that wasn't there in the legal tradition itself. Thus law school catalogs are now filled with interdisciplinary offerings to provide powerful new ways of analyzing why the law is labile, taking on meaning from new circumstances instead of preserving something immutable from the past. The appointment of professors of literature, such as Stanley Fish and Martha C. Nussbaum, to law school faculties invites the application of deconstructive techniques to its tradition.

In such an intellectual climate, the law becomes progressively deauthorized and its once stable authority is undermined. Martin Redish of the Northwestern University Law School applies a line from *Dr. Strangelove*—"There will be no fighting in the war room"—to suggest that there will be no law in the law schools.

Monetization is a by-product of the decentering and diffusion of the law's once sharp focus of authority. The financial model provides a new basis for and measure of what the law does, an identity based on markets and on the economic rather than the philosophical analysis of human behavior. Through monetization, the law, as with other professions, transforms its identity, its ideals, and its way of practicing. Such translation into monetary incentives is a classic example of the experimentation that follows the diffusion of institutional authority. The slogan of such experimenters is perennially seductive: "Let's put this on a business basis."

Perhaps no profession in America has so actively embraced the business model as the law. The boast that the law is not "a trade or a business" is, according to the lawyer Alexander Forger, "a hysterical note from the past." Monetization is the engine for the tasteless advertising, exemplified by such legal entrepreneurs as the Philadelphia lawyer who spread his phone number, INJURY-1, on broadcasts, benches, and buses, at bus stops, on magnets and ballpoint pens as well as in newspapers. The plunge into the money pit is captured by, "Just Call toll-free, 1-800-EX-JUDGE. . . . Let the ex-judge help you get everything you're entitled to."

Such aggressive placing of capitalistic rather than judicial goals at the heart of the law has led to marketing associations for lawyers and the use by many firms of the business corporation and its profit motive as an alternative to the traditional professional partnership and its ideals of justice. A 1987 Milbank, Tweed market study advised that "potential clients were not looking for 'quality and integrity' when choosing their counselors. . . . In fact, executives were looking for entrepreneurial lawyers who took initiative and made a discernible impact on transactions."[4]

As a result, law firms clouded their identities, the foundation of their authority as well as the standards and the ethical principles authorized by them. Aping the conglomerates they helped to create, they adopted the forms of commercial enterprises, redefining each of a firm's elements as "profit centers." They also developed commercial subsidiaries that enabled them to engage in business without concern for the ethical standards that would forbid them, as lawyers, to do so.[5]

In 1992 the ABA House of Delegates reversed Model Rule 5.7, condemning such subsidiaries, which it had passed the year before. Such ambivalence about nonbinding rules is evidence of the internal conflicts of the law about the exercise of its authority and its identity. The ease with which arrangements can be altered suggests that there is nothing at stake here but a business negotiation, that monetization has flattened and overridden principles and ideals. Such a diffuse state follows the erosion of the hierarchical structure with which the law had become so intermingled. Generative legal authority transcends those structures, and the law's rehabilitation depends on its rediscovery.

Lawyers feel in themselves the difficulties in their practice that are symptoms of the breakdown of their legal authority. After noting that lawyers have never had greater power, influence, or wealth than they do at present, Mary Ann Glendon notes that their work satisfaction plummeted by 20 percent between 1984 and 1990. If they are so central to American culture, Glendon asks, "Why are so many lawyers so sad?"[6]

Lawyers regularly confess their woes publicly. Sam Benson stated his case for quitting the law in *Newsweek:* "I am astounded that I was able to practice law. . . . I was tired of the deceit. I was tired of the chicanery. But most of all, I was tired of the misery my job caused other people."[7]

"The net result," Derek Bok, the former President of Harvard, writes, summing up the diffusion of traditional legal authority, "is a massive diversion of exceptional talent into pursuits that often add little to the growth of the economy, the pursuit of culture, or the enhancement of the human spirit."[8]

17

The Law as Authority Surrogate

America has not sought a cure for the effects of its authority deprivation but has settled for a crutch instead. It leans heavily on the law to
support or, in many cases, to authorize its functions. Placing all its
weight on the law, the culture accepts a handicap in place of wholeness. Dependence on the authority of the law not only confesses
weakness but unfairly and ultimately unhappily drains the law of its
best energies.

The law and lawyers have gotten into everything in the post-hierarchical interval. The fact that the law has become the surrogate authority for other institutions is understandable. It has been invoked
through regulation, lawsuit, precedent, and, perhaps most subtly of
all, a transplanting of the legal mind into the republic's central nervous system. The Frankenstein myth, of whose telling we never tire,
has been reenacted by us, bereft of authority, in the monstrous creature we have made of the law. That is why, like Dr. Frankenstein, we
are so threatened by what we have set loose and now want to kill it.

During this fluid period in which institutions experience authority
default, many Americans now perceive the Supreme Court as a secular counterpart of the Vatican, a temple within whose sacred precincts

every cultural matter, including those that are moral and ethical as well as legal, is defined and resolved.

Once the branch of government concerned with judicial review, that is, deciding the constitutionality of legislation, the Supreme Court has perforce become a substitute authority for other branches of government and other authority-impoverished institutions. Analyzing its 1991–92 rulings on issues related to prisoners' rights, Linda Greenhouse observes in the *New York Times:* "So far, Congress has either rejected these changes outright or, locked in partisan combat, remained stalled on them. So, in contrast to the concept of judicial restraint . . . the Court has taken an activist approach. It has, in effect, assigned itself the role of rewriting the Federal statute to its own taste."[1]

Indeed, the deliberations of the Supreme Court are covered by major American media as if they were the religion substitute for a secularized society. The selection of justices is treated as if the sacred mysteries of America were in their hands. The power of appointment to the Supreme Court is an issue of apocalyptic proportions in presidential campaigns. So reverential is Linda Greenhouse's court coverage in the *Times* that her name, as "the Greenhouse Effect," is used to describe the acolyte devotion of activist journalists to judges whose opinions meet with their approval.

Neither the law nor the Supreme Court can be blamed for being regarded so grandiosely. Where governmental authority falters, judges intervene to fill the authority vacuum. Anthony Lewis explains in the *New York Times* how Federal Judge A. David Mazzone forbade Massachusetts from hooking up any new sewer lines that would empty into Boston Harbor until the state cleared the legal way for a new landfill: "That we have to look to judges to focus our minds on pollution and decayed hospitals and overcrowded prisons is not a happy fact. But it will go on—it must go on—until we regain the ability to decide such issues for ourselves."[2]

Sometimes by default and sometimes by overestimating their own abilities, judges also intervene in situations aggravated by the general cultural problems with authority, responsibility, and accountability. Thus, of Queens, New York, Judge Edwin Kassoff's role in deciding a matter involving an Alzheimer's disease patient, the *Wall Street Journal* reported:

"Hundreds of similar cases are inundating the nation's courtrooms, as judges are being asked to assess whether an elderly person has Alzheimer's or another debilitating condition. . . . Difficult as these questions are for doctors, they are even more complicated for judges with no medical training."[3]

Such situations, in which incidents, events, science, and even religious mystery are translated into legal terms, announce that we are willing to play by the law's rules even when the latter cannot encompass adequately the names of the subjects entrusted to them. As a result, music is not music, art is not art, and life is not life until represented by a lawyer and validated in the language of the courts. Although some lawyers may relish the idea of being the contemporary wise men, judges and lawyers who take a longer historical view understand that there is more danger than comfort to the country and to the law in this dependence on legal authority to bolster or supplant the compromised authority of other institutions.

The culture groans like a litigator's overstuffed briefcase because the medium and the restrictive thought processes of the law have been invoked, with such little serious reflection, in an attempt to manage and monitor an atmosphere deprived of natural authority. The complaints that ordinary people register about the intrusion of the law into their lives are laments about the malaise that results from long-term deprivation of even the idea of natural or healthy authority. The results are bad for everybody, lawyers included.

With the authority of other institutions in default, that of the courts has been invoked much as jerry-built behavior codes and sexual harassment rules have been in education's vacuum of ethical and moral authority. The law is also pressed to reinvent common sense and common courtesy, which mean nothing unless people author them from within themselves.

So, too, the law has been drafted into the service of reforms by institutions whose authority is so enfeebled that they can no longer carry them out for themselves. If you depend on legal-like procedures, however, you get legal-like products that may not adequately house or honor the traditions of either the common law or common sense. Regulations are the fuel of the bureaucracies that multiply when natural authority doesn't work well any more. Thus, the Harvard Law School professor Richard H. Fallon, Jr., who chaired the faculty committee that drafted the school's sexual harassment guidelines, asks, "[A]re sexual harassment guidelines necessary at all? In fact, Harvard Law School is required by law to protect its students and employees against sexual harassment."[4] One might add, by the Ten Commandments as well.

Court calendars are not clogged because judges and lawyers want them that way. The situation is a result of employing the law for purposes that threaten to snap its own tautly stretched authority. Suits are filed in so many matters that were once dealt with informally or through others, including teachers and pastors, now themselves the subject of many lawsuits, that the character of American life seems greatly altered and its continued workability is doubted by some social critics.

The enormous preoccupation with legal actions, draining of physical, psychological, and financial resources, is a characteristic that flows from estrangement from true authority. It is a defense—unhealthy, short-term, and doomed—against the chaos that will threaten until generative authority is rediscovered. That, along with our fundamental problem with authority, is a spiritual, not an economic or legal, problem.

Thinking Like a Lawyer

The transfer of practical authority to the law leads to a lawyer-dominated culture—in effect, a legal state—and is less a sign of our intellectual commitment than of our spiritual impoverishment. Reviewing the consequences of making everybody "think like a lawyer" allows us to understand how little it has relieved and how much it has exacerbated the rawness in our souls and in our relationships with each other. This resort to the law is an unconscious reflex for many leaders. It may have been a serious obstacle for the presidential candidate Robert Dole, whose immersion in legislative detail had narrowed his vision, causing him to respond to questions by saying, "We have a bill about that. We can handle it. We'll work it out in conference."[5]

If there is a bill or a legal solution to everything, then it is clear that the other institutions need to rediscover their authority. When law dominates a culture, these are the effects:

- Everything becomes *adversarial,* challenging, and confrontational, subverting the idea of trust and the conditions necessary for it to exist. People mourn trust as a moribund virtue in contemporary culture. With the best of intentions, the law does not substitute for but extinguishes trust.

- *Advocacy* overwhelms objectivity. The notion that a lawyer should be included in deliberations of a nonlegal sort, such as those of an ethics committee, as proudly announced by the American Psychological Association, to insure "fairness" is foolhardy. Advocates *advocate* a position chosen beforehand; they do not dispassionately await the discovery of the truth.

- "Thinking like a lawyer" does not promote *justice.* The objective is to win, whether that outcome is authentically just or not. In pursuit of that goal, clever maneuvering, smokescreen distraction, and trying the case in the media are commonplace.

- "Thinking like a lawyer" often *makes the healthy elements of life seem bad or dangerous.* The healthy task of *risk taking,* for example, is considered an unnecessary and imprudent step in liability claims against various products. That works against innovation and invention in industry, pharmaceuticals, and medicine. It frustrates an admirable human quality. It also rewards those who act in an impulsive manner by abusing or misusing the products. For example, the person who stood on a rolling desk chair to adjust the window shade and fell was awarded damages on the grounds that he was not explicitly warned about the danger of using the chair for that purpose.

Such a use of the law to promote safety decreases human responsibility by shifting the emphasis to environmental factors and allowing them to overshadow the role of individuals in being responsible for, that is, being the authors of, their own safety within the work environment. This *estrangement from the human* is found as well in product liability and other cases in which legal thinking proposes a standard of zero-defect behavior that fails to match, as the law should, the fallible, imperfect human condition.

- *Telling the truth,* transformed by excessive legal thinking, comes to be regarded as dangerous, imprudent or unnecessary. Here one detects the influence of the advertising–public relations complex that is committed to "image" and "perception" more than "reality." *Spontaneity* is penalized by legal thinking and is made to seem rash and impulsive in many situations when, in fact, it is one of the signs of healthy personality.

•   "Thinking like a lawyer" leads to *dead-end obsessiveness.* Larger meanings are missed because of a focus on small details, "loopholes," or "technicalities" that confuse *accidents with substance* and trivialize common sense and justice at the same time.[6] This tugs at the thread of *indecisiveness* that, in its endless rumination over phrases and fine points, threatens to rend the garment of justice.

•   Legal thinking also results in other dangerous psychological consequences. For example, it fills the air with the fumes of *paranoia* by emphasizing suspicion, mistrust, and attack strategies against opponents.

•   Legal thinking invokes *euphemisms,* a sign, according to the historian Paul Johnson, of the rise of the modern in our thinking. Referring, as the courts did for many years, to slavery as "that peculiar institution" blurred its real meaning. There are a hundred contemporary equivalents that distort the significance of what happens to and between people.[7]

•   "Thinking like a lawyer," perhaps to the surprise of many, is the source not of protecting but of breaking *confidentiality.* The latter concept has been undermined *by legal means* in every profession but the law. Confidentiality, for all practical purposes, has been broken open in every relationship and institution, including medicine, psychotherapy, education, pastoral care, and even the confessional in the recent use of a secretly taped confession to prosecute a man accused of murder. The same applies to tax records, occupational files, military records, journalistic sources and the intimate communication of spouses.

•   "Thinking like a lawyer" stresses belief in the *literal* much like that of extreme fundamentalists in the bible. But the literal application of legal authority cannot construct a happy marriage, a successful business partnership, or the flowering of the imagination into works of art, nor, for that matter, can it turn the soil in which justice and truth grow. The most dangerous possibility of "thinking like a lawyer" is its becoming the biblical "letter that kills" instead of the "spirit that gives life."

Glendon sees that "the extended orgy of legal hubris is winding down," grimly concluding that this interlude and its excursions have not been fulfilling and have bred disillusionment in a coming-of-age legal generation whose members will seek very different values. Those will include, in Christopher Lasch's words, "decent, honorable work, the kind of work that confers self-respect and a sense of being useful."[8] For the Harvard professor the law suffers as a widow does who has not yet mourned and so cannot get on with a new life. Authoritarianism has died but the new life of healthy authority has not been discovered. It is striking that Glendon looks to traditional professional ideals as possessing the generative authority to command the attention and admiration of those now aspiring to the law.

Those ideals are undeniably spiritual values. So, essentially, are the self-discipline and professional craftsmanship that Glendon views as necessary if the law is to triumph over the threatening chaos and enter a new and vigorous phase of life.

18

Rediscovering the Authority of the Law: Recommendations

> I often wonder whether we do not rest our hopes too much upon constitutions, upon laws, and upon courts. These are false hopes: believe me, these are false hopes. Liberty lies in the hearts of men and women; when it dies there, no constitution, no law, no court can save it; no constitution, no law, no court can even do much to help it. While it lies there it needs no constitution, no law, no court to save it.
>
> —Judge Learned Hand[1]

The crisis of the law and the courts aches like a phantom limb lost in a war we can't remember; the authoritarian tyrants fell but authority has not yet been restored. In fact, we have not yet named America's crisis of healthy authority. The first task is therefore to identify and define the problems of the legal system.

What has been obscured tells us what needs to be rediscovered. In the universe of the law, that is justice itself. But justice cannot be recovered unless we examine its true nature. Otherwise we do not know what we are looking for. And we cannot proceed far in that direction without encountering authority as a healthy and indispensable spiritual quality.

Lawyers and judges need to affirm justice, in the light of the authentic meaning of natural authority, as a spiritual value, the responsibility, sacred trust, and distillate of the institution of the law. These authoritative values are foundational to the idea of justice, traditionally described, by Aristotle for one, as a virtue that inheres in human beings.[2] Others, including Rawls, see justice as a quality residing in a situation or state of affairs. These distinctions lie beneath the current debate about the values of socialism. For if justice is a virtue, it is authored only by individuals and the social order is reshaped around the lives and through the actions of those who pursue justice personally. Rawls and others see justice as a criterion for the distribution, in a supposedly equitable way, of social goods. The pursuit of a specific social order—socialism—authors justice. Do you live a good life and make the world more just, or do you impose an order on the world that distributes everything "justly"? That is, in fact, the debate of the interim. It has many faces, political as well as philosophical. The question of the age is, "How do we author justice?"

Imposed socialism has failed in Germany, Russia, Great Britain, and dozens of other states. It remains on the American agenda of debate about whether government or individuals are the best authors of a just society. Clearly, the condition of the law, and therefore of justice, during what we call the interim—decentered, diffused, experimental, monetized—argues that it cannot be rehabilitated until it rediscovers its own nature. Our argument is that justice is a manifold personal virtue, in other words, that it follows the nature of authority itself as a function of human relationships ordered to growth and to the benefit of the common good. The recovery of the natural authority of justice depends on the recovery of the idea and ideal of that authority. Only then can it re-authorize the institutions of the law, including the practice of law and the administration of the legal system.

Unsettled contemporary institutions, from the Congress to the Vatican, have become disconnected from their own spiritual traditions, the source of their dynamic authority over their specific fields. Their pragmatic experimentation in the authority void immersed them in greater difficulties. Trial-and-error improvisations, such as operating with no authority figure at all in such settings as classrooms, dormitories, and monasteries, quickly proved unworkable. Having overdrawn their own authority, they borrowed that of legal-like structures and, finally, that of the law itself *as a literal authority* to supply for their authority default. It is becoming apparent in American culture that a generalized effort to translate every human experience into the language of the law not only distorts the law but exhausts it at the same time.

Across a wide range of human activity, it is clear that generative authority, that which creates rather than controls, is the indispensable energy of personal and public life. The core of authority's function is spiritual and therefore profoundly human. It depends on our capacity to see and forge relationships in a manner proper to persons rather than to machines.

Justice is not a code of regulations but the spiritual reality authored and honored by the creative activity of the law. On recovering this sense, to which poets point more clearly than reductionist theorists, does the future of the law depend.

Nor is it impractical. A rediscovery of the spiritual dimension in life, work, learning, the arts, the professions, and commerce is essential to their regaining their independent moral authority. Each has a role to play—and these individual callings cannot be filtered through the law for validation—in carrying out their responsibilities for cultural generativity. That challenge is the very opposite of narcissistic self-absorption. It involves the creation and renovation of a symbol system, handing on what has been termed "the mind of a culture" to our descendants.

Each person—the judge, the lawyer, the professor, the philosopher, the concerned citizen—must work in ways proper to his or her position and function to restore the misplaced but not destroyed authority of the law.

Our common calling of authorship includes but is not exhausted by the only subject with generative resonations that is presently discussed: whether the generation that comes of age in 2010 will be able to pay the bills this generation has piled up for them, as, for example,

in the financing of the Social Security program. Generative authorship insists that we also be concerned about the kind of life that we
bequeath to the future and whether it will increase the opportunities
for true human experience. We leave our heritage better in metaphor
than in money, better in the spirit than merely in hard currency.

*The law should recognize and protect the values of the independent author-
ity of, among others, the arts, education, religion and the press.* Our national reacquaintanceship with healthy authority cannot be arranged by
the law as matchmaker. Because their tissues differ so, legal authority
transplants will ultimately be rejected.

What is lost for both parties when institutions drain off the authority
of the law to substitute for their own? Does art disown its integral authority and tradition, pleading bankruptcy when it justifies its creations
almost entirely on legal grounds, as it does when it defends them as pro-
tected free speech under the First Amendment? Does literature recognize
or stand by its own authority when it depends on the courts and the
First Amendment to rationalize itself as art? Can the voice of law, so limited in range and timbre, speak above a whisper compared to the commanding voice of an authentic creation? The law may speak well against
authoritarian censorship, but that does not make the law a replacement
for the soul and nervous system of art or of any other institution that
tries to use it as a foundation for its existence and function.

Art, education, and other institutions must ultimately speak for and
justify themselves. America's overall problems with authority demand
a rediscovery and reimplementation of sensible authority within the
great institutions of society. Nobody can do that for them, least of all
the courts and the government, from which solutions come in a one-
size-fits-all: bureaucratic regulations bundled and dumped like newspapers on America's streetcorners.[3]

Obviously, this culturewide problem cannot be solved solely by the
law or its practitioners. Yet, just as it is for religious and educational leaders in their respective institutions, lawyers and judges need to revitalize
and redefine their understanding of the authoritative professional ideals
that transcend the broken language of hierarchical authoritarianism that
no longer expresses them well. Spiritual reality survives outside the cus-

toms of religious devotion that may be popular at any given period. So too does justice survive and live outside its misuse and misappropriation during this interim period. Our deeper entry into the Space/Information Age will pressure the legal profession, of all the professions, to rediscover justice as its justifying goal. Once it has rediscovered the root and purpose of its own authority, it will see and sustain more clearly the authority of other institutions. That task, however, is not yet well in focus. People, including lawyers, are still too preoccupied with the symptoms of this transforming period to address fully their causes.

Summation

The rediscovery of authority in any institution, including the law, begins within individual men and women. Character is crucial, because the morally mature personality generates healthy authority as it does the healthy "mores" of the country.[4] Like common sense, healthy institutions are a function of healthy people who understand the extraordinary demands and remarkable rewards of authoring rather than borrowing their own identities. So, too, they author their friendships, love, work—the whole of their lives as individuals and as members of the communities they build together.

A temptation to fascism can easily arise when institutions no longer function well, when the bone marrow authority of the law is dangerously thinned by transfusing it into so many other anemic structures. The temptation is to restore authoritarianism, perhaps of a subtler but no less pseudo-populist sort than the swaggering Mussolini's promise to make the trains run on time.

This longing for a savior from outside ourselves may lead some people to follow a demagogue for a while, as they did in 1992 when the extraordinarily manipulative H. Ross Perot promised, in his down home way, that he could balance the budget and reduce the deficit without "breaking a sweat." In the long run Americans will reject all demagogues, no matter how wealthy or temporarily persuasive, as they rediscover the hard but highly moral work of restoring generative authority in their personal and public lives.

The shift of the cargo of our woes onto lawyers and the courts has resulted from a breakdown in our capacity to make the relationships with ourselves that are the model of our relationships with each other—to form, sustain, and, if necessary, mend them when they are under stress or are damaged without resorting immediately to lawsuits, which, successful or unsuccessful, institutionalize enmity. The culture of victimhood, which has spawned an industry of narcissistic confession and claims, is a further side effect of our unwillingness to be accountable for our own intentions and behavior.

Healthy authority flows from within us, that is, from leaving self-absorption behind and becoming mature, an imperfect but reliable state. A broken or immature relationship, like a snapped or poorly soldered wire, cannot transmit the energy of natural authority. Wanting to look mature but perhaps unwilling or unable to author inner maturity, also known as character, we want the law to be the wire, solder, and energy of lives for whose happiness we have come to claim a legal right instead of a human responsibility.

We may define the moral theory of a world lacking authority as feeling good without really being or doing good. That occurs when the slogan, whether it is pro-choice or pro-life or any passive profession of tolerance, is confused with and accepted in place of the hard work of authoring real-life virtue. That is why one of the most popular questions about almost any issue in American culture is not "What do you think?" or "What do you choose?" but "How do you feel?" That is the question not of the unexamined but of the unauthored life.

The law that casts a reflected glow of being good in this passive environment also replaces the individual as an instrument of doing good. To this end the law is routinely politicized or enlisted in the cause of ideology.[5] Not entirely new in the American experience, this tendency, to the ultimate frustration of the do-gooders and to the eventual harm of the law, has flourished during the post-hierarchical era.

Americans cannot get their own authority back until they understand that it is spiritual rather than legal. The great human issues in American history have always depended for their favorable resolution on convincing a majority of the population of their rightness according to spiritual values. Slavery's abolition in the nineteenth century was the outcome of a generations-long spiritual crusade to help white Americans perceive black Americans as equal human beings rather than as property. The mid-twentieth-century civil rights campaign to give full citizenship rights to African-Americans was driven by spiritual conviction and dependent for its success on conversion of heart.

This latter campaign, in no small part spiritually authored by the churches, moved Americans to look again at the injustices of racial segregation. Lyndon B. Johnson is described as having experienced a "conversion" on the matter of civil rights before he led the political battle to recognize and validate by law the spiritual transformation that had already taken place in the hearts of large numbers of Americans.[6] The legendary civil rights activist Rosa Parks views her refusal to give up her bus seat to a white man as "an act of faith."[7]

The courts never lead, indeed, they cannot lead, but always follow in such grave matters as civil rights and equality. The law cannot author the concerns that come from within the men and women who, implementing their own spiritual beliefs, seek to implement equal justice for all. The impulse for change cannot and does not originate in the law or the courts. Laws, such as the Fourteenth Amendment, are passed only after the great causes, led by people of character and convictions, have been resolved in the American heart.

"To maintain a democratic republic," Tocqueville observes, ". . . physical circumstances are less efficient than laws, and the laws infinitely less so than the customs of the people." Those customs he identifies as the "whole moral and intellectual state of the people."[8]

So, too, the rediscovery of generative authority is a great cause that will be successfully led in this new time, as in times long gone, by men and women in whose hearts its longing now burns and on whose character its recovery depends.

Notes

Epigraph Pages

Yves R. Simon, *A General Theory of Authority* (Notre Dame, IN:, University of Notre Dame Press, 1980), p. 13.

Joseph T. Shipley, *The Origins of English Words* (Baltimore: Johns Hopkins University Press, 1984).

Chapter 1. Why We Need to Rediscover Authority

1. Tim Weiner, "Finding New Reasons to Dread the Unknown," *New York Times,* Section 4 ("Week in Review"), March 26, 1995, pp. 1, 3.
2. William Morris, ed., *The American Heritage Dictionary* (Boston: American Heritage Publishing/Houghton Mifflin, 1970), p. 89, for Indo-European Roots, see page 1507.

    The derivation of the word "authority" includes that from the Latin word *auctoritas,* "authority," the Latin *auctor,* creator, from *augere,* to create, to increase. The root is the Germanic *aug,* to increase, as in the Germanic *auchan,* and the Old English, *eacan,* to increase.
3. For a discussion of the *relational* concept of authority see the chapter entitled "Authority: Its Nature and Locus," in *Authority: A Philosophical Analysis,* ed. R. Baines Harris (University, AL: University of Alabama Press, 1976).
4. Joseph Campbell, *Myths to Live By* (New York: Viking, 1973), pp. 250–51. Emphasis added.
5. Joseph Campbell, *Historical Atlas of World Mythology,* Vol. II: *The Way of the Seeded Earth,* Part I, "The Sacrifice" (New York: Harper & Row, 1988), p. 38.
6. Eugene Kennedy, *Tomorrow's Catholics, Yesterday's Church: The Two Cultures of American Catholicism* (San Francisco: Harper & Row, 1990), p. 74.

233

7. Paul Johnson, *Modern Times: The World from the Twenties to the Nineties* (New York: HarperCollins, 1992), p. 1.
8. Kenichi Omahe, *The Borderless World* (New York: Harper, 1990), pp. 82–101.
9. As subjectivity has come to be the measure of almost everything, some people are surprised that certain philosophies of art, such as that proposed by James Joyce, even exist. The author of *A Portrait of the Artist as a Young Man* borrows the Italian physician Galvani's phrase in describing the spiritual state of our response to genuine or authoritative art as "enchantment of the heart." Such art demands the qualities of wholeness, harmony, and radiance. Improper art leads to desire (possession) or loathing (abandonment) but proper art arrests the mind in that moment and raises it above desire or loathing (pp. 143, 241).
10. Hannah Arendt, *The Origins of Totalitarianism* (San Diego: Harcourt Brace, 1973), p. xvi.
11. Interview with Richard M. Daley, Mayor of Chicago, December 3, 1995.

Chapter 2. The De-authorization of Marriage

1. Mary Ellen Strote, "Magical Sex: Something Worth Waiting For," *Cosmopolitan*, September 1993, p. 88.
2. David W. Murray, "Poor Suffering Bastards: An Anthropologist Looks at Illegitimacy," *Policy Review*, no. 68 (Spring 1994), p. 9.
3. "Notebook," *Chronicle of Higher Education*, May 19, 1993, p. A32.

Chapter 3. Rediscovering Authority in Marriage: Recommendations

1. Arendt, *Origins of Totalitarianism* (ch. 1, n. 10 above), pp. 475–76. Arendt notes that similar to authority, common sense is a function of relationships. "Even the experience of the materially and sensually given world depends upon my being in contact with other men."
2. Walter Goodman, "On the Many Splendors of Long-lasting Love," *New York Times*, July 13, 1993, p. B13.
3. George Eliot, *Middlemarch,* ed. David Carroll (Oxford: Oxford University Press, 1988), p. 682.

Chapter 4. The De-authorization of the Family

1. Alexis de Tocqueville, *Democracy in America,* ed. Phillips Bradley (New York: Vintage Classics, 1990), II: 192–97.
2. Larry L. Bumpass, "What's Happening to the American Family? Interactions Between Demographic and Institutional Change," *Demography,* 27, no. 4 (1990): 483–97.
3. Paul Popenoe, "American Family Decline, 1960–1990: A Review and Appraisal," *Journal of Marriage and the Family,* 55 (August 1993): 527–42.
4. Barbara Dafoe Whitehead, "Dan Quayle Was Right," *Atlantic Monthly,* April 1993, p. 47. The author's ideas have been further developed in *The Divorce Culture,* New York: Alfred A. Knopf, 1997.

5. *Ibid.,* pp. 40, 80.
6. *Ibid.,* pp. 80–84.

Chapter 5. *Rediscovering Authority in the Family: Recommendations*

1. Jerry M. Lewis, M.D., *How's Your Family?* revised edition, (New York: Brunner/Mazel, 1989), p. 86.
2. Freedom's root is discovered to be *pri,* which means "to love" and appears, for example, in the Germanic *frijaz,* "beloved, belonging to the loved ones." To be out of bondage meant to be loved, as in the Old English freo, which survives in our word "friend." William Morris, ed., *The American Heritage Dictionary* (Boston: American Heritage Publishing/Houghton Mifflin, 1970), p. 1536.
3. Arendt, *Origins of Totalitarianism* (ch. 1, n. 10 above), p. 466.
4. Albert Camus, *The Fall* (New York: Knopf, 1957), pp. 132–33.
5. Meditating on John F. Kennedy's funeral, Joseph Campbell reflects on the origin of its rites in the legends of ancient heroes and of the Civil War funeral of Abraham Lincoln, also assassinated in office: "The force of the contemporary rite was enormously enhanced by these symbolic overtones—unheard by outward ears, perhaps, yet recognized within by all—in the slow, solemn beat of the military drums and the clattering black hoofs of those horses of King Death through the absolutely silent city." Campbell, *Myths to Live By* (ch. 1, n. 4 above), pp. 54–55.
6. *Ibid.,* pp. 45–46.
7. Daniel Goleman, "Family Rituals May Promote Better Emotional Adjustment," *New York Times,* March 11, 1992, p. B6.
8. William Safire, "What Fathers Want," *New York Times,* June 16, 1994, p. A15.
9. Ann Landers, "Mom has 'some' concern over girl, 11, having sex," *Chicago Tribune,* November 16, 1993, *Tempo,* p. 4.
10. Christina Hoff Sommers, "Teaching the Virtues," *Chicago Tribune Magazine,* November 15, 1992, p. 18.
11. James Trelease, *The New Read Aloud Handbook* (New York: Penguin Books, 1989), p. xv.
12. Christopher Lasch, *Haven in a Heartless World* (New York, Basic Books, 1979), p. 123.
13. William Raspberry, "Making Miracles with Young Fathers," *Chicago Tribune,* May 11, 1992, p. 12.
14. Ellen Graham, "My Father's Bridge to the Saturday Girls," *Wall Street Journal,* May 11, 1992.

Chapter 6. *Rediscovering the Source of Moral Authority*

1. The psychiatrist Robert Jay Lifton has poignantly described his observations of an evolving personality structure of modern man, a function of this period of upheaval and disruption. He writes, "Without quite realizing it we have been evolving a sense of self [which he calls the protean self] appropriate to the restlessness and flux of our

time" (page 1). Central to this concept is a feeling of the loss of our "psychological moorings," the older and more familiar version of personal identity characterized by stability and sameness and the acquisition of a personality consisting of "odd combinations." In this state, protean man necessarily experiences feelings of fatherlessness and homelessness, free-floating emotions and restless work patterns. Protean man questions whether moral principles can be either sustained or adhered to in the midst of such psychological flux. Many who suffer its effects have difficulty in their intimate relationships, exhibit a variety of symptoms, and lack a sense of satisfaction in their personal and professional lives. Robert Jay Lifton, *The Protean Self* (New York: Basic Books, 1993).

2. Note the derivation of the word "law" from the root *legh*. "Indo-European Roots," *The American Heritage Dictionary of the English Language,* ed. William Morris (Boston: American Heritage Publishing Company/Houghton Mifflin, 1970), p. 1525.

3. See the derivation of the word "ethic" from the root *seu*. *Ibid.,* p. 1538.

4. Sidney B. Simon, Leland W. Howe, and Howard Kirschenbaum, *Values Clarification* (New York: Hart Publishing, 1972).

5. William Kilpatrick, *Why Johnny Can't Tell Right from Wrong* (New York: Touchstone, Simon & Schuster, 1992), pp. 80–81.

6. "An R.C. Document," *The Responsive Community,* 4, no. 1 (1993–94): 93.

7. Andy Abrams and Kristine Herman, "Antioch Is Not Legislating 'Sexual Correctness'," *Chronicle of Higher Education,* January 26, 1994, p. B3.

8. Dorothy Collins, ed., *Lunacy and Letters* (New York: Sheed & Ward, 1958), p. 97.

9. Paul Johnson, *A History of Christianity* (New York: Atheneum, Macmillan, 1976), p. 484.

10. Jane Gross, "Where 'Boys Will Be Boys,' And Adults Are Bewildered," *New York Times,* March 29, 1993, p. A9.

11. Yves Simon, *A General Theory of Authority* (Notre Dame, IN: University of Notre Dame Press, 1980), p. 28.

12. "The superego, so Freud pointed out, is the internalization of all the restrictions to which the ego must bow. . . . He looks for models by which to measure himself, and seeks happiness in trying to resemble them. Where he succeeds he achieves self-esteem." Erik Erikson, *Identity and the Life Cycle* (New York: Norton, 1959, 1980), p. 19.

13. Arthur Schopenhauer, *Die Bieden Grundproblemen Der Ethik,* II. *Uber das Fundament der Moral,* (1840), in *Samlichewerke,* 12 vols. (Stuttgart: Verlag de Ctta'schen Buchhandlung, 1895–98), 7: 253–54, 292.

14. Tocqueville, *Democracy in America* (ch. 4, n. 1 above), I:64.

15. Samuel Oliner and Pearl Oliner, *The Altruistic Personality: Rescuers of Jews in Nazi Europe* (New York: Free Press, 1988).

Chapter 7. The De-authorization of Education

1. Douglas Martin, "Law School Dean Wanted: A Man for All Reasons," *New York Times,* May 6, 1988, p. 23.

2. CBS News, *60 Minutes,* April 3, 1994.

3. Denise Grumney, "Immokalee High Students Stage Walkout to Protest Tardiness Policy Change, *Naples Daily News* (Florida), March 22, 1994, p. 1A.

4. Carl Rogers, *Freedom to Learn* (Columbus, OH: Merrill, 1969).

5. Lillian Katz, "Reading, Writing, Narcissism," *New York Times,* July 15, 1993, p. A15.

6. Susan Swartzlander, Diana Pace, and Virginia Lee Stamler, "The Ethics of Requiring Students to Write About Their Personal Lives," *Chronicle of Higher Education,* February 17, 1993, pp. B1, B2.

7. Sonia L. Nazario, "Move Grows to Promote Failing Pupils," *Wall Street Journal,* June 16, 1992, pp. B1, 18.

8. William A. Henry III, *In Defense of Elitism* (New York: Doubleday, 1994), pp. 54–59.

9. Lynda Richardson, "Public Schools Are Failing the Brightest Students, a Federal Study Says," *New York Times,* November 5, 1993, p. A23.

10. Christopher Shea, "Fewer Test Takers Get Top Scores on the Verbal SAT," *Chronicle of Higher Education,* January 13, 1993, pp. A29, A30, A33.

11. Ron Grossman, "A School System That's Fail-Safe," *Chicago Tribune, Tempo,* August 2, 1993, pp. 1, 8.

12. Laura Mansnerus, "Mediocrity in the Classroom," *New York Times,* education supplement, August 2, 1992, pp. 22, 23.

13. Stephen Burd, "Critics Say Cancer Institute Hid Fraud in Breast-Cancer Project," *Chronicle of Higher Education,* April 13, 1994, p. A28.

14. Kilpatrick, *Why Johnny Can't Tell* (ch. 6, n. 5 above), p. 14.

15. Eric Schmitt, "Inquiry Recommends Expulsions in Naval Academy Cheating," *New York Times,* April 1, 1994, p. A1, A8.

16. Karen Grassmuck, "Big Increases in Academic-Support Staffs Prompt Growing Concerns on Campuses," *Chronicle of Higher Education,* March 28, 1994, p. A32.

17. Edward Shils, "Do We Still Need Academic Freedom?" *The American Scholar,* Spring 1993, pp. 200–209.

18. Johnson, *Modern Times* (ch. 1, n. 7 above), pp. 555–56.

19. Noretta Koertge, "Scrutinizing Feminist Critiques of Science," *Chronicle of Higher Education,* November 9, 1994, p. B3.

20. Joan Hoff, "The Pernicious Effects of Poststructuralism on Women's History," *Chronicle of Higher Education,* October 20, 1993, pp. B1–2.

21. Sarah Lubman, "More Schools Embrace 'Full Inclusion' of the Disabled," *Wall Street Journal,* April 13, 1994, pp. B1, B7.

22. George F. Will, "A Trickle-Down Culture," *Newsweek,* December 13, 1993, p. 84.

23. Wes Smith, "Trial and Error?" *Chicago Tribune Magazine,* May 1, 1994, p. 20. Emphasis added.

24. Edward B. Fiske, "Colleges Playing Larger Role in Guiding Lives of Students," *New York Times,* February 22, 1995, pp. 1, 14.

Chapter 8. Rediscovering Authority in Education: Recommendations

1. Scott Heller, "Left-Wing Journal 'Goes Legitimate' with Move to University Press," *Chronicle of Higher Education,* February 24, 1993, p. A6.
2. Michael Kimmelman, "The Art Critic Whose Viewpoint Remains Central," *New York Times,* May 10, 1994, p. B4.
3. Dinesh D'Souza, "Pied Pipers of Relativism Reverse Course," *Wall Street Journal,* July 27, 1993, p. A16.
4. William Celis III, "Beyond the PTA: Parents Seek More Power,"*New York Times,* October 24, 1994, pp. A1, A10.
5. Carin Rubenstein, "Success in School Called Family Effort," *New York Times,* September 8, 1994, pp. C1, C12.
6. David Armor, "Families Spur Black Students' Gains," *Wall Street Journal,* June 30, 1992, p. A14.
7. Rochelle Sharpe, "To Boost IQs, Aid Is Needed in First Three Years," *Wall Street Journal,* April 12, 1994, p. B1.
8. T. Friend, "Many Parents Resigned to Kids' Drug Use," *USA Today,* September 18, 1996.
9. Roger Scruton, "The Higher Meaning of Food" (a review of *The Hungry Soul* by Leon Kass), *Times Literary Supplement,* September 30, 1994, p. 13.
10. Debra Chira, "Where Children Learn How to Learn: Inner-City Pupils in Catholic Schools," *New York Times,* November 20, 1991, p. B8.
11. David Gonzalez, "Poverty Raises Stakes for Catholic School," *New York Times,* April 17, 1994, p. 10.
12. Steve Stecklow, "Fed Up with Schools, More Parents Turn to Teaching at Home," *Wall Street Journal,* May 10, 1994, pp. A1, A12.
13. Edward Wynne and Kevin Ryan, *Reclaiming Our Schools: A Handbook on Teaching Character and Discipline* (Columbus, OH: Merrill, 1994).
14. Eric N. Berg, "Argument Grows That Teaching of Values Should Rank with Lessons," *New York Times,* January 1, 1992, p. 36.
15. Peter Drucker, "The Age of Social Transformation," *Atlantic Monthly,* November 1994, pp. 53–80.

Chapter 9. The De-authorization of Work

1. Robert Hogan, Gordon J. Curphy, and Joyce Hogan, "What We Know About Leadership, Effectiveness and Personality," *The American Psychologist,* 49, no. 6 (June 1994): 503–4.
2. Edwin P. Hollander and Lynn R. Offerman, "Power and Leadership in Organizations, Relationships in Transition," *The American Psychologist,* 45, no. 2 (February 1990): 179–89. This article provides a review of the pertinent literature.
3. Jude Wanniski, "Macro-Economics: The Enemy Within," *Wall Street Journal,* June 27, 1991.
4. "Hostility Taints Postal Service, Congressional Report Finds," *New York Times,* October 28, 1994, p. A14.

Chapter 10. Rediscovering Authority at Work: Recommendations

1. Gilbert Fuchsberg, "Study Delves into Causes of Failures in Downsizing," *Wall Street Journal,* October 1, 1993, p. 9.
2. Harlan S. Byrne, "Ready to Accelerate," *Barron's,* March 21, 1994, p. 19.
3. Diane Riggan, "Re-parent the Young Workers? Not on Your Life," *New York Times,* Sunday business section, December 1, 1991, p. 12.
4. Keith H. Hammonds and Kevin Kelly, "The New World of Work," *Business Week,* October 17, 1994, pp. 76–87.
5. Peter Drucker, *Managing in a Time of Great Change* (New York: Truman Talley Books, Dutton, 1995). See especially ch. 21, "A Century of Social Transformation," which describes the emergence of the knowledge worker.

Chapter 11. The De-authorization of the Professions

1. Kenneth L. Lynn, "Introduction to the Issue 'The Professions,'" *Daedalus,* 92, no. 4 (Fall 1963): 649.
2. Edmund D. Pellegrino and David C. Thomasma, *The Virtues in Medical Practice* (New York: Oxford University Press, 1993).
3. In a contemporary defense of the professional claim, Henry argues that "there are differences from birth, not only of class and privilege, but of brains and drive—qualities that can only be enhanced, not instilled, from the outside. Still, we persist that everyone finish even. . . . The defense of elitism that our society so sorely needs is ultimately nothing more than the defense of common sense." He further notes: "As the novelist Robert Stone observed on the op-ed page of the New York Times in March 1993, 'In our radical interpretation of democracy, our rejection of elites, our well-nigh demagogic respect for the opinions of the unlearned, we are alone.'" Henry, *In Defense of Elitism* (ch. 7, n. 8 above).
4. Everett C. Hughes, "Professions," *Daedalus,* 92, no. 4 (Fall 1963): pp. 655–58.
5. This objective is not so clear in professional relationships restyled in the present "consumer–provider" model, which ignores common good spiritual values in favor of a professional universe as a Wal-Mart of sorts, in which service is equated with courtesy and value with the lowest price. The merchant–buyer relationship is necessarily brief, functional, easily terminated, and essentially economic. Freidson observes: "When at least some of the consumer's needs are reduced to standard categories, thus reducing the consumer to a standard object, this may seem oppressive and disabling. . . . [T]he producers of some goods and services should be able to exercise discretion and judgment not only for the sake of their own humanity but also for the sake of the humanity of the consumer." Eliot Freidson, "Are Professions Necessary?" in *The Authority of Experts: Studies in History and Theory,* ed. Thomas L. Haskell (Bloomington: Indiana University Press, 1984), p. 22.

    For a contemporary overview of health care models and the professional conflicts they generate see George Anders, *Health Against Wealth: HMOs and the Breakdown of Medical Trust* (New York: Houghton Mifflin), 1996.
6. *Ibid.,* p. 4.

7. Writing of this claim in the light of the antiprofessional movement of recent years, Freidson observes that many writers "have reserved the label for a relatively few well-established, prestigious and strongly credentialed, exclusive professions like medicine. . . . Other writers, like myself, have emphasized the capacity to control and regulate itself as a mark of such occupations." Furthermore, he concludes: "There is what I regard to be the center of professional autonomy—sufficient authority to undertake discretionary action as a matter of choice." *Ibid.,* pp. 10, 21.

8. Drucker, *Managing in Time of Great Change* (ch. 10, n. 5 above), pp. 226–33. "Knowledge workers will not be the majority in the knowledge society, but in many countries, if not most developed countries, they will be the largest single group in the population and the workforce. And even if outnumbered by other groups, knowledge workers will be the group that gives the emerging knowledge society its character, its leadership, its social profile. They may not be the *ruling* class of the knowledge society, but they already are its *leading* class."

9. Drucker, "Age of Social Transformation" (ch. 8, n. 15 above), p. 68.

10. *Ibid.*

Chapter 12. *Rediscovering Authority in the Professions: Recommendations*

1. Gerald F. Seib, "Military Reform Has Given Field Commanders Decisive Roles and Reduced Interservice Rivalry," *Wall Street Journal,* January 24, 1991, p. A12.

2. John J. Fialka, "Allies' Battle Plans Changed Fast and Often, Confusing Friends and, More Important, Foes," *Wall Street Journal,* March 11, 1991, p. A16.

3. See Stephen E. Ambrose, *D-Day June 6, 1944: The Climactic Battle of World War II* (New York: Simon & Schuster, 1994): "[W]hat Hitler regarded as the greatest German assets—the leadership principle of the Third Reich, the unquestioning obedience expected of Wehrmacht personnel from field marshal down to private—all worked against the Germans on D-Day. The truth is . . . the performance of the Wehrmacht's high command, middle ranking officers, and junior officers was just pathetic. The cause was a simple one: they were afraid to take the initiative. They allowed themselves to be paralyzed by stupid orders coming from far away that bore no relation to the situation on the battlefield." (p. 579)

4. Elisabeth Rosenthal, "Insurers Second-Guess Doctors, Provoking Debate over Savings," *New York Times,* January 24, 1993, pp. 1, 10.

Chapter 13. *The De-authorization of the Institutions of Government and Business*

1. Meg Greenfield, "The 'Just Folks' Pantomime," *Newsweek,* October 10, 1994, p. 78.

2. Susan B. Garland, "Too Many Advisers Could Spoil the Broth," *Business Week,* January 25, 1993, pp. 34, 36.

3. "Washington Wire," *Wall Street Journal,* April 29, 1994, p. A1.

4. Evan Thomas *et al.,* "Under the Gun," *Newsweek,* October 3, 1994, p. 29.

5. Maureen Dowd, "Inquiry Is Putting First Lady at Center of Ethical Troubles," *New York Times,* March 6, 1994, p. 12.
6. Michael Rothschild, "Why Health Reform Died," *Wall Street Journal,* September 22, 1994, p. A14.
7. Joseph A. Califano, Jr., "Imperial Congress," *New York Times Magazine,* January 23, 1994, p. 40.
8. Interview with Donald Rumsfeld, July 18, 1990, Chicago.
9. Michael Kelly, "Rip It Up," *New Yorker,* January 23, 1995, p. 32.
10. Address to a January 1995 Washington seminar on "Democracy in Virtual America," quoted in *ibid.,* p. 33.
11. *Ibid.,* p. 35.
12. Quoted in *ibid., p.* 36.
13. John A. Byrne, "Requiem for Yesterday's CEO," *Business Week,* February 15, 1993, pp. 32–33.
14. John A. Byrne, "The Horizontal Corporation," *Business Week,* December 20, 1993, pp. 76–81.
15. Jim Manzi, "Address to the Council on Competitiveness," Washington, D.C., September 7, 1994, p. 4.
16. Byrne, "Horizontal Corporation," p. 77. Emphasis added.
17. "A Master Class in Radical Change, *Fortune,* December 13, 1993, p. 83. Emphasis added.
18. Manzi, "Address," pp. 16–17.
19. *Ibid.,* p. 4.
20. John R. Wilke, "Computer Links Erode Hierarchical Nature of Workplace Culture," *Wall Street Journal,* December 9, 1993, p. A1.
21. Peter H. Lewis, "Executives Unmask Computer Fears," *New York Times,* October 5, 1994, pp. C1, C3.
22. Joanne S. Lublin, "Turning the Tables: Underlings Evaluate Bosses," *Wall Street Journal,* October 4, 1994, p. B1.
23. Sue Schellenbarger, "Reviews from Peers Instruct—and Sting," *Wall Street Journal,* October 4, 1994, p. B1.
24. "Master Class," *Fortune,* p. 83.

Chapter 14. The De-authorization of Religious Institutions

1. David Remnick, "The Pope in Crisis," *New Yorker,* October 17, 1994, p. 51.
2. Among the many articles analyzing, for general readership, the inexorable change in Roman Catholicism from historical, theological, and philosophical perspectives, see Thomas F. O'Meara, "Leaving the Baroque: the Fallacy of Restoration in the Post-conciliar Era," *America,* February 3, 1996, p. 10, and Walter J. Ong, S. J., "Do We Live in a Post-Christian Age?" *America,* February 3, 1996, p. 16.
3. Gustav Niebuhr, "Many Protestant Faiths Face Financial Binds," *New York Times,* October 23, 1994, p. 10.
4. Gustav Niebuhr, "Tradition Pulls Episcopalians Back to Rome," *New York Times,* October 23, 1994, pp. 1, 14.

5. Joseph Campbell, *The Inner Reaches of Outer Space: Metaphor as Myth and as Religion* (New York: Alfred Van Der Marck, 1986). Campbell writes: "One cannot but ask: What can such tribal literalism possibly contribute but agony to such a world of intercultural, global prospects as that of our present century? It all comes of misreading metaphors, taking denotation for connotation, the messenger for the message; overloading the carrier, consequently, with sentimentalized significance and throwing both life and thought thereby off balance. To which the only generally recognized correction as yet proposed had been the no less wrongheaded one of dismissing the metaphors as lies (which indeed they are, when so construed), thus scrapping the whole dictionary of the language of the soul (this is a metaphor) by which mankind has been elevated to interests beyond procreation, economics, and 'the greatest good for the greatest number'" (p. 58).

Chapter 15. Rediscovering Institutional Authority: Recommendations

1. Quoted from *Taste: The Secret Meaning of Things* (New York: Pantheon, 1992), in *New York Times Book Review,* March 31, 1992.
2. Bruce G. Posner and Lawrence R. Rothstein, "Reinventing the Business of Government: An interview with Change Catalyst David Osborne, *Harvard Business Review,* May–June 1994, pp. 134, 139.
3. Bill Richards, "Test of Virtual Reality Spans the Pacific," *Wall Street Journal,* November 16, 1994, p. B1.
4. John Noble Wilford, "Moon May Save Earth from Chaotic Tilting of Other Planets," *New York Times,* March 2, 1994, p. B5.

Chapter 16. The De-authorization of the Legal Profession

1. Mary Ann Glendon, *A Nation Under Lawyers: How the Crisis in the Legal Profession Is Transforming American Society* (New York: Farrar, Straus & and Giroux, 1994), p. 37.
2. *Ibid.,* p. 288.
3. Liva Baker, *The Justice from Beacon Hill* (New York: HarperCollins, 1991), pp. 607–8.
4. Ellen Joan Pollock, *Turks and Brahmins: Upheaval at Milbank, Tweed* (New York: Simon & Schuster, 1990), pp. 263, 264.
5. The famous Washington law firm of Arnold & Porter pioneered subsidiaries in 1984 with a lobbying firm later sold to Grey Advertising. The firm's current subsidiaries "include the Secura Group, one of the largest bank consulting organizations in the country, headed by a former chairman of the Federal Deposit Insurance Corporation." Sol Linowitz with Martin Mayer, *The Betrayed Profession* (New York: Scribner's, 1994), p. 163.
6. Glendon, *Nation Under Lawyers,* p. 15.
7. Sam Benson, "Why I Quit Practicing Law," *Newsweek,* November 4, 1991, p. 10.
8. Derek Bok, "A Flawed System," *Harvard Magazine,* May–June 1983, p. 41.

Chapter 17. The Law as Authority Surrogate

1. Linda Greenhouse, "A Window on the Court," *New York Times,* May 6, 1992, p. A20.
2. Anthony Lewis, "Why Judges Act," *New York Times,* May 13, 1991, p. A13.
3. Edward Felsenthal, "Judges Find Themselves Acting as Doctors in Alzheimer's Cases," *Wall Street Journal,* May 20, 1994, p. B 1.
4. Richard H. Fallon, Jr., "Ideological Fog at Harvard Law," *Wall Street Journal,* February 11, 1996, p. A 15.
5. Ruth Shalit, "Uncle Bob," *New York Times Magazine,* March 5, 1995, p. 57.
6. See Harold J. Rothwax, *Guilty: The Collapse of Criminal Justice* (New York: Random House, 1996). "Judge Rothwax argues that criminal justice has been rendered ridiculous by what he calls 'formalism,' which he defines as applying 'rigid principles' to law enforcement even when they undermine the cause of justice." Richard Bernstein, "Judge Worries that Excess in Rights Foils Justice," *New York Times,* February 14, 1996, p. B16.
7. Johnson, *Modern Times* (ch. 1, no 7 above), p. 313.
8. Christopher Lasch, "The Baby Boomers: Here Today, Gone Tomorrow," *New Oxford Review,* September, 1993, pp. 7, 8, 10.

Chapter 18. Rediscovering the Authority of the Law: Recommendations

1. Irving Dilliard, ed., *The Spirit of Liberty: Papers and Addresses of Learned Hand* (New York: Knopf, 1953), pp. 189–90.
2. Roger Scruton, *Modern Philosophy: An Introduction and Survey* (London: Sinclair-Stevenson, 1994), pp. 297–98, 424–32.
3. The Harvard Law professor Randall Kennedy, for example, asks whether scholarly excellence depends on First Amendment authorization: "Judges are the arbiters of the First Amendment. But they are not academics committed first and last to advancing the mission—perhaps the peculiar mission—of a lone, distinct scholarly institution." "Should Private Universities Voluntarily Bind Themselves to the First Amendment? No!" *Chronicle of Higher Education,* September 21, 1994, Section 2, p. B1.
4. Glendon, summarizing the conclusions of James Boyd White and Yale Law Dean Anthony Kronman, notes that they "reject the idea that the activity of the law can be understood apart from the character of the persons engaged in that activity. In the search for law, it seems, as in folk tales of other sorts of quest, prowess is not enough. What the searcher discovers may depend as well on how he or she has lived." Glendon, *Nation Under Lawyers* (ch. 16, n. 1 above), p. 240.
5. Of Justice Anthony Kennedy's 1992 assertion that the American people's "very belief in themselves . . . was not easily separable from their understanding of the Court," Glendon observes that "it's quite a leap from John Marshall's emphatic insistence on the Court's power and duty 'to say what the law is' to the notion that the Court should tell us what our constitutional values should be. Ultimately (or so the Framers

repeatedly insisted) the voice that is privileged 'before all others' in our system of government is the voice of the people, expressed in a variety of ways." *Ibid.,* p. 114.

6. Bernard Schwartz, *The Law in America: A History* (New York: McGraw-Hill, 1974), p. 264.

7. David Briggs, "Rosa Parks, Mother of Civil Rights Movement, Tells How Religion Shaped Her Life," *Naples Daily News* (Florida), February 4, 1995, p. D1.

8. See Tocqueville, *Democracy in America* (ch. 4, n. 1 above), I: 319, 322.